THE

POLITICS

OF

COACHING

A Survival Guide To Keep Coaches From Getting Burned

CARL J. PIERSON

DOUBLE NICKLE PRESS

Published by Double Nickle Press
Printed in USA – CreateSpace

Cover design by Brad Weiss

Interior format by Jodee Kulp

For more information visit
www.politicsofcoaching.com

ISBN-13 978-14610974-5-7
ISBN-10 14610974-5-2

Dedicated to the spouses

and children of

coaches everywhere,

but most of all

to my beloved Jean and Boston

Table Of Contents

"If you don't turn on to politics,
politics will turn on you."
−*Ralph Nader*

Introduction

L ate March is a magical time in Minnesota. Once magnificent snow banks have been reduced to puddles in most places, hints of green are returning to the grass, and the months of being confined to a dimly lit gym during the winter sports season give way to the rejuvenating sunshine of spring sports. While this transitional time of year has historically been a pleasant and exciting period in my coaching career, my emotion on this particular March evening was one of relief.

Our team's end of season awards night had just concluded, marking the official end to one of my most challenging seasons as a coach. After cleaning up the auditorium I climbed into my car, exhaled a deep sigh, and took a moment to silently celebrate surviving a season that had been consumed by controversy. Then my brief moment of solace was shattered by the sound of my cell phone.

The call was from a fellow girls' basketball coach, a man that was also one of my best friends in the world. We chatted for a couple of minutes about how my teams' awards ceremony went and then he dropped the bombshell.

"I got fired today."

I was beyond stunned. In the conversation that followed we deliberated over the how and attempted to understand the why of this shocking development. It was shocking because my friend had just completed his eighth season as a head coach and his team posted winning seasons in six of the eight years. His only losing seasons were his first, when he inherited a 4 and 20 team and brought them to the brink of a .500 season and his last, when his do everything all-state player suffered a season ending injury in the first game of the year condemning his team to a mediocre 11 and 13 record. It was also shocking because my friend was absolutely the most dedicated coach I had ever encountered. He worked with his players extensively in the offseason, he was active with his youth programs, and his commitment during the season was unsurpassed.

But on a certain level, the news from my friend was not entirely surprising. He coached at an average sized school in an average sized Minnesota town where, after only eight years, he was by far the longest tenured head coach on staff. His school, like so many other high schools in America, disposed of head coaches with the frequency that a baby disposes of diapers. After seeing a string of head coaches at his school get fired in wrestling, football, hockey, baseball, and volleyball I warned him that he was living on borrowed time. I told him he needed to get out.

However, my friend was adamant that because he had established an excellent program and because his teams were very successful for several seasons in a row, what happened to those other coaches could not and would not happen to him. And then it happened to him.

Not long after the news, I drove down to spend a weekend with my friend. During our time together we attempted to dissect all the factors that contributed to his dismissal. As we talked, it became clear to me that he had been oblivious to what I considered clear warning signs that his job was in jeopardy. Perhaps these signs seemed apparent to me because I had been a student of politics for longer than I had even been an athlete or a coach. I grew up in a politically active family and was so intrigued with the subject that I made political science my undergraduate major in college. My political pedigree had equipped me with the ability to read people, recognize their motives, and anticipate how they would react in a given situation. In nearly 20 years of coaching football, baseball, and basketball this understanding of politics and people has allowed me to navigate the often treacherous terrain that has become youth and high school coaching. I had always taken for granted this understanding was intrinsic in most coaches. That is, until my friend was fired.

After spending the weekend with my fallen friend and exploring the events leading up to his dismissal, it became obvious that he was not fired because he was an incompetent coach. He lost his job because of politics, pure and simple. His lack of exposure to the nature of political maneuvering left him powerless to derail the campaign that some powerful parents had waged against him. On the drive home from my friends' house, I contemplated his experience and recognized that it was all too similar to the story shared by thousands of former coaches across the country. Every day good coaches are fired, not because they are inadequate coaches, but because they are not trained or prepared to manage the very political aspect of their coaching position.

It is for my friend, and for the thousands of coaches that have suffered his same fate, that I was compelled to author this book. My sincere hope is that the information, anecdotes, and advice offered in the pages that follow will empower coaches of all ages and all sports to win the political battles that have become so common place in the current coaching climate.

The attrition rate for coaches in America today is enormously high. While there are next to no definitive studies citing specific numbers on average length of tenure, coaches need only look around their conference or league and they will find adequate evidence. If a person has had the privilege to coach for four or five seasons there is an excellent chance that within their league there are more than a few new faces prowling the opposing sideline.

And while it used to be that coaches of so called "low profile" sports like golf, track, or tennis could count on greater job security and less parental or public pressure, in recent decades several new dynamics have developed that have increased the pressure on coaches in all sports.

Among those dynamics that are driving the deluge of political pressure is the increased financial investment made by parents. As more and more parents pursue an athletic scholarship for their child, they are making a significant monetary commitment and naturally, they expect a return on their investment. When parents hire personal trainers or coaches for their child, they expect that their child will become one of the top players on their team. When parents shell out thousands of dollars for their son or daughter to play on an "elite" club team that travels nationwide in an effort to gain exposure to college coaches, they are going to expect that the club and high school coaches will showcase their child appropriately.

Also adding to the political mine field that has become coaching is the advent of youth associations with governing boards populated by parents, each with their own agenda. When these parents spend their child's formative years with the power to hire and fire coaches, they often expect that level of influence will continue when their child moves on to the high school level.

Combine these relatively new developments with the traditionally toxic political issues of picking teams, picking starters, and playing time and it is clear that a coach has far more to juggle than how to help their team win games. While it is beyond a coach's control to alter or eliminate many of these obstacles, all coaches can become more adept at navigating the political pitfalls these situations can create. Clever coaches can even use politics to their advantage rather than becoming victims of it.

The best indicator of which coaches will survive and thrive in the current climate is not career wins and losses, but rather, how honed and how keen a coach's political instincts are.

Anyone that has been around athletics for any length of time can cite examples of coaches at the high school or college levels that have produced championship athletes or championship teams for years on end only to find themselves pushed out of their position for political reasons. There are thousands of books intended to help coaches win the games played on the field. This book intends to prepare coaches to prevail in the political games that take place when the other games are over.

Politics is analogous to sports in a number of ways, many of which you will be exposed to in the pages that follow, but for the purpose of this introduction allow me to indulge in just one example. In politics there is a great deal of focus on poll numbers. Politicians examine poll numbers in the same manner coaches pay attention to the scoreboard. While the score and time remaining can dictate the strategy a coach elects to employ, so too can it impact a candidate's next move. When John McCain selected Sarah Palin as his vice presidential candidate in 2008, his staff acknowledged that it was a decision driven largely on polling data. The numbers showed McCain needed to make a bold move to have any chance of beating Obama. This is no different than when a hockey coach is forced to pull their goalie late in the game or when a defensive coordinator in football recognizes they must gamble with a blitz in an effort to create a turnover when their team is trailing in the closing minutes.

When a presidential candidate surges into the lead after their national party convention, you see a change in the "scoreboard" or the polls. Then after the debates, the other candidate may pull into the lead. There are distinctive junctures during a campaign that signal the end of the first period, or the first half, and polls tell us who is winning. Of course, as in sports, the only time you have to have the lead is when the final buzzer sounds, and in the political world election day is that final horn.

Coaching is also strikingly similar to politics in the sense that no matter what decision a coach makes, they are likely to have one group endorse it and another group outraged by it. When a senator makes a key vote in favor of stricter environmental regulation, they immediately win the approval of a block of voters and create the condemnation of another group. When a coach decides to play Billy at quarterback instead of David, you can be sure there is a constituency for both quarterbacks that extends beyond both boys' parents. The very nature of the position of both elected officials and head coaches is such that they will always anger some people while pleasing others. And just as political figures need to be aware of their approval ratings, coaches must be cognizant of what allies they are creating and what people they are alienating with every decision they make.

Don't get me wrong. As coaches, we always want to make the decision that is best for our team and make the move that gives us the best chance to win. I would rarely, if ever, suggest a coach should do otherwise. But to be oblivious to the implications of each important decision we makes leads us to lose in the increasingly political arena that is the coaching profession.

Since the tender age of 10, I have known that I wanted to run for political office at some point. I can imagine no better training ground than coaching. Whether it is the public relations aspect of creating partnerships with area businesses to sponsor a summer camp or responding to questions from the local media, dealing with disgruntled parents (part of a coach's constituency) or making the tough budget choices on whether to buy new balls or new uniforms, the parallels are too numerous to ignore.

In this book, you will read about how to better understand the political nature of head coaching positions from the youth through varsity levels. Some coaches suggest they don't want to play the political games and that they just want to coach. I would suggest that if they really want to coach, playing the political games, or at the very least acknowledging that politics play a role in their job, is the only way they will get to coach or survive in the profession for any length of time.

There are techniques and suggestions in this book that will almost certainly be considered controversial. This is not a playbook about how to reach the moral high ground in every political dispute. This book provides coaches with options to consider and solutions to problems. These options and suggestions are intended to help coaches prevail in the increasingly cut-throat world of youth and high school sports. Ultimately, even if you disagree with some of the principles put forth, hopefully the suggestions will cause you to consider how you will respond when confronted with these situations that all coaches encounter. If you want to be among the handful of coaches that buck the trend and last in the profession, then you will learn to embrace and understand *the politics of coaching*.

ONE
***

The Campaign

*"I don't make any apologies
for what I do on the campaign trail."*
— George W. Bush

A t first glance, it may appear that this opening chapter is
targeted only at aspiring head coaches or current head coaches
about to apply for a new position. However, whether it is due
to school budget cuts creating staff reductions, being fired, or
having a better opportunity present itself elsewhere, the current
coaching climate is such that even established head coaches are likely
to find themselves applying and interviewing for a new position in the
not too distant future. With that in mind, it is prudent for all coaches
to understand the intricacies of the campaign.

Pursuing a head coaching position can be remarkably similar
to running for elective office. Granted, there are no bumper stickers,
parades, or TV commercials, but this much is certain; an astute and
aware aspiring head coach will run a modified version of a campaign.

Recognizing who the key decision makers are in the hiring process
and who exerts the most influence over those decision makers is the
beginning of running a successful campaign. But before we dive into
those areas there are several factors one must consider before applying
for a head coaching position.

Throwing Your Hat In The Ring

The first thing an aspiring coach must attempt to discern is what
kind of coach the school is looking for. In arriving at that answer, there
are some key questions to ponder:

* Is it a program that just had a hard line, disciplinarian head
coach that is looking for a more laid back, people person or
are they turning the page from a coach that lacked discipline
leading them to look for someone to provide structure?
* Has the program had a lot of success and do they have the

luxury of luring a "big name" coach with an established track record?
* Has the program been bottom feeders and are they looking for a person that can reinvigorate the program?
* In the case of female sports, are they going to do their best to hire a woman as their head coach?

In addressing the first question, knowing what kind of a coaching style a school seeks can be a determining factor in deciding whether to apply for a position in the first place. If a coach is a hard line, "my way or the highway" type and that is the kind of coach the school just ran out, a hard nosed coach would be well advised to keep looking for other jobs. If you have not heard it yet, you will hear it often that a coach has to "be themselves." If a coach is so anxious to get a job that they try to be someone they are not, they might get a job, but they will not keep that job for very long.

The knowledge of what kind of coach a school is looking for is exceedingly valuable when heading into an interview. Armed with this information, the prospective coach can answer questions in a manner that makes it clear to those doing the hiring that they have the temperament and philosophy the school seeks.

In the case of the second question, if the school has a history of success it is likely they will make the safe play and hire someone from within their school that is familiar with the traditions that made the program great or that they will hire a big name, established coach from another school. This does not mean an inexperienced coach cannot or should not apply. It merely means the inexperienced coach is likely a long shot and should prepare themselves as such.

The school a young or inexperienced coach is likely to get a chance at is the perennial bottom feeder. These schools tend to get far fewer applicants and they are in a much better position to take a chance on an unknown coach. These types of jobs are the best targets for young, aspiring head coaches.

The answer to the final question of those listed previously is one that impacts male and female coaches differently. With more and more former female athletes pursuing a career in coaching, it has become the definite preference of many schools around the country to try to hire a woman to guide their girls' sports whenever prudent or possible. If a coach does a little asking around and finds that hiring a woman is the preference of the school in question, it can either save the male coach the cost of a stamp or inform a female coach that she will have a much better shot at the position than she may have otherwise expected because the pool of potential applicants is essentially reduced by half or more.

Another dynamic that can impact a coach's application is whether the aspiring head coach currently works at the school they are applying at or if they are applying in a district they have never worked in.

Some key questions to consider in these situations include:

* If you are applying for a position at a school you already teach or coach at, who among the decision makers can you count on as an ally?
* What kind of support will you generate from current or former players, parents, and others associated with the program?
* If you apply and do not get the job, does it threaten your ability to continue coaching in that program?[1]
* If you are applying for a position at a place you don't currently work, do you have any connections to help get your foot in the door?
* Does the school have any strong internal candidates?
* Are there other factors such as the finances of the school that would limit their ability to hire someone from outside the district?
* Does the administration prefer to have their coaches be teachers in the building or have they demonstrated a willingness to hire people outside of their district or even people that are not teachers at all?

After considering the various key questions, if you decide to pursue the position you had better polish up your political skills because the second you submit your application and announce your candidacy, the campaign has begun.

If a coach is applying for a position and they are not currently

---

1 *This third question is an important consideration because when a new coach is hired and later learns that the 9th grade coach or the JV coach was among those that pursued the head position, it can lead the new coach to feel threatened right off the bat. They may elect to cut loose the members of the previous coaching staff and get a fresh start rather than deal with what could turn out to be an assistant coach that questions their every move. When a coach that has been involved at some level of the program applies for a head job they have to be prepared to cut ties with the program completely if they are not promoted to the position because a new head coach will often elect to hire an entirely new staff.*

a part of that school district, their campaign begins by demonstrating to the school just how serious they are about winning the job. That signal is sent with the materials the coach submits. Simply submitting a cover letter, resume, and letters of recommendation will rarely get you an interview. You need to do something to make yourself stand out from the other candidates, whether you are competing against dozens or just a few. Standing out begins with submitting a legitimate and comprehensive presentation.

In addition to all the usual application materials, I have always included an athletic philosophy statement, my parent policy (see appendix 1 and 2), and a 10 plus page outline detailing how I go about building and running a program from the elementary level through the varsity. The mere act of including these materials has earned me interviews at schools I had absolutely no connections in. When an athletic director sees the attention to detail and the organization and planning devoted to my mere application for the position, they tend to get a strong impression that I am more than equipped to handle the many administrative aspects of leading a program.

Once you have submitted your materials, the next thing to do is to try to find someone on the inside that will put in a good word for you. Go to the school district website and scour the names of teachers at the school or coaches in the district, searching for anyone you might know. Look for an old acquaintance from college, someone you played in a softball league with or against, essentially anyone that might be able to tap the athletic director on the shoulder and say "you should bring this person in for an interview." When it is ultra competitive for a position, having a person working for you on the inside is not just nice, it is necessary.

In the absence of an insider, a coach needs to initiate contact with the athletic director themselves. In the old days, that meant picking up the phone and making a call. Today, e-mail allows us to make a more subtle gesture that demonstrates our interest to an AD while gauging theirs. Below is an example of a short, informal e-mail that a coach could cast out just as a fisherman might cast a line.

Dear Mr. Johnson,

My name is Carl Pierson and I am writing to express my interest in the head football coaching position at Douglas High School.

I was immediately intrigued when I saw the position posted because I have always admired the strong tradition of academic and athletic excellence at your school.

While I have enjoyed my years as the head coach at Mitchell High School and I am proud of the success we have achieved, I have reached a point where I am seeking a new challenge and I would be excited for the opportunity to help build on the great tradition at Douglas High School.

I hope you received my application materials and I would welcome the opportunity to discuss with you in greater detail my ideas for building a championship caliber program.

Sincerely,
Carl Pierson

Some administrators will not respond at all to a query like this. They believe it falls outside the parameters of how a professional search should be conducted. Others will give you a nibble. They might respond that they have received your materials and that they will be setting up interviews later that week. Of course, they might leave out whether you will be one of those asked to interview. A select few athletic directors will bite hard on the line you cast and tell you they are anxious to sit down with you. Sometimes they share the bad but beneficial news that they already have a strong candidate they expect to hire. At any rate, it is good to cast a line if for no other reason than it gets your name in front of the administrator's eyes again and helps to emphasize your sincere interest in the position.

It's Who You Know, Not What You Know

Most of us have heard or even lived the famous line listed above. When it comes to securing a job in coaching, those words could not be more true. The longer I have coached, the more I have learned that in the coaching fraternity we develop relationships. Perhaps more accurately we cultivate connections. When a job opens up that we are interested in, we can call someone that knows someone and have them put in a good word for us. Without these connections getting a foot in the door for that first head coaching job can be a tough task.

Every head coaching position I have been offered was the direct result of an important connection I had developed. For my first head coaching job, the superintendent of the school district I was hired in had been the superintendent of my home town school district. I had been active in student government and served on a few committees with him while I was in high school.

When I went for my teaching interview at Red Wing High School (this superintendent's new district) before I was even asked a question the Principal took me on a tour of the school. I distinctly remember him saying "and this will be your classroom." I was a bit surprised by his phrasing and I thought perhaps the principal had made a Freudian slip, but when the Superintendent decided to sit in on the interview I was pretty confident the job was mine.

A year later, when I was engaged in a contest with the longtime JV coach for the head girls' basketball position I am confident the superintendent helped push the AD in my direction based on his past experiences with me and the reputation I had developed in my hometown.

My next head coaching job was similar in the sense that the job was mine before I even interviewed. The AD at Red Wing was friends with the AD at the school that was about to offer me a job. The two visited about the opening and about me. My current AD gave me a ringing endorsement. That was all the other AD needed to hear. I was the only person they "interviewed" for their coaching position, if one could even call it an interview.

In landing my most recent head coaching position, the connections were not as clear, but proved to be just as fortunate and fruitful. The bottom line is that connections in the coaching fraternity make all the difference. Without a connection, an aspiring head coach is usually left on the outside looking in.

It Never Hurts to Apply (Almost Never)

As we just covered, without a connection it can be very difficult to even get an interview, much less get hired for a head coaching job. Even with that said there is usually little to lose by applying for a job. Even if you do not get the job, the mere act of applying can be of some assistance.

It can help you because athletic directors that are looking for good head coaching candidates will often call other athletic directors that have recently hired a coach. The AD that is about to begin his search will ask the AD that recently hired if they encountered any strong candidates they could recommend. Even if you feel like you have no shot at getting a particular job or if you feel there is no point to going in for an interview because you have heard through the grapevine that another candidate is likely to get the job, you should always accept the interview and put your best foot forward. A great interview can land you a job elsewhere because of the collegiality that exists between athletic directors.

Perhaps the best lesson I can share of why it never hurts to apply comes from my own personal experience.

Four years into my head coaching career I had four losing seasons to my name. Granted, what we did at my first stop (Red Wing High School) was widely applauded because of how low the program had been, but still, to an AD on the outside looking in it would be hard to look at my track record and say "this is a guy we have to interview".

So when the head girls' basketball job at Champlin Park High School was posted, I first looked to see how good they had been in previous years. The team was 24 and 5 in the season that had just concluded and what is more, they graduated only one key player from that team. "What a fantastic job that would be!" was my first thought. "I don't have a snowball's chance in hell at getting it" was my second thought.

But my fiancé lived in a town just four miles away from the school and it would have been a perfect fit personally and professionally. I sent an e-mail to the athletic director just to feel things out. I expressed that I was interested in the job but that I did not see a corresponding teaching position. His reply was very professional, merely saying there were no teaching positions at that time but that they were willing to consider applicants that did not teach in the building. I went back and forth for the next two weeks on whether to even waste the paper to submit my application materials. Finally, the day before the application deadline, I decided to drop my materials in the mail.

You might imagine my surprise when I received a phone call about 10 days later asking if I would like to come in for an interview. I was happy to accept, but I knew I would have to keep the interview quiet as I was just finishing my first year in a new position at Chisago Lakes High School and I did not expect my administrators would look too kindly on their new coach shopping around for a job already.

I was quite concerned when a day before my interview I was stopped in the hall by the Chisago Lakes head boys basketball coach. He pulled me aside and said he had heard I was interviewing for a job in the "big time".[2] I was shocked and a little nervous that he had heard about the interview. I asked him how he found out.

He went on to explain that the coach that was on his way out at Champlin Park was an old buddy of his from their days as graduate assistants at North Dakota State. This guy had called our boys basketball coach to get some background on me. Fortunately, the boys coach had nothing but good things to say (which was very nice

---

2 *Champlin Park was the second largest school in Minnesota at the time with an enrollment of over 3,000 students in grades nine through twelve.*

considering we had just finished a miserable 8 and 19 season). After my conversation with our boys coach I was suddenly optimistic that I may indeed have a shot at the job because of a connection I did not even know I had.

My conversation with our boys coach compelled me to call the former Champlin Park head coach to learn more about the school, the program, and who would be interviewing me. During our conversation my hopes were diminished all over again when he explained that his top assistant coach from the previous season was one of the people being interviewed. This was revealed to me when I had asked him if he would put in a good word for me with the AD. He explained that he could not do that out of loyalty to his longtime friend and assistant coach.

So now, just a day before my interview, I was utterly convinced that I was just a "token" interview. Big school districts often have policies that they have to interview at least three people for any position. There was no reason for this program to make a major coaching change after experiencing the level of success they had the year before, especially when they had nearly their entire team back. It was clear to me that hiring a coach that brought continuity was a no brainer and I certainly did not blame them for going that route.

While I did not have any expectation of being offered the job, I agreed to interview and decided to go in and give my absolute best effort. I approached it with the attitude that I could still get the job. In truth, my motivation was that a good interview there may parlay itself into a good job elsewhere in their district.

I was the last of the three candidates interviewed. The AD, the recently resigned head boys coach (like the departing head girls coach, he too had resigned to take a job in administration), and a female science teacher that had coached at various levels of the program until recently, comprised the interview committee. I fielded the usual questions and gave my usual answers. One question I had not encountered previously asked for me to draw up what my team would do against a 3-2 zone. I was very excited to get into X's and O's because I had always considered that area one of my strengths.

Then came what I feel proved to be the key moment in the interview. It was not one that I had deliberately prepared for, but the most sincere answer I could give just happened to be the perfect response.

The athletic director explained that the expectations for the team amongst the players, parents, and school community were extremely high for the season to come. He said "in fact, I would suggest that if this team does not make it to the state tournament and win at least one game, the season will be considered a failure."

I showed no hesitation or trepidation. I immediately responded "that is <u>exactly</u> the kind of job I have been looking for!" I went on to explain that in the town where I grew up, winning was absolutely an expectation. If we lost a game it created a major controversy throughout the community for at least the next several days. My hometown considered it their natural born right to watch their team play in the state tournament every year. People would literally reserve all of the rooms at a major hotel a full year in advance in the city the state tournament was held. My hometown of Mitchell, South Dakota casually called the state tournament "the Mitchell Invitational" and anything short of a state title was cause for weeks of remorse in the community. I told the three person interview committee that I had desperately wanted to coach in a place that cares as much as the people in my hometown did. I told them that I wanted to coach somewhere that insisted on that same level of excellence I had always known. I explained that I would not feel pressured by the expectations, rather I would embrace them fully.

I walked out of the interview feeling good about my performance, but still certain I would be getting the "thank you for coming in but we have offered the position to someone else" call.

I nearly fell over when the next day I answered my cell phone and heard the Champlin Park AD offer me the job. I barely knew how to respond because I had not prepared myself for the possibility that I would actually get the offer.

I told him I would love to accept but there was no teaching job available and I could not commute 40 miles one way every day. He replied that Champlin Park was part of a huge school district with five high schools and six middle schools and that "something will open up to get you in the district." I decided this coaching job was just too good of an opportunity to pass up. Without the guarantee of a teaching job, I accepted the coaching position. It would be seven scary weeks waiting for a social studies job to open up, but eventually one did. We went 27 and 5 that season and took 4th place at the state tournament. Not bad for a job I almost didn't apply for and was sure I could never get!

Another example of how it never hurts to apply would be an opportunity I was presented as I finished my year as a graduate assistant coach at Northern State University. The head women's basketball job opened up at a small upper Midwest NCAA division

III school in late March. There were no high school teaching jobs advertised for me to pursue yet and though I had decided during my time as an assistant college coach that I much preferred the high school level, on a whim and for something to do, I applied for the D-III job.

I was brought in for an interview and got to experience all the bells and whistles that go with it. An interview for a college job is a completely different animal than an interview for a high school job. They are often an all day affair, meeting with professors, the university president, alumni, and the team. I thoroughly enjoyed the experience. I was a bit embarrassed when I was offered the job because I knew before I applied there was little to no chance I would accept. I asked some specifics about salary and other compensation and that helped solidify my decision. I turned down the position and I have never regretted it for one second. But the experience further demonstrates that you just never know what can happen when you throw your hat in the ring.

However, there are a couple of specific situations where it may not be wise to apply for a job. One such scenario is when you would find yourself competing against someone at your school that is well qualified and well liked. Notice I used the word "and" to join those two criteria. If a candidate fits just one of those descriptors, an aspiring coach may have a chance. But, if the competitor possesses both characteristics our aspiring coach is similar to the sacrificial lamb selected to run against an immensely popular ten term incumbent Congressman that has won every election by a wide margin. Running in that situation does next to nothing to further a person's political career and in many cases, it can prove to be the end of their career. The same is true of applying for a head coaching job at your current school when the odds are nearly insurmountable. It can make you appear rather clueless to those that do the hiring and to anyone in the public that learns of your application.

The other way applying for a long shot position can damage you is by taking you out of consideration to be on the newly hired head coach's staff. Not all, but many head coaches are leery of having a person that publicly coveted their job on their staff. The chances that such an assistant undermines them as a head coach are often too great. So by applying in a situation where you are more than a long shot, you not only look foolish and damage your chances of being hired for the head position down the road, you might also bring a pre-mature end to your coaching career altogether.

Another scenario where an aspiring coach should think long and hard about whether to apply or not is when they are new in a school district or on thin ice in a district, and they decide to apply for a position outside that district. A coach that elects to do this must be very discreet and they should be quite confident that they will be offered the new position they are applying for.

If administrators discover that their recent hire is already shopping around for a new job, that will not sit well with most athletic directors or principals. And if they had already been thinking about dropping the axe on you, the knowledge that you are applying for other jobs may give them that little extra push they needed to decide to let you go.

It can be awkward asking prospective employers not to contact your current employer in an effort to maintain discretion. When I was interviewed at Champlin Park at the end of the interview I asked that they not contact my current administration unless they were almost certain they wanted to offer me the job. It was awkward to ask, but at least my administrators would only know of my intention to leave when I was about to be offered the new position. It may not be the most comfortable way to handle things, but it is the way that protects you professionally.

The Interview

I have interviewed for head coaching positions over a dozen times. I have been offered the job in just under half of those interviews. I have been interviewed by committees, by a panel of parents, teachers, and administrators, and I have had an informal "interview" with an AD at a pizza parlor. Though every interview has its own dynamics there are some commonalities one can expect regardless of what type of coaching job they are campaigning for.

Before I share and then dissect the common interview questions, let me first tell you that I would strongly advise you to <u>never</u> formulate an answer for the sole purpose of telling the hiring committee what you think they want to hear. If you answer one way, then go out and do things differently, you have already damaged your relationship with some of your most important allies. The prudent move is to be completely honest with your answers in an interview. Show them who you really are. If they are not comfortable with your responses it would not have been a good place for you to coach anyway. If they respond positively to your replies they will like what they see when you begin to implement the ideas you articulated in the interview. In the case of a head coaching interview, as in most cases, honesty is the best policy.

Why did you get into coaching?

This seemingly easy question can be one that trips a coaching candidate up if they have not really reflected on it ahead of time. Just before Ted Kennedy announced his candidacy for President in 1980, in a nationally televised interview journalist Roger Mudd asked him "Why do you want to be President?" Kennedy's stumbling, rambling response to this exceedingly relevant and important question had a major impact in the minds of voters and Kennedy never completely recovered.

My response to this question (and most questions for that matter) is best given through a story. I tell the committee that I first started coaching during my junior year of high school. I coached 5th and 6th grade parks and recreation boys' basketball and I loved every second of it. I enjoyed designing practices, teaching skills and offenses, and motivating kids. I explain that I consider coaching an extension of my teaching and that I appreciate how we can learn life lessons in athletics that we could never convey within the confines of the classroom. Things like self discipline, teamwork, the value of competition, work ethic, and how to handle success and defeat are just some of the values I attempt to instill in the kids that I coach. Teaching those lessons compelled me into coaching as much or more than anything else.

I would be remiss if I did not also mention that I love the competition. I love the teaching aspect of coaching but I thrive on the competition as well. If you convey to a hiring committee that you got into coaching for the kids and for the love of competition, you can't go wrong.

How would you describe your coaching style?

This question is full of potential pitfalls. Perhaps more than any other question, it is one that can lead a coaching candidate to try to craft their reply to what they think the hiring committee wants to hear. If you attempt to tailor your response it is very important to know definitively what the hiring committee is looking for. This is often difficult to discern from the posted job description.

If a coach is going to try to score points with the hiring committee via their answer, they had better do some research. Ask some people around town or from the school what the previous coach was like and how well they were liked. You may find out that the previous coach was a hard nosed disciplinarian that got run out because the parents and players hated them. In that case, it is probably not helpful to tell the committee that you are a "Bobby Knight type." That could immediately end your candidacy. That being said, if you are a hard nosed kind of coach it would do you no good to suggest you are something otherwise. If you were to get the job then go out and be yourself, you would find everyone turning against you almost immediately anyway.

An excellent answer a coach could offer that would appeal to a hiring committee in nearly any situation is to express that you expect your teams and your players to be disciplined on the court and off, but that you have always been able to have those expectations of your players because your players know first and foremost that you care about them as people. When players know that their coach cares about them and has their best interest at heart, coaches can be demanding and players will always respond.

This is the type of answer a politician might offer to a tough question because it is crafted in such a way that it is appealing to the two main interest groups (those that want a hard nosed coach or those that want a softy) without saying anything that might alienate either side.

What has been your proudest moment as a coach?

This is a loaded question. If you tell a hiring committee "when we beat our arch rival" or "the night we won the conference title" you can appear to be focused on the wrong things. That may, in fact, have been your proudest moment, but if you only tell them about the state title you won or the time your athlete set a state record it can look rather shallow.

Try to tell them a story that tugs at the heart strings. Doing so demonstrates that you have the big picture in mind and that you are not just all about wins and losses. I respond to this question with a story about a time I convinced several of my players to do the right thing and confess to their parents and to our administration that they violated training rules.[3]

I have told that story during an interview several times and I have even gotten emotional at times when I have told it. Every time those feelings have been completely sincere. It remains my proudest moment as a coach to this day. But it is also the perfect answer to give in response to this kind of a question because it demonstrates that coaching is about helping kids be winners in life, not just in sports.

If your proudest moment is the time your team won the state title, then you can't just leave it at that. You have to explain that the way the kids overcame adversity or how they worked so hard to make it happen is what makes you so proud. That humanizes what could

---

3 *You can see the full story on page 237.*

otherwise be construed as a less than appealing answer.

How do you deal with disgruntled parents?

In my experience, coaches fall into one of two main categories when it comes to dealing with parents. You are either a coach that invites parents to ask questions and that has an "open door" policy or you are what I identify as a "call and click coach." If you are call and click, your attitude is in the event a parent calls to talk to you about playing time or why little Billy didn't get into the game last night, you will hang up on them. Some coaches have that approach and it works for them. Conveying that you are a call and click coach is rarely a good answer to give in an interview though. Administrators and hiring committees want to hear that their prospective coach will communicate with parents and that they are not adversarial. If the coach won't listen, that means the upset parents will be calling and bothering the athletic director or other administrators. No administrator wants that.

But again, you need to be honest about who you are and how you deal with things. If you are a call and click coach (there is a chapter later in the book that will encourage you to reconsider that approach as it tends to be toxic to your longevity) then you can convey your policy diplomatically by telling the hiring committee that you establish strong boundaries with parents and make it clear what subjects are acceptable to discuss and which are off limits. That answer sounds far more palatable to an administrator than someone saying "I don't talk about playing time, period."

The perfect answer for most hiring committees is the coach that says they welcome inquiries by parents and they are happy to explain why things are happening in the manner they are. This signals a few things to the committee. First, it demonstrates that you are comfortable with the confrontation that is so often a part of any head coaching position. Second, it communicates to the committee that you have the ability to put out your own fires and to deal with potentially difficult situations. Finally, it conveys that you are confident in what you are doing. You are not so insecure or defensive that you refuse to field parent phone calls or consider complaints. When you say that you welcome a parents' comments or concerns it implies a confidence that you are doing what is best for the player or best for the team and that is a huge plus to a hiring committee.

What is your policy on cutting players or promoting younger players to varsity?

This is another question where the answer can make or break you. If you have any knowledge of the previous coach and how things went that can provide major insight on how to best answer this. At two of the schools I have coached at the previous head coaches were notorious for promoting younger players and cutting juniors and seniors or leaving upperclassmen on the bench. As a result, the administration in both cases was looking for a coach that would demonstrate a loyalty and a commitment to the older kids.

That just happens to be my philosophy so my response resonated. I am a believer that a ninth or tenth grader should not be on a varsity team unless they can make a meaningful impact. I tell the committee that a younger player can't be as good as an older player, they have to be noticeably or demonstrably better. In general, this response is going to be what a hiring committee wants to hear nine times out of ten. They want to hire a coach that, among other things, is going to prevent a lot of headaches and problems for them. Moving up younger players creates <u>far</u> more problems and complaints than playing older kids and letting the younger kids develop at the lower levels.

If you have a different philosophy, it is best to share it. But don't be surprised when you find yourself as the runner up for head coaching jobs time and time again.

What kind of role would you play with the youth programs?

I have never heard of a hiring committee that was looking for a coach that would be "hands off" with youth programs. You need to explain that you recognize youth programs are the lifeblood of your high school program and as such, you intend to be visible and available to the youth teams and coaches.

Things I highlight when asked this question are that at every school I have been at, I hand out an extensive drill and playbook to all of our youth coaches. I do this to ensure they are teaching fundamentals the way we expect them to be performed at the varsity level, that they are incorporating the same terminology that we use at the varsity level, and that they begin to implement our offensive and defensive concepts. I point out that there is no substitute for a group of kids that have been running the same offense for six or seven years. When these players reach varsity the comfort level those years of continuity create for them is priceless. I emphasize my commitment and my ability to get all the coaches in our program on the same page.

Further, I tell the hiring committee that after distributing the youth coach's resource guide, I host a fall clinic for our youth coaches. I invite them into the gym to see the drills that are diagramed on the pages of their handbook come to life. I ask 10 or 12 of our varsity kids go through the important drills and plays on the court so the coaches are afforded a first hand look at what it is we emphasize and execute. There is also a chance for them to ask questions or get clarification on various concepts.

Your primary goal is to convince the hiring committee that you will be a visible presence at youth games and even practices. I still make it a point to go to at least one tournament for each of our youth traveling teams every winter. And when a coach has asked me to come to a practice to help them implement their full court press or get better at an aspect of the offense, I have always jumped at the chance.

If you convey a willingness to do all the things I have listed above and more, you can make yourself a top candidate based on your response to this question alone.

What is your philosophy about your athletes participating in other sports?

This is another question where I can assure you that the answer a hiring committee seeks is almost universally the same. Athletic directors and other administrators typically want to hear that a coach is going to encourage their athletes to participate in other sports and other school activities. Perhaps you want them playing your sport nearly year round, but to state that publicly or to share that with a hiring committee can become a major strike against you.

You can temper your comments by saying that if one of your athletes is clearly going to earn a college scholarship in your sport you can understand and would support their interest in specializing. You can also add that if a kid simply loves the sport and has no interest in any others you would not discourage them from participating in off-season leagues, etc. But you should always follow those words with "in most cases though, my first choice would be to see my athletes competing in multiple sports."

To further emphasize my feelings on this issue, I tell the hiring committee the story of my two basketball players that were also on our school's state championship golf team. I loved the fact they were golfers because I knew that when they were at the free throw line with 2 seconds left and our team down by one, they had been in that pressure packed position before. They had lined up a 15 foot putt with the state golf title at stake. The competitive atmosphere derived from that experience is not something that can be duplicated in an empty gym playing a meaningless spring league basketball game. Sharing a story like this with the committee only accentuates your sincerity when responding to this question.

What kind of a plan do you have for your athletes in the offseason?

The vast majority of committees want to hear that you are going to work like crazy in the off-season and be incredibly committed. Outline your expectations for strength training, conditioning, and what kind of camps or clinics you intend to offer to help your players improve their skills.

Open gyms, summer leagues, weekend tournaments, etc. should all be part of your answer. Make it clear that you are going to be as active and involved as your state's high school association rules allow you to be. Explain that all offseason activities will be designed to get an edge on your competition and they will be offered because you know they are necessary to build a championship caliber program.

What is your offensive/defensive philosophy?

Obviously this question would only come up for those that coach a team sport. I have my offensive and defensive philosophies in the form of handouts, available to leave with the committee should that question come up, (See appendix 3 and 4). You will notice the statements in the philosophies are not specific. They do not say "we are a 2-3 zone defensive team" or "we run the flex offense." Instead, they highlight key concepts and principles we teach and promote to our players.

I then share with the committee that while I have certain things I prefer to run (i.e. the motion offense and man to man full court defense) I recognize that as a high school coach we cannot recruit kids to fit our system the way a college coach can. Often, we need to adapt our system to fit the strengths of the kids we have. If the skill set of our current group of players suggests we should run a lot of zone on defense, I am not too proud or stubborn to do that. I make it clear to a hiring committee that we will implement the offenses and defenses that give us the best chance to win, period. I have found that to be a diplomatic and honest answer that is hard for a hiring committee to frown on.

What is your biggest weakness as a coach?

This can be a dangerous question, but it is one that could come up in as many as 50% of the interviews you experience. I believe it is best to have a ready or rehearsed answer to this question in an effort to prevent any major mis-steps.

Try to come up with something that is honest, but that could not be construed as too damaging or negative. If I were asked that question as a basketball coach I would probably say something like "I am too stubborn to call a timeout when the other team is going on a run. I hate to call timeout in that situation because it is like admitting that the other team is getting the better of us at that juncture of the game. I always instruct my coaching staff to remind me to take a timeout if the other team is going on a run because I despise doing it."

That is an honest answer and it speaks to a weakness, but it is certainly not a weakness that would eliminate anyone from consideration for a job. In fact, if said in the right manner it can even come across as a strength of sorts because, as I say above, I refuse to admit the other team has us on the run. That conveys confidence.

Try to devise an answer that is honest, that can't be damaging, and if you are really good, an answer that actually makes you appear stronger in the midst of describing a weakness.

How much experience do you have with fundraising?

Unfortunately this is becoming an increasingly common and important question in head coaching interviews. With school districts nationwide being asked to do more with less, athletic department budgets have been cut considerably. Coaches are expected to fundraise for even basic needs like balls, practice jerseys, and even game uniforms.

One thing I have been proud to announce in interviews is that my athletes have never had to sell cookies or candles or anything else for us to raise funds. We have raised all the money we need and then some through basketball related activities. We run a week long youth camp in the summer that raises a few thousand dollars for our program. We also run a 24 team summer league that generates several thousand more. Once every winter we host a youth tournament and ask our players to help out running scoreboards or working in the concession stand. That weekend has generated upwards of ten thousand dollars at times.

If you can tell the committee that you are able to fund your program without asking your athletes to sell anything, that is a huge plus. If you can tell them you can raise funds even as your athletes are getting better at their sport (i.e. playing in our summer league) you will have made an immensely positive impression.

Questions you need to ask at an interview

One thing I always remind myself before I go into an interview is that I am interviewing the school more than they are interviewing me. Rather than approach the interview nervous and hopeful they offer me the job, I put myself in a frame of mind where I think that I may not want the job and at all and that they are the one that have to impress me! This approach is a good way to calm the nerves, but it is also true. A wise coach will be evaluating their prospective bosses during an interview as much as the boss is evaluating the coach.

If the questions below do not come up during the course of your interview, you need to ask these questions before you leave so you can get in your car knowing whether or not this school is a place you really want to coach.

What does this school or athletic program hang its hat on?

To clarify, I might say "If you had a visitor from another state come in and ask what your school is proudest of or most well known for, what would the answer be?" The answers I have got to this question have varied but all have been interesting. Perhaps the best thing about asking this question is it is one that always impresses the committee as it demonstrates a genuine interest in the school community. It is also a question they usually have never been asked before.

What kind of off-season program do other sports offer?

This will give you a gauge into several things. You will learn if you are going to have to compete with the soccer or softball coaches for your athletes' time in the summer. You will discover if there is a local organization that tends to administer the off-season program like your local parks and recreation or community education department. It will also afford you the chance to share an idea with the hiring committee that may impress them even more.

When I was at Red Wing we had a summer program that I thought was nothing short of outstanding. Created by our head football coach, we had a gender neutral, non-sport specific "strength and agility camp" that met four days a week, all summer long. We had coaches from volleyball, hockey, track, basketball, tennis, football, etc. all in attendance and running stations. Kids were divided into groups and put through plyometric drills like box jumping, agility ladders, and harness running. The idea of the camp was to build better athletes to benefit all sports. By the time I left Red Wing, we routinely had 100 kids in attendance every morning. It was a wonderful program that built camaraderie and a sense of community between coaches and athletes. It worked well at a school with 1000 students in grades 9-12. I have found it would be nearly impossible to offer at my current school with 3000 students. But if you can suggest a program comparable to this, the committee will see that you are innovative and that you are not just interested in making your program better, but that you would like to see all of the athletic programs at the school succeed.

What is the most popular sport or team at the school amongst the student body and the community?

The committee's answer to this question will give you a great feel for where you would be in the athletic pecking order at your school. Usually the program that is most successful at the time will be their answer to the question, but at a school where several teams are successful, the answer can be particularly insightful.

Let's imagine they respond that football is the most popular sport in town. A good follow up question might be "how did it get to be that way?" or "what does the football coaching staff do that helps elevate the interest in the program amongst the students and the community?" Again, the answer will be good information for you, but merely asking the question can score nice points for you as well.

How do you, as an athletic director, deal with parent complaints about coaches?

As much as anything, the answer you get to this question will tell you whether you should accept the job or not. The trouble is, most athletic directors are going to give you the answer you want to hear. They are going to tell you that they support their coaches and that they have your back.

Things you should be looking for them to say include:

"I don't talk to parents unless they have gone up the chain of command. They need to talk to their kid first, then to the coach, and if they are still not satisfied then they can come to me. But if they haven't talked to the coach first, I will not talk to them."

Or

"I tell parents we will talk about anything but playing time. That is why we have a coach run the team and not a parent, to make those kinds of decisions. I trust that our coaches do what is in the best interest of our team. If you want to talk about other things I will listen, but I won't listen to complaints about playing time."

Or

"Any complaint a parent comes to me with is something I am going to eventually share with you. I don't believe in secrets. I'm going to keep you in the loop and keep you involved in everything. All I ask is that there are no surprises. I need communication from you. If something comes up give me a heads up so I can be prepared to defend you and have your back."

But more than their words, trust an athletic director's record. Do some research. Stop by a local coffee shop and ask about the local teams. Poke around and see if you can find out how many coaches have been let go in the last few years. Above all, make sure you know exactly why the position you are applying for is open. Did the previous coach leave on good terms, move on to a better job, get pushed out by parents, or get in trouble with the law? It is important to know what kind of a situation you would be walking into because taking a new job is a decision that alters the course of your life. You want to be totally certain you know what you are getting yourself into.

How much fundraising is our program expected to do?

If the committee doesn't bring up this topic during their time to ask questions, it is something you need to ask. When I completed my first year as head coach at Red Wing I was shocked to learn my school did not pay for team uniforms. The uniforms we had been wearing were already over five years old and it was clearly time for some new ones. I was told every team had to fundraise to buy new uniforms. That knowledge would not have led me to turn down the job, but it is always good to know what is expected of you before you accept a job.

What kind of access do players have to the weight room in and out of season?

I have encountered two schools where athletes do not have access to the weight room in the offseason. At one school, it is because the football team monopolizes the weight room and they just don't want any other athletes in there. At the other school, the athletic director actually bans athletes from the weight room when they are not in season. I know that one is hard to believe, but one of my fellow coaches shared her disgust with her athletic director's policy and I never forgot it.

These two situations are likely exceptions and not the rule, but it is important to know just how involved you can get your athletes with strength training. And again, merely asking the question demonstrates to those doing the hiring that you are motivated, that you have a plan, and that your players are going to work.

Who is the school's biggest rival and why?

This is kind of a creampuff question, but it usually brings a smile to the committee's faces and it can lead to some light hearted discussion. I would not consider this a mandatory question by any means, but it can be a fun one to ask. It can also be helpful for a new head coach to be equipped with this information when they meet with their team for the first time. You can score points with your players and parents right away if in your first meeting you announce that you're going to do X, Y, and Z and conclude your comments by saying "and we're going to beat the Cougars this year!"

If you could change anything about the school/athletic program, what would it be?

The answer to this question can shed light on some of the athletic department's blemishes. Typically in interviews, both sides try to present their best face. This question forces the committee to honestly assess the things their school or their athletic program need to improve. Just as you can expect a committee to ask what your greatest weakness is, you have the right to probe the same of your prospective employer.

It is impossible for me or anyone else to predict what you might get for an answer to this question, but again, I think merely asking the question demonstrates your intense interest in the school and the position. It also demonstrates that you are a thoughtful, analytical person keen on gathering as much information as you can.

The Underdog

In my first successful campaign to become a head coach I was an immense underdog on paper. I was 24, had taught in the school for just one year, and had spent only one season as the 9th grade girls' basketball coach. The only other candidate had taught in the district for 10 years, was a former women's college basketball player, and she had spent the past several years as the program's junior varsity coach. The fact that she was a woman applying for a head girls' basketball job was already enough to put me at an immediate and distinct disadvantage, but her resume was also very impressive. Despite these circumstances, my ascension to the head coaching position was a classic example of how one coach played the political game while the other was utterly oblivious to it.

The girls' basketball program in Red Wing had been in the cellar of their conference for the better part of a decade. Two years before I arrived at the school, things had bottomed out. None of the five teams at the high school level, (varsity, jv, sophomore, 9A, or 9B) had a single win all season. The five teams combined that year to finish 0 and 100! The program was in this position due to a confluence of factors but ultimately the most pressing problem facing the program was a complete absence of enthusiasm, and that was true from the top down.

The gentleman that was the head coach when I arrived was pushed into the position. He was appointed head coach because no one else in the district would accept the job and he had previous experience running a program at his prior school. He did an admirable job but he had little interest in working with the girls in the off-season. In short, he was not interested in investing the time, effort, and energy that would be required to resurrect the program.

During my first season on his staff, he promoted two of the top 9th graders to the JV team so it was widely assumed my 9th grade team would struggle. But I found my freshman team was left with a core of four good players and we put together a nice 14 and 8 season. The success our team had that winter made the 9th graders, and by default me, the celebrities of the program. We were all christened the great new hope for Red Wing girls' basketball. Of course, ambitious young coach that I was, I did little to deflect this praise and adulation.

That season, I did not spend much time with the varsity team at practice or at games due to time conflicts. In the end, that probably proved to be a benefit. I would sometimes sit on the varsity bench for home games, otherwise my interaction with the varsity players and coaching staff was quite limited. This proved helpful because I did not have the stench of "loser" on me that I otherwise may have had if I had integrated myself fully with the varsity team.

At the end of the season, the head coach approached me and said that he was going to resign and that the job was all mine if I wanted it. My level of excitement shot through the roof! Not only did I see the chance to take over a program as had been my aspiration, but I saw the chance to gain a reputation for "resurrecting" a program. Clearly my 9th grade team had some talent and it seemed there was a bit of talent mixed in with the grades above and below them. I had all of my application materials ready to submit before the head coach's resignation letter was able to settle on the athletic director's desk!

When the head coach first told me that he would be resigning, I asked him about his JV coach and her potential interest in the job. He said "She could have had the job three years ago and didn't want it then. I have no reason to believe she would want it now."

That was the consensus among the people in the program as well. The JV coach was well liked, friendly, personable, and positive, but no one expected that she had any designs on becoming the head coach. I am not sure what led her to have a change of heart but while parents and players were busy asking me if I would be the next head coach, the JV coach suddenly declared her intention to apply for the position.

Her announcement created something of a divide amongst the parents and players in the program. Naturally the 9th graders were squarely in my corner and I had some of the older players in my camp as well. But as one would expect, there were players and parents that felt a sense of loyalty to the woman that had just been their coach during the recently completed season.

To offer a political analogy, initially it looked as though I would be running unopposed for an open seat. However, the race became an extended and dramatic confrontation for the head coaching position of a program that no one had wanted to touch with a 10 foot pole just a few years before.

The head coach's resignation became official in April. I expected a new coach would be named by the end of May so the coach could lead the players through a summer program. Soon it became evident that the administration was going to drag things out so I decided to take a bold step. I had the benefit of being at the high school while my opponent was an elementary PE teacher. I recognized the opportunity this fact afforded me and I took full advantage of my easy access to the players.

I began to post sign-up sheets outside my classroom door for players to register for various summer tournaments and team camps. I also organized open gyms and communicated to players and parents when these opportunities would be available. While orchestrating these events, I knew I could be accused of being presumptuous so I was careful to maintain a politically correct stance in promoting all of the off-season activities. I stated that I would take on this role "until a new head coach is named." I added that the program could not afford another off-season of inactivity. Opposing teams were already well ahead of us in terms of skills and fundamentals.

This proved to be a monumentally important move. It improved my position in the minds of people in the program through the demonstration of my willingness to work with the kids in the off-

season. My initiative also highlighted the primary weakness of my
opponent. She had never been involved with the girls outside of the
season and she had showed little to no interest in spearheading any
off-season activities at present. Nearly all of the parents and players in
the program understood that to catch up with the competition the kids
would need to have a rigorous off-season program. While my opponent
had the edge in terms of her resume, my assertiveness was propelling
me into the lead in the court of public opinion and that would prove
pivotal.

My actions compelled several players and parents to lobby the
activities director on my behalf. Without asking anyone or campaigning
directly, I had created a group of vocal supporters. These players and
parents essentially became my campaign staff. They handled the day to
day politics while I was able to assume the politically correct position
of maintaining a low profile until the new coach was announced.

The two head coaching candidates were scheduled for interviews
during the final week of May, just before school got out. I expected
there would be an announcement about which of us would get the job
by the last day of school. But June came and went and there was still
no decision by our administration.

The administrators found themselves in a precarious position.
They likely knew I was the best person for the job given my work ethic
and enthusiasm, not to mention my growing support amongst players
and parents, but they also knew that if they were to hire me they
could conceivably have a lawsuit on their hands. With the JV coach's
far superior experience and background if I were hired instead of her
she could certainly claim discrimination and would have excellent
grounds to gain a nice financial settlement. So our administration
waited, probably hoping one of us would withdraw our names from
consideration. They had no such luck.

In late June I took a group of varsity players to a tournament at a
local college. They had a great time and we won a couple of games.
The on court success only helped to keep my momentum rolling. But
the key moments in the campaign did not transpire on the court or at
an open gym. The key moment, like so many in politics, took place in
the traditional "back room" situation.

As a young, single guy, I had nothing to do all summer but focus
on coaching. So in addition to my role administering the girls' summer
program, I was also serving as an assistant coach to the Red Wing VFW
baseball team. The athletic director's son played on the team and while
the AD and I had plenty of chances to visit during the summer, we

kept things very professional and kept any discussion about the girls' basketball position to a bare minimum. In fact, I don't know that we discussed it at all beyond a brief conversation in June when I asked him when he expected to make a decision. He quoted hall of fame football coach Bud Grant as saying "the best time to make a decision is when you absolutely have to." By this, he was trying to tell me there was no reason for him to rush into a hire. He added that he wanted to wait and see if any applicants from outside the district with previous head coaching experience would step forward. I responded that if the national coach of the year were to apply I could certainly understand his desire to explore that option.

By late July the VFW team was on an overnight trip for a weekend tournament. The team and the parents were staying in a hotel together. That evening the AD invited me to his room for a beer. We visited for a few minutes about the days' games, then the subject turned rather abruptly to basketball. I remember him broaching the subject by saying something like "you're a young guy and you'll have plenty of opportunities to become a head coach at our school." Immediately I knew what he was getting at and it did not sit well with me. He discussed how I would make a fine head baseball or head football coach. As he explained that the coaches in both of those sports were near retirement. I started stewing.

It was clear that he was trying to let me down easy. In a very friendly, fatherly, diplomatic way, he was telling me that he was going to hire the JV coach. I could feel the anger starting to brew inside of me. If I thought she would do a better job than me I would have been content to step aside and "wait my turn." After he was done with his monologue, I made a bold but calculated move.

"I appreciate your comments, but I can tell you I have no interest in being a head football or baseball coach. I intend to be a head basketball coach." He had been lying on the bed with his head propped up against the head board, sipping his beer, but upon my saying that he sat up. I continued "and while Jennifer (the JV coach) is a good person, she is not the person this program needs right now. More than anything this program needs someone that will be committed to getting the kids to work in the offseason. We are light years behind the other teams in our conference and that is not going to change with her as the head coach. If you want a program that continues to finish last in the league every year, that is what you are going to get with her. If you want a winner I am the person that is going to get you there."

I could tell he was uncomfortable and he didn't really know what to say in response. But I had planted the seed that I needed to plant so I bailed him out by breaking the silence and saying "but I know you can't really discuss these things with me right now, so let's put the business aside." I asked him about a story I had heard about him back when he was the head hockey coach. We shared coaching stories for the next hour or so and called it a night.

I left his room still angry that it seemed I would not be named the head coach, but at least I had made my point. I had also played a card I would not have been able to play in a more formal setting. I was able to make a negative attack on my opponent and it was one she would not be able to defend against. I also knew the AD was a competitive man by nature. I had appealed to his competitive side and his ego. He wanted all of his sports programs to be at the top of the conference. Flat out saying that I was the only way he was going to get there was a key thing to do. But it still wasn't enough to get me over the top.

When the calendar turned to August I was getting frustrated. There were no more teaching positions to be filled. I could not understand why administration continued to drag out the decision. I decided to take another calculated risk.

I had seen a posting for a head boys' basketball position at a small town in South Dakota. I had no connections to this school and had no reason to believe I would be interviewed, much less hired, but the administrators at Red Wing did not know those things.

I knew the principal wanted to keep me as a teacher and that I was valuable to the school because I coached three sports in addition to serving as the student council advisor. I understood that in August the last thing any administrator wants to do is have to search for a new teacher and a person to replace all of those extra-curricular positions.

I went in to meet with the head principal and told him about "an opportunity" that had been brought to my attention back in South Dakota. I explained that while my overwhelming first choice was to continue teaching and coaching at Red Wing, if I was not going to be the head coach I didn't think I could pass up the opportunity in South Dakota. I was bluffing. I wasn't going anywhere. But they didn't know that.

About an hour after meeting with the principal, I was in the weight room at the high school when the AD came downstairs and offered me the head coaching position I had coveted for months. My bluff had paid off and forced their hand.

While I never asked, I have no doubt it was my conversation with the AD in the hotel room that turned the tide. After that encounter I suspect the primary reason for the delay in hiring me was a result of the administration and the superintendent covering all their bases in the event there would be a discrimination lawsuit brought against them. My refusal to concede the job and my beers with the AD got the wheels turning in my favor, but they likely had some legal factors to consider before making a formal offer.

This story is instructive to an aspiring head coach in many ways. Lessons to be learned include:

1. Be proactive. Fill the leadership vacuum that is created in the absence of a head coach. Take the lead on organizing the team.
2. When the parents and players are already advocating for you, step back and let them do it. You don't need to toot your own horn if they are willing to do it for you.
3. If you feel things slipping away, you can either withdraw your name from consideration or you have to up the ante and play hardball.
4. Use any and all leverage you have if you feel it necessary to win the position. But be prepared for them to call your bluff and live with the consequences.

Know Your Strengths

Young coaches tend to be particularly ambitious when it comes to pursuing a head coaching position, but it is important to be able to accurately identify your strengths and accept a position that you can ultimately be successful in. By successful, I don't necessarily mean win a state championship. Often, the first head coaching opportunity one will get will be with a program that has been struggling. But consider what the program needs and what the administration's expectations will be, then determine whether you are equipped to meet those needs and expectations. If you aren't, passing on that particular head coaching job could actually save your career.

When I was 23 and still finishing up the spring semester of my final year of college, I went for my first job interview at a very small school in Southern South Dakota. The town had a population of about 500 and the school may have had 80 kids in Kindergarten through twelfth grade. The school had a great track record of athletic excellence though, winning numerous state championships in a variety of sports. They were best known for their success on the basketball court. I applied for a social studies opening as well as their head boys basketball position. When I was called for an interview I was very excited as I thought I could be walking into a powerhouse program with a great tradition. I also recognized that if I were to get the job it would serve as an excellent spring board to get me where I really wanted to be; head coach at a large school.

The interview was going well when suddenly the line of questioning took an unusual turn. Questions veered away from teaching and basketball and turned to football. I had been an assistant varsity football coach at Aberdeen Central High School during my final few years of college so I thought that perhaps they were interested in having me help out as an assistant. In a small school I recognized that even a head coach would be expected to help out coaching other sports.

I left the interview optimistic that I would be offered the job. When my phone rang the next day I was surprised at what the principal had to say.

"We would like you to be a social studies teacher and our head football coach" he said. I remember being confused and at a momentary loss for words. I responded that I appreciated the offer, but that I thought I had interviewed for the head boys basketball position. He said they brought me in with that intention but during their interviews they found someone they thought would be a better fit. They would love to have me as their head football coach though and as an assistant to the new boys basketball coach.

I knew who I was and what I was best at. I was not a great football coach. In football, I was more of a rah-rah motivator type. I had never developed an interest in the X's and O's of football. While I was honored to be offered a head coaching position I also knew that by accepting it I would be putting myself in a bad position.

I told the principal "I really appreciate the offer, but I don't feel that having me as your head football coach would be in the best interest of anyone involved. I like coaching football, but I am not cut out to be a head football coach." He spent a moment or two trying to twist my arm but shortly after that the conversation ended. In my first job interview I was offered a head coaching job, just not the right job. Little did I know it would be almost four months before I would be offered another job. I spent much of those four months fretting that I had made the wrong choice. I shouldn't have been so picky. I began telling myself that I could have learned to become a great head football coach. But the benefit of hindsight has convinced me that I made the right choice.

Know your strengths and acknowledge your weaknesses before you begin your campaign for a head coaching position. It will help you avoid making poor choices that could bring a premature end to what could otherwise be an outstanding career.

Never Use Negative Campaigning Publicly

Here is one realm where electoral politics departs from coaching politics. In campaigns for elective office, it has been demonstrated time and again that the side that runs the first negative ad against their opponent wins the election a great percentage of the time. While voters insist in poll after poll that they despise negative ads, the evidence indicates that negative ads are extremely effective. The only poll that really matters in politics is the one pitting the respective candidates against each other. In that most meaningful of polls, the candidate that launches the first negative attack wins frequently.

The reason negative ads work in elective politics is two fold: First, running a negative ad allows you to paint whatever picture of your opponent you would like. You can label them in a manner that leads the public to see them through the lens that you have chosen. This is a very difficult thing for the person that has been labeled to overcome. Second, throwing the first "punch" puts your opponent on the defensive. Rather than talking about their ideas and their agenda they are constantly responding to your charges. By running the first negative ad you get to frame the debate.

But in the politics of coaching, when pursuing a head position there is enormous risk in being publicly negative toward your opponents. This is particularly true when you are campaigning for a position within the school you are already a part of.

If you publicly announce reasons why your opponent is not as qualified as you, this will mobilize your opponent's supporters. When they may have otherwise been content to let the search process play out, by attacking their preferred candidate these people now feel compelled to voice their support for your opponent in a more public way. This can directly damage or undermine your chances.

There is another great danger in going negative. By calling out the shortcomings of your competition you indirectly invite their supporters (and others) to publicly criticize your own weaknesses. When pursuing a head coaching position it is never a good thing to invite others to publicly criticize your flaws. By taking the high road and refraining from public critique of your opponent you also protect yourself from public criticism.

Some reading this might say, "I can afford to go negative because there is nothing anyone could criticize about me." First I would caution that this is a dangerously arrogant attitude to have, but for the sake of argument, let us assume you are right. If you, in fact, have a pristine reputation and none of the parties involved could find a flaw with your candidacy that is all the more reason to avoid going negative. Let the public do the dirty work for you. If your opponents have obvious flaws others will identify them. Stay above the fray.

There is a time and a place to convey why you feel you are more qualified than the other candidates, but talking about these matters with players, other teaching staff, or parents is a recipe for trouble. A situation like the one I described in "The Underdog" where you have a private audience with an influential person is a prime example of a situation where launching a negative attack could be effective. But even then, going negative should only be used as a last resort as the risks for backlash are still significant.

Running a Campaign Against an Incumbent

Historically incumbents (officials currently serving in elected office) have an enormous advantage when running for re-election. It is a rare occasion when one loses an election. Just as in electoral politics, unseating a sitting head coach is a remarkably difficult thing to do. In the world of coaching politics I would also caution it is potentially career suicide.

An ambitious, aspiring head coach may consider an incumbent head coach weakened or wounded because they just experienced a losing season or perhaps some parents have been complaining publicly. Do not be fooled. Every head coach has their allies. They would not have been put into their current position if they didn't. What you need to ascertain is precisely who is on the current head coach's side.

If it is administration, then running a campaign against the sitting head coach would be folly. If administration is luke warm to the coach, but a moderately sized group of respected current and former players and parents are ardent supporters of them, again you would be foolish to try to manufacture a mutiny.

The only scenario where it might make sense to attempt a coup against a current head coach is if you know the administration and a strong majority of the players and parents are considering the coach's ouster. But again, in that situation you would be better served to stay out of the muck and let the situation play out. It may require being patient for another year or so, but let the parents and players in the program do the dirty work for you. If you get involved in trying to take down the current coach people will recognize your personal ambitions and it usually does nothing to enhance your reputation.

Of course there are exceptions to every rule.

A friend of mine shared a story with me several years ago about a coach that was forced out after just a year on the job. That aspect of the story was not all that memorable. The manner in which this new coach had their career come to an end is what burned the story into my brain.

A young man had been hired to lead a girls' soccer program that was on the rise. The program had been in the basement of their conference for many years, but in the years prior to him taking the helm the program had a re-birth of sorts. The number of kids participating was growing. The commitment of the players in the offseason was much improved. The benefits of both of these trends were beginning to show up on the field. To top it off, there was a very talented group of sophomores that had experienced a great deal of success all through their youth years. Expectations were growing and enthusiasm was high. After a few years of steady improvement and with this group of talented sophomores on board, the people in the program, at the school, and in the community were convinced that the varsity team would have its first winning season in several years.

A slow start to the season immediately damaged the credibility of the new coach, but that was not what ultimately led to his demise. It was a crafty, calculating, politically astute opponent that would end his remarkably brief head coaching career.

The head boys' soccer coach at the same school had been very successful for several years. His teams had been to several state tournaments, but for a year or two he had made it known that he may be interested in moving over to coach girls' soccer in the not too distant future. He shared with some key community members that he would love to coach his two young daughters and their friends someday. But someday needed to come sooner rather than later for this gentleman because he was also wise enough to know the talent pipeline he had enjoyed with the boys program was about to run dry.

Though he had publicly announced his intentions to switch to the girls' program, the boys' coach did not apply for the girls' job when it opened up. As a result, a young man with no prior head coaching experience was hired. To some in the community it was confusing that the boys coach didn't apply because it seemed like the ideal time for him to make the switch. What likely made the timing less than ideal was the fact that this boys coach had a very talented team returning. He recognized he would have one more chance to win a state title with the boys so he didn't apply for the girls' position. It turned out the coach was right. He made it to the state tournament with his boys' team that year, losing in the semi-final game.

Even as he was in the midst of this stellar season with his boys' team, this coach continued working towards his goal of becoming the girls coach. While piling up wins with the boys, the coach started a subtle campaign to unseat the girls' coach. This would allow him to slide over to that program just in time to continue his string of success. During the season, when the girls' soccer team would lose a game, the boys' coach would visit quietly with some of the girls on the team and say things like "I can't believe you guys didn't use a stop and go play on that corner kick." Or he might tell a player that wasn't entirely happy with her playing time that "you should be playing a lot more."

When a coach that has been to the state tournament several times says things like that, kids listen. Then those kids go home to their parents and tell them what the successful boys' soccer coach said. This compels parents to call the AD and suggest that the girls' coach he just hired does not know what he is doing. And so, in a very subtle, quiet way, the boys' soccer coach was waging a campaign to undermine the current girls' coach and pave a path for him to take over the program.

Sure enough, at the end of the season the young man that had just completed his first season as head coach was told by the AD that he may want to consider resigning. He shared with him that it seemed there was a large group of players and parents that did not believe he was the right person to lead the program and that he did not make wise decisions during games.

What the AD should have shared is that this poor young man never had a chance. He had his legs cut out from under him before he had an opportunity to win the players and parents over. The shadow campaign waged by the boys' coach had done exactly what it was intended to do.

This young man knew that if he stayed on as coach it would be nearly impossible for him to convince the players to try to execute the things he taught them because they didn't believe in him. He knew that with every loss the parents would pile on and say that the girls would have won if only he had done this or that differently. He recognized that when you lose the faith and confidence of your constituency, it is difficult, if not impossible, to win it back. So he resigned. His final state tournament run with the boys' program behind him, the boys' soccer coach promptly applied and was given the head girls' job. To the surprise of only a few, in his first season the girls' team went on to have a great year, even making it to the girls' state tournament.

There is no doubt the boys' coach was a good coach, but there is also no doubt he was exceedingly opportunistic. He recognized the time was right for a coup. He had a young head coach with no track record as his target and he was campaigning with a remarkable resumé on his side. He also understood that if he did not make his move at that moment the maturation of the talent on the current girls' team might be such that they would have become successful even without him, and that would have made it very difficult for him ever to make the move to the girls' program.

At the time of the coup, the coach's daughters were in elementary school. They were years away from being varsity players. But if he didn't make his move soon, he also knew that he would be saddled with a suddenly poor boys' soccer program. If the girls were winning while his team fell from grace, he likely recognized that <u>he</u> could end up being the coach on the hot seat.

While some might look at this story and say the boys' coach in this case was unscrupulous and corrupt, it is important not to lose sight of the political brilliance he demonstrated. This was a very clever move and it is an example of someone that intrinsically understands the politics of coaching. Few would condone this coaches actions, but the fact of the matter is his actions were simultaneously an act of career advancement (taking the reigns of an up and coming program) and self preservation (escaping a soon to be sinking ship). Condemn him if you must, but there is no question this scenario is extremely instructive and the politics were absolutely well executed.

TWO
***

Director of Communications

"In real estate they say it's all about location, location, location. In coaching I can tell you
it's entirely about communication, communication, communication."
– Anonymous

The State of the Program Speech

Every coach of every sport should have a mandatory pre-season
meeting for all players and parents. This meeting allows you to
manage some menial tasks like collecting contact information
and getting other paperwork turned in but it also allows you
to get policies in your parents' hands and set the tone for the
season. To insure attendance and to communicate the importance of
the pre-season meeting, I would recommend not allowing players
to try out if they were not in attendance with at least one parent/
guardian.

Our coaching staff hands out contact forms to every parent on
their way into the meeting along with our "Important Policies and
Procedures" form, our "Rebel Way," another handout explaining tryout
policies and procedures, and season long practice and game schedules.
(see appendix 1 and 2)

The meeting always begins with an introduction of the coaches.
Then I go through common expectations like being on time for
practice, no cell phone conversations on the bus to a road game, etc.
Next I will typically cover some concepts about tryouts to make sure
that everyone is on the same page and knows exactly what to expect.
Finally I will tailor my comments to whatever our team might need
that particular season. One year I had a group of young, ambitious
players that all thought they were going to get athletic scholarships.
Perhaps more accurately, their parents expected that their kids would
get athletic scholarships. I knew this could be a problem as the season
progressed as "so and so is shooting too much and I never get the
ball" kind of issues were likely to crop up. I attempted to diffuse this
with a 15 minutes presentation detailing how difficult it is to earn an

athletic scholarship. I also pointed out several players from our area who earned scholarships that did not have prodigious scoring averages. I proved that the thing these scholarship players shared in common was that they played on winning teams. I presented this to educate the parents as much as the players. With one exception, our players and parents seemed to understand the message and our group played very unselfishly that season.

During a different pre-season, I used the meeting to show the players and parents the massive numbers we had trying out and to soften the blow a bit by explaining it meant that "good players were going to get cut" because we had such a glut of talent. In short, make it a point to include a segment of your pre-season meeting that addresses an issue you anticipate being a potential problem so you can cut it off ahead of time.

To close the meeting I typically talk about my expectations for our on court performance in the season to come. Doing this is important because it allows the coach to control expectations to a degree. I always try to be honest. When we have had a team that was going to be good, I would say so, but I would also point out some of the challenges in our schedule to make it clear that there was always the potential for things to take a bad turn.

In years when we did not have much talent, I would "sugar coat" it some. Obviously the head coach cannot announce the season will be awful before it begins so I would instead say "All the pre-season publications expect us to be at or near the bottom of the league." That way it isn't me saying we will be awful, but the parents became aware that people outside of our program do not expect much from our team. This technique helps to inhibit the ability of those parents that would attempt to rally the others against me when we go on a five game losing streak. Our 9th and 10th grade parents will recall the meeting and respond "They weren't supposed to be that good this year anyway. That isn't the coach's fault." When a coach sets realistic expectations, it helps protect them from potentially meddling parents.

Almost as important as beginning the season with a meeting is closing the season with a gathering of some sort. Of course, it is hard to make this mandatory, but nearly everyone shows up when you have an awards night. Most teams already have an end of season evening of some sort, but if the coach is not using it as a spring board into the offseason and the season to come they are not maximizing the night's potential. I always refer to my comments at the end of the season as my "state of the program" speech, obviously patterning it after the

President's annual state of the union speech. I highlight what we accomplished in the season that just ended but I also look ahead to the things we expect to do in the future. I attempt to set the tone for the off-season and outline specifics about what we will need to work on in preparation for the next season. By the end of the evening I have dozens of players already signed up for off-season activities. I always endeavor to send them out more focused on the season to come than on the season that just concluded.

As a head coach, you have to be a strong communicator and you cannot shy away from public speaking. If you do, you will miss out on several wonderful opportunities to influence your parents and players in a way that encourages them to buy into your plan and your vision for the program.

Individual Player Meetings

These are also a must for every coach in every sport. I recognize it is considerably more challenging in track or football because of the large number of athletes involved, but I know coaches in both sports that find a way to get it done. These individual meetings can help you avoid problems and they can help you improve as a coach.

I would recommend having a round of individual meetings as tryouts are winding down or at the start of your season. During the early season meetings there is usually not much give and take. It should involve the coach explaining to the player what role they anticipate them filling on the team. One of the quickest ways to derail a team is to have a handful of players that do not understand their role or what is expected of them. Just as bad is having players that know their role but do not accept it. The start of season meeting allows a coach to head off both potential problems.

I hold my meetings just before announcing the team. I do this so I can visit with those kids that I know may not necessarily embrace the role I assign to them. After I inform them of their role, I tell them that if they don't like it, it would be best for all involved for them to go find another activity to take part in. Very few kids choose this option. I then follow up with a statement explaining that we would love to have them play that specific role. They are our first choice to play that role. But I also make it clear that if we get a month or two into the season and suddenly they are complaining and causing drama they will be off the team. In nearly 20 years as a coach I have only had one player that claimed they could accept their role go back on their word. Players can appreciate and accept a coach being upfront and honest with them.

Kids can play a role, even one they do not prefer, if they know what is expected of them and they know they are valued in that role.

When conducting individual meetings it has become critically important that the head coach not be alone in the room with the player when the conversation happens. We live in an increasingly litigious society and coaches need to protect themselves from players or parents that may see an opportunity to take the coach down. If you have another adult present to corroborate everything that is said and the tone with which it is said, you can effectively eliminate potentially damaging accusations.

A few years ago we had been conducting a team fundraiser and we had excellent participation amongst all groups except our sophomore team. I was not all that worked up about it though until one of my varsity players said that a sophomore player was yelling at her about how the sophomores were not going to help with the fundraiser because all the money was going to be spent on the varsity players. That is when I got fired up. It was an incredibly selfish perspective for the sophomores to adopt and it simply was not true.

I knew I would not have a chance between the sophomore game and the varsity game to talk to the sophomores as a team so I asked their coach if I could have a word with them at half time of their game. I talked to the team for about 90 seconds, explaining my level of disappointment with the attitude apparently adopted by many of them. I said that while fundraising is not mandatory, everyone else in the program was doing their part and I thought it was fair for the players to ask themselves, "what have I done to help this program?" I concluded my remarks by saying that whoever was barking at one of our varsity players a few minutes ago went after the wrong person and that anyone that has a problem with the way we do things had better come to me because I make the decisions. During this visit I spoke in a stern tone but I never raised my voice. Fortunately the sophomore coach was a few feet away from me as I talked to the team because the next day a sophomore mother e-mailed our AD and our principal demanding that I apologize to her daughter and the entire team for "screaming at them and insisting that they must participate in a fundraiser."

This was a parent that already had it in for me. The mother demanded a meeting with our administration. If I did not have another adult to corroborate what was said and the tone with which it was said, this mother would have wounded me just as she had intended to. Instead she was the one that was left looking like a fool. The sophomore coach (and a couple of sophomore players) corroborated my version of the story. This is just one example of why a coach must always have another adult present at any meeting involving a player.

End of season individual meetings should be conducted in an entirely different manner than the early season meeting. Players should do most of the talking and coaches should primarily listen and learn. Below are questions I always ask my players at our end of season meetings.

Tell me about the season.

Obviously not a question, this is deliberately open ended so they can touch on whatever aspects of the season jump out at them. I also think it is interesting to see if they talk about their individual performance/experience or if they speak from a team point of view.

What was the highlight of the season for you or your favorite moment?

This is where I typically get an individual accomplishment mentioned but they may also reference the day our team went bowling or something to that effect.

What was the low point of the season for you?

I love this question because this is where I really begin to learn things as a coach. Players tend to reveal more about themselves and the things about the season they did not enjoy in response to this question. As coaches, I think one of our goals should be to do our best to help every kid have a good experience when they participate in our sport. A players' answer to this question often reveals how successful we were in helping make that happen.

What are some things I do as a coach that you like, that you think I should continue to do?

What are some things I do as a coach that you don't like, that you would recommend I try to change or improve on?

These two questions combine to be the most instructive and constructive for you as a coach. You have to be open to criticism and you have to be willing to really listen if you ask these questions. You can become a better coach if you listen and take to heart the responses offered.

We always close our end of season individual meetings the same way. If the player is a senior, I tell them what I appreciated about them during their career and we discuss their future plans. I also make it known that I will always be happy to serve as a reference or author a letter of recommendation should they need one. I think it is important players know that they don't stop being important to you just because they are out of eligibility.

To our returning players I will ask what role they hope to fill on the team in the season to come and what they think they need to improve on to make that happen. I will offer my thoughts on what I feel they need to focus on and where I see them fitting in and then we close with a quick look ahead to offseason opportunities.

Again, these meetings are important for a multitude of reasons, but from a political perspective they help you to take the pulse of the players on your team and they help you learn your strengths and weaknesses in the eyes of your constituents.

Open Door vs. Call and Click Policy

In my deliberations with coaches about their policy toward phone calls or contacts from parents I have found that coaches tend to gravitate toward one end or the other of a philosophical spectrum. Some coaches elect to be very open and approachable. They encourage players or parents with concerns to contact them directly. I will refer to this as the "open door" approach.

The other group of coaches lay out very clear guidelines and restrictions about how they are to be contacted or if they are to be contacted at all. Because I have heard many of these coaches suggest that if a parent calls them about playing time they simply hang up, I will term this the "call and click" philosophy.

Both philosophies have their appeal. Some would suggest that you need to adopt the philosophy that best fits your personality. However, I would argue that to merely adopt a policy based on what makes you most comfortable would be ignoring the political ramifications that come about through the adoption of your preferred policy.

Those that advocate for "call and click" would say that it lays out very clear ground rules for parents. Some of the rules I have heard include:

*   No phone calls or contact for 24 hours after a game.
*   Any mention of playing time ends the discussion.
*   Any mention of a player other than your child ends the discussion.

*   If the parent says "Billy doesn't know I'm calling and please
     don't tell him I called" I am definitely going to tell Billy

And the one I consider most gutsy of all...

*   Any correspondence complaining about your son/daughters
     playing time will be posted in the team locker room for the
     entire team to see.

The idea behind all of these ground rules is to convey to the
parents that the coach runs the show. I think the coaches that embrace
these philosophies do so with the genuine belief that taking a hard
line will reduce the number of angry phone calls they have to field.
That may be true. But these angry parents are not simply going to
stew in their own juices if they aren't able to vent their frustrations to
the coach. They will complain to other parents in the program about
"that damn coach." As a result, they will begin to pollute the other
parents with their frustration. They are also far more likely to take their
complaints to administrators, and administrators can get tired of taking
calls complaining about a coach. What "call and click" coaches may not
realize is that by failing to offer an adequate means of communication
they are not making life easier for themselves. Instead they are sowing
the seeds of their own demise.

To help illustrate the point, allow me to share a story.

When I was 20 years old, I was coaching a baseball team of 14
and 15 year old kids. We had a very good team anchored by one stud
pitcher named Chad. Chad was absolutely our ace, but in an unusual
twist for such an accomplished young pitcher, pitching was all he
excelled at. He was a marginal position player, below average hitter,
and he pulled the proverbial plow on the base paths. But Chad had a
rocket fastball and he had pin point control. As a result, by late in the
season he was 8 and 0 with a miniscule ERA leading us to first place in
our league. It was a night late in the season, in the heat of a conference
title race, where I learned precisely why coaches should always
encourage open communication with parents.

We were playing a non-conference double header. We had a big
double header against the second place team in our conference the
next day. With that in mind Chad was going to be an observer for the
evening so we could save him to pitch as we attempted to clinch the
league crown. The first game of the double header was pedestrian
enough. As I recall we won by a comfortable margin. In the second
game, we found ourselves down 10-2 in the fifth inning. I went out to
the mound to make my third pitching change of the game. I brought in
one of my worst kids just to eat up the last couple innings and save our

best arms for the next day. Then in the 6th inning (of a 7 inning game) we rallied. Several big hits and a couple of errors by our opponents started a big comeback. Miraculously we found ourselves up 12-10 needing three outs to secure an astounding come from behind win.

When we took the lead, I told Chad to go warm up. He had a very durable arm and I knew I could use him to close out the game and still count on him to throw a gem the next day. As expected, he mowed the opposing team down in the seventh inning to earn a save. It was a fun win for our team and after the high fives were finished, Chad's dad came down to greet me from the stands.

What came out of his mouth next absolutely stunned me. He said "Why do you hate my son?"

I didn't even know how to respond at first but the dad's demeanor made it evident he was not kidding around. My head was racing. How could this man possibly think I hate his son?

"Hate your son?" I said with a quizzical look. "Are you kidding me? I love your son. He's my best pitcher! What could possibly ever make you think I hate him?"

The dad responded "Some of the parents told me you yelled at him in practice the other day, and then he doesn't pitch at all tonight until the last inning! In the 2nd game you put two other pitchers in before him! Clearly, you have something against him!"

Again, I was shocked, but now my shock was at the father's lack of baseball acumen. After hearing his explanation of how he had arrived at this wildly erroneous theory I knew how I could remedy the situation.

I explained to the father that yes, I barked at his son at practice the other day because he had his ass hanging out of his pants in the middle of a drill, trying to get a chuckle out of his teammates. "I told Chad there is a time and place for that, but we have a big week coming up and we need to get to work. I told him and the team that they can save their screwing around until after practice."

And to the point about Chad not pitching, this was simply a lack of understanding about baseball and I was happy to educate the father. I explained that Chad was without question our best pitcher and for that reason we deliberately held him out of the games that evening so he would be able to pitch in the big games the next day and win us the league championship. I then explained why he didn't pitch until the final inning that evening, pointing out that there was no point in wasting Chad when we were already down eight runs. I added that when we came back to take the lead and were in position to win, "look who we put on the mound!"

The dad was quite agreeable to everything I had outlined and he apologized for his accusation. I was happy to forgive him as I recognized it was nothing more than a father going off of what he had heard other parents saying and having a limited knowledge of baseball. Those two facts combined to create a heated moment where a father felt compelled to protect his son. I can respect that. But from that point forward I learned that I needed to convey to parents that if they ever have a question about why I am doing something, they need to come to me with it.

The way I phrase it in our pre-season meetings is something like this:

"If you ever have a question about how or why we are doing something, rather than pontificating with other parents in the stands, please come to me. I am happy to tell you. I have a very good reason for everything I do. I do not make 'gut decisions'. Everything I do is for a reason and again, I will happily explain it to you. You may not like the explanation or the reason but you will get an answer and you will know exactly why. When you ask other parents in the stands you get speculation and conjecture. The fact of the matter is those other people you ask are only guessing. They don't know! If you really want to know, come directly to me because I am the only one that really knows the answer."

I have often incorporated the story of Chad and his dad during this passage to parents in an effort to demonstrate what can happen when speculation runs amok. It also illustrates how a simple question and conversation can diffuse what could otherwise evolve into an explosive situation.

The whole situation is a bit reminiscent of the Cuban Missile Crisis and the events that followed. A lack of communication, information, and then rampant speculation was a major reason our world reached the precipice of nuclear annihilation. It was only when Kennedy and Kruschev started communicating through teletype that the situation began to be resolved. In the weeks immediately following the crisis both sides agreed that a 24 hour phone line needed to be created so the two nations could communicate more immediately and directly. It is not a coincidence that we have never again had such a dangerous nuclear showdown with the Russians.

A coach that refuses to communicate with the players and parents in their program is creating the breeding ground for a coup. Rather than confronting problems when they are minor, by putting up barriers

the coach forces players and parents to look elsewhere for answers or
to go to others to vent their frustrations. When they do that, the parents'
questions and their contempt only fester. The disgruntled members
of your program are like a disease. Sometimes you have enough anti-
bodies (players and parents on your side) to fight off the disease or
to keep it at bay for a time. But as soon as you get weak (have a
losing season for example) the disease starts to spread and before
you know it, the coach is consumed by it and it leads to their demise.
Communication is the only real inoculation from such diseases.

As I tell parents, they may not always like the answer they get
but they will always get an honest answer to their question. While
sometimes people don't like the answer, on some level, they almost
always respect it. Perhaps more important, they tend not to run their
mouth to many other people after venting their thoughts and feelings to
me. It unburdens them to a degree.

That is not to say I have ever allowed a parent to yell at me or
be belligerent in any way. I would discontinue our discussion until
they decided they could conduct themselves in a civil manner. But in
40 seasons of coaching three sports it has never come to that volcanic
confrontation because of another thing I share with all parents and the
start of each season.

I tell them that if or when they contact me about their son/
daughter I will never begrudge them for doing that, for they are
defending their child. I recognize that if they did not defend their child
they would be delinquent in their duties as a parent. I will always
respect their position as a parent.

Then I point out that as a head coach I do not have the luxury of
looking out for just one kid. I have the responsibility of doing what is
best for our entire team. While I always endeavor to do what is best
for each individual player on my team, I can never do something for
an individual if it comes at the expense of the rest of the team. I will
always respect a parent's responsibility to defend their child. All I ask
is they reciprocate and respect my responsibility and my position as
a coach. While I have not had more than 15 or 20 disgruntled parent
phone calls, e-mails, or meetings in my 40 seasons of coaching, I can
tell you that every encounter was remarkably amicable due in large
part to my approach. It is an approach built on a foundation of mutual
respect.

In my efforts to foster open and direct communication I will
concede there are some limits to what we can say as coaches. As much
as I can, I work to restrict the conversation to the player in question

and leave other names out of it. At times though, when it is the parent's child and one other kid in direct competition for playing time, everyone knows precisely who the parties involved are so I do not pretend to attempt to protect anyone's anonymity. I just tell it like it is.

I find no joy in telling a player they are not as good as they think they are. I do my best to stay positive and avoid hurting a player's feelings. But when those meetings have occurred where a parent and player want to know why "so and so" is playing and they aren't, I will not tip toe around the answer. My belief is if a player or parent asks a question, they had better be prepared for the answer. Sometimes people just don't get it and they need to hear the unvarnished truth.

I will always remember the '08-'09 basketball season because of the carnage that took place the week of tryouts. We had 14 players returning from an 18 win team. We carry 18 players on our combined JV and varsity roster. It would be reasonable to expect that most of the girls trying out would look at the number of returners, realize there are really only four spots open, then look around at the crowd and come to the conclusion that they don't have what it takes to make it.

In November of 2008, no girls reached that conclusion. We had a total of 30 juniors and seniors tryout for 18 spots, 14 of which were essentially spoken for. Add a handful of talented sophomores and freshman to the total number trying out and we had 40 players competing for four spots. 30 of these players had no business being in the gym for tryouts. How they could possibly believe they had what it took to play on a team that would spend a good portion of the season ranked in the top 10 in the state was beyond me. But they all believed they were going to make it and when the cuts came down, the level of shock and devastation exhibited by the players was like nothing I had ever encountered as a coach. The epitome of these cuts was a junior I will call Erica.

Erica was one of the least athletic players I had ever seen. She was a 5'8" post player that played limited minutes on a brutal 5 and 18 sophomore team the year before. In fact, the soon-to-be junior class was so bad that the summer before the tryouts they competed in a summer tournament where they got crushed by two soon-to-be 9th grade teams and a team full of girls that were going into 8th grade! And when I say crushed I mean by 20 plus points.

By the time they played in that summer tourney it was clear most of these kids had not yet figured out there was no chance of them making our varsity team so I decided their performance against these much younger teams gave me an opportunity to paint a specific picture for them. I called the juniors in after the third game and with one of my assistants by my side I said "Ladies, what just happened today should never happen. A group of girls that are about to be juniors should never lose to 8th and 9th graders. By this age you should all be faster, stronger, and more skilled than them. But what happened today? You lost by 20 and in one game you even lost by 30!"

Then I turned to my assistant. "Coach V, how many airballs do we see in a week of practice and games at the varsity level?"

"Maybe one or two?" he replied.

"Ladies, how many airballs did you shoot per game today? At least 9 or 10! The bottom line is this; you are going to have to improve enormously between now and November to have any chance of making the varsity team."

Apparently all of them felt I was talking to the other girls on the team and not them. Or they felt they had done just as I said and improved dramatically in the three months leading up to tryouts because every single one of them was there in November. I had done everything but tell them "You are too shitty to play basketball at the varsity level!" I went to the absolute limits of political correctness in my diatribe to them and they still did not get it.

So when they were cut and they wanted to know why, I had to tell them. My first choice was always to be diplomatic and hopefully keep the kids dignity intact. When Erica learned she was cut she approached me in tears and said "I just don't understand. Why?" I explained that she was rather undersized for a post. Her response was "I can move to a guard." Bear in mind, this girl could not dribble from one end of the court to the other or make a shot from one foot away much less from the perimeter. But instead of giving her the unvarnished truth I tried to be kind yet again and say that we had a number of skilled guards that had played the position for years and she was just too far behind them.

When her father sent me an e-mail conveying his rage and shock at her failure to make the team I resisted the temptation to show him the numbers from tryouts. We tested all players in vertical jump, bench press, and a timed sprint course. His daughter was dead last out of the 55 players that tried out in two of the three categories and second to last in the other category. Had he pursued it any further I would have been forced to bring up those damaging facts. A coach should do their best to convey a players' faults without being heartless, but if diplomacy does not work you have to take off the gloves.

To recap, invite and encourage communication. While it may

make you uncomfortable to be questioned or confronted about certain things, encouraging communication avoids larger problems down the road. Always be as direct and diplomatic as possible. When it becomes obvious that your attempts at courtesy and politeness are muffling the message, just be brutally honest.

The Magic of E-mail

The advent of e-mail has been both a blessing and a curse to coaches. We will begin by examining the positive attributes of e-mail.

When I started coaching in the early 1990's, a rainout or a schedule change meant triggering a phone tree or me personally calling 20 different phone numbers. It would take 45 minutes to an hour to leave messages or explain to each parent the details of the change. E-mail allows coaches to convey this kind of information remarkably quickly and efficiently. What used to take an hour can now be done in two minutes.

But if we only use e-mail for situations such as the one just described, we are not deriving the maximum possible benefit from it. The players and parents in our program get an e-mail from me almost weekly during the season and at least bi-weekly during much of the offseason. This constant flow of communication from a coach serves several purposes.

1. It keeps the people in your program in the loop on various upcoming events.
2. It keeps your sport and your program in the forefront of the players and parents' minds. This helps you when you are competing for the attention of a multi-sport athlete.
3. It provides a quick and easy way for parents to correspond with you.
4. It can end up being a way for you to receive positive feedback and even better, positive feedback you have in writing that you can file away for a time when it might be needed.
5. It allows a coach to carefully consider everything they intend to convey before doing so. Face to face meetings or phone conversations can be damaging when something is said in the heat of the moment.
6. It allows a coach to set the agenda and dictate the discussion in their program through something of an electronic "bully pulpit."

No parent or player in my program can ever offer as an excuse for missing an event "I didn't know about it." With my constant flow of e-mails, everyone is always aware of upcoming events and the expectations that go with them. This flow of information is particularly helpful when it comes to player/parent planning for the offseason. Coaches are often competing for their athletes' time and attention in the summer months. With this in mind, I e-mail our summer schedule to players and parents by early March, well ahead of the summer softball or soccer schedules. This has helped increase our offseason participation and has led players to pick basketball over other summer activities because they were informed early and mom or dad wrote it right onto the calendar. If you give players a handout to take home there is a 50/50 chance the handout ever makes it there. E-mail allows coaches a direct pipeline to the parents so everything a coach wants to communicate is sure to reach home.

Offering these semi-frequent e-mails also provides an easy avenue for parents to communicate with you. They can quickly respond with a question and you can give them a nice, direct answer without having to deal with all the uncomfortable small talk that accompanies the average phone call. Further, I have found parents are far more likely to offer an encouraging word or a thank you to coaches via e-mail rather than in person. That is how coaches should want it! You can print and save those e-mails to offer as evidence of the positive perspective the parents in your program have for you should it ever be called into question by a combative parent or by administration.

I have a tendency to be very blunt and direct in my face to face meetings. I am also somewhat emotional and even volatile at times. E-mail allows me the chance to measure my words when responding to a parent or dealing with an emotionally charged issue. In a face to face meeting where everything demands an immediate response, coaches can sometimes speak from the heart or the gut and they end up saying things that come back to haunt them. Addressing a politically pervasive issue via e-mail helps coaches keep their emotions in check and it allows them to address issues in a more thoughtful, deliberate, and diplomatic way.

Finally, and perhaps most importantly, the mass e-mail can allow a coach to "frame the debate" to use modern political parlance. If there is a program wide issue that needs to be addressed you have the ability to do so with the push of a button rather than trying to gather everyone together in a room at the same time for a big meeting.

One example of a time I found this particularly effective was in the fall of '09. After a run of three very good seasons, graduation had left us with a group of players that were not particularly talented but even worse, they were not particularly motivated. They tended to play basketball for the social aspect of it rather than a love of competition or the love of the game.

We had scheduled a handful of open gyms in the fall prior to the open of practice. While I typically look over the fall sports schedule to make sure our open gym does not conflict with soccer, swimming, or other female fall sports, I failed to consider the chance there may be a football game on a night other than a Friday. Late in the season our football team had a Wednesday road game scheduled. In a gesture that would shed all kinds of light on what kind of a season we were about to have, one of my captains asked if we could cancel open gym that night so they could go to the football game. Of course I said no.

I explained that it is an open gym. No one <u>has</u> to come. I was going to make sure it was open for those that would rather improve at basketball than travel to watch a football game.

I was very interested to see what the turnout would be. In the three previous open gyms that fall we had around 40 players show up. I knew the numbers would be down on this night but it turned out to be a very cold, unpleasant evening. Freezing rain was falling by about 6pm and the forecast was for things to get worse, not better. I thought the terrible weather would mean we would have more girls opt for the relative comfort of a gym rather than icy metal bleachers at a football field in freezing rain with a bitterly cold wind.

Nine players showed up for open gym that night. I was not happy. I was stunned so many players would choose to freeze at a football game rather than join us in the gym. But I also knew this bunch was not as devoted to basketball as previous teams so I was not going to say a word. I was disappointed with the turnout but I was content to leave it alone.

The next day I visited with one of our football coaches and asked him how the crowd was at the game. He told me it was horrible. He said there might have been 30 students at the game. I sarcastically asked him if all 30 were girls' basketball players and he laughed out loud and said "Not a chance." While I was already disappointed, this information got me flat out fired up. If my players were not at the football game then why in the heck were they not in the gym!?!

I decided to express my displeasure with the group at large by sending out an e-mail. In our state, there is pretty strict enforcement of a rule called "undue influence." Coaches cannot exert any influence or in any way insist that a kid attend an offseason opportunity. I knew I would have to choose my words carefully (see the chapter on political correctness for instructions on how to master this skill) but I had to get my point across.

First, I had to find some ulterior motive for the e-mail that did not pertain to the massive absence from open gym. Then I had to concoct a sentence or two that would convey my disgust for the lack of commitment without violating the state's rule. Below is the text of my e-mail:

> *Rebel Players and Parents,*
> *I'll begin by saying thank you to the nine high school players that showed up for open gym last night. It's always interesting to see who shows up on a night that there is a football game. I really appreciate those nine players that made the decision to join us in the gym.*
> *We have three more open gym opportunities before tryouts begin, with one of the three being tonight.*
> *Now, on to other business...*
> *Next Tuesday, Oct. 27th we are hosting our annual Youth Clinic from 6:30-8pm in the CPHS Fieldhouse. We are hoping we can get 6 to 10 players in grades 10 through 12 to volunteer to help run the kids through drills at the clinic. Also, at 8pm we run a brief clinic for CPTBA and CDAA coaches where we do some on court demonstrations of drills that they can use with their teams. So if you volunteer, please plan on sticking around until about 8:45pm.*
> *If you are able or willing to help out, please respond to this e-mail.*
> *Finally, this reminder to players: all interested in trying out need to attend a meeting during advisement next Wednesday, Oct. 28th in the South Lecture Hall (next to the activities office). Have your advisor sign your travel card and come directly to the lecture hall. The meeting will take the remainder of advisement. As always, please contact me with any questions.*
> *Just 25 days until tryouts!*

This e-mail elicited an angry response from two parents. One parent was the father of our captain that wanted to lead players to the football game rather than lead them to the gym. Apparently he did just as I intended for all to do and he read between the lines of my message. He pointed out that open gym is not mandatory to which I agreed. He suggested that my e-mail was taking a "swipe" at his daughter and those that did not attend. Below is most of my reply.

*It is precisely because it's not mandatory to attend, and because
so many people that had been attending previously elected to
be somewhere else that night that I thought those few kids in
attendance deserved a tip of the hat.*
*I've been thinking about your suggestion that I took a "swipe" at
kids. While I will continue to respect your right to believe that,
I found myself wondering if something like recognizing the
National Honor Society kids in our team program is somehow a
slap in the face to the kids on our team that aren't in NHS?*
*I think it is wise to recognize people that do extraordinary things.
That is not a condemnation of those that don't.*
At least that is my perspective.
But I've had my say on this issue, as have you.
Thank you for communicating with me directly on this matter.

What you have just read above is politics personified. I conveyed
the message I intended while insulating myself from parental attacks.
Rather than lashing out at those that took the night off, I instead
applauded those in attendance. Players and parents were able to
interpret my gesture just as I hoped they would. My e-mail got the
message across. Ten hours after I sent the e-mail we had another open
gym and over 40 players attended. We also had more than enough
volunteers for our youth clinic as some kids came to the realization that
with tryouts just 25 days away it is probably not the best time to piss
off the head coach!

At the end of that season I used the e-mail bully pulpit again to
confront what was proving to be a growing collection of grumbles.
It started with a small group of conspiratorial parents but during my
end of season individual player meetings I learned the movement was
gaining members. Rather than make our end of season awards night
a forum for me to squash this attempt at rebellion I let a mass e-mail
stage the debate on my terms.

Before I share the story, let me first emphasize the absolute
importance of using the blind carbon copy option when sending a mass
e-mail. The primary reason for this is that some people are protective of
their e-mail address and they do not want others to have it. There have
been instances where a parent that is a salesperson will "reply all" to a
mass e-mail sent by a coach, seizing on a chance to make a sales pitch.
Obviously this is frowned on. But the other reason to send a team
wide e-mail using the "bcc" button is to prevent a massive retaliatory
response.

By sending a well crafted e-mail a coach might convey a message in precisely the way they intended but an antagonistic parent has the ability to steal the bully pulpit away with a click of "reply all." Every mass e-mail you send must have the e-mail addresses hidden and you must make certain that the receivers do <u>not</u> have the ability to reply all. This protects your parents but in particular it protects you!

Now back to my story. The "8th grader issue" is how our coaching staff referred to this conspiracy kerfuffle. At previous schools I had coached at, we sometimes had younger players stop by practice to see what a varsity practice was all about. Sometimes they would come once every week or two and we would include them in a shooting drill or some other non-contact situation. When I had a couple of 8th graders that would soon be a part of our Champlin Park program approach me and ask if they could come to practice from time to time, as I had always done previously, I said yes.

In mid January one 8th grader showed up and joined us for a couple of drills. A few days later another showed up and did the same. Shortly after these two occasions an assistant coach approached me at practice and shared that a parent had come to him with a concern and they insisted on remaining anonymous. This parent wanted the assistant to convey to me that they did not feel the 8th graders should be at our practices because they were "stealing reps" from the older players. I thought such a suggestion was petty and ridiculous, but considering our players have to pay an activity fee of over 300 dollars to play I thought I would honor the anonymous parent's suggestion and modify the 8th graders participation.

That night in the weight room I announced to the team that we may have some younger players showing up from time to time. We typically had a side court open during the final 30 minutes of practice while we scrimmaged. I explained the 8th graders would be welcome to do some shooting on that court. I also mentioned that we may also incorporate them in a drill from time to time if a varsity player was absent that day. As I said to the players, "if a younger player asks me if they can come in the gym and get better, as a head coach I would be stupid or crazy to tell them no."

I thought that approach would diffuse any possible complaints. I could not have been more wrong.

I didn't hear much about the issue again until our end of season individual player meetings. During these meetings, several players shared that they did not feel the 8th graders belonged at our practice, even though they attended for only 30 or 40 minutes and even though they rarely participated in drills. I was flabbergasted by this. As I probed the topic with the players further I discovered two things.

First, I found that much of this sentiment was driven by parents, and in particular the "anonymous" parent that had lacked the courage to contact me directly with their issue. Second, I found that part of the reason this complaint took hold is because the 8th graders that were coming to our practices were very talented players. Some of our older players felt threatened by them.

I was getting more and more angry with each suggestion that the 8th graders might end up taking an older players' "spot." I recognized the situation for what it was; a group of jealous players and parents that saw this thing they thought they were entitled to, a spot on varsity, threatened by some young, talented, hard working players.

When I did a little asking around and discovered the 8th graders had become a big issue not just with our JV or Varsity players and parents, but also with our sophomore and 9th grade players and parents, I knew that I could not afford to leave the subject alone. I crafted what amounted to three full pages of a mass e-mail and sent it out to everyone in our program, 8th graders included. In the letter I shared my shock that anyone would object to the presence of younger players, especially when they took no time or opportunity away from current players. I explained that the occasional attendance of younger players had happened at every other school I had coached at and not only had it been accepted, it was actually universally applauded. It was applauded because as the head coach I was not just focused on the varsity team, but I was also demonstrating an interest in the development of players at all levels of our program. The other thing I shared was that in the three previous years I had coached at Champlin Park, I appreciated the fact that when people had a problem or a question about how we did things they had the courtesy and the courage to approach me. I followed that by conveying in no uncertain terms that anyone that tries to further their own personal agenda by anonymous messages and by talking to anyone and everyone other than me would no longer be a part of the program.

This mass e-mail elicited two negative replies. A dozen parents responded that they agreed with my perspective and that they supported the policy. At the very least those that didn't respond learned that if they have a problem they better have the guts to talk to me about it because if they don't, I will call them out in a very public way.

E-mail can be a magical, wonderful thing for coaches. It can save you time. It can deliver your message to the masses fast and in just the way you want it conveyed. It can be read by your parents when it is convenient for them. It really is a magnificent tool that has helped make a head coach's job easier. Of course, there is a dark side to e-mail as well.

The Danger of E-mail

While the advent of e-mail has done much to improve our condition as coaches, it is the proverbial two edged sword. In addition to all the ways it has enhanced our ablity to communicate with players and parents in a convenient, quick, and efficient manner, it can also be used as a weapon against us like nothing that has ever existed before.

One of the great dangers of e-mail is that whatever coaches communicate is documented in writing. If a coach e-mails something that is inappropriate or that violates a rule or a policy there is no "he said, she said." There can be no suggestion that someone is mis-representing what was said or taking it out of context. The coach's words are in black and white for all to see and review. That is why, more than ever before, coaches must choose their words very carefully.

If I think there is even a chance that what I would like to communicate could be misconstrued, I pick up the phone or ask for a face to face meeting. I am always careful not to make promises in writing that could be thrown back in my face in the way a contract could be. While I certainly advocate for the frequent use of e-mail, I would be remiss if I did not also emphasize the importance of prudence. Before a coach clicks send they should read through their message a second time and attempt to read it from the perspective of a person that may be looking for ammunition against them. Have you written anything that could eventually be held or turned against you? If the answer is no, click send. If there is even the slightest possibility your words could somehow be used to hurt you at a point in the future you had better find a different way to word your message. Or you could pick up the phone. A phone call doesn't leave a written record of what was said.

The other danger that e-mail has created is it has provided an outlet for parents to air their complaints in an incredibly easy way to a large number of administrators in very rapid fashion. Not that long ago a disgruntled parent used to have to take the time to make several copies of an angry letter, address the separate envelopes, etc. Now with a simple click they can include the AD, principal, superintendent, and the entire school board when they send their vitriolic, hate filled letter. This is a harsh new reality I got familiar with fast during my first year at Champlin Park.

During a mid-season road contest I called a late game timeout. During the timeout I became particularly animated. I was yelling loudly and demonstrably at my team for getting beat to loose balls in what was a very important game. Our point guard was having an unusually poor game and during the time out I saw her with her head down, pouting. I poked her in the shoulder and shouted "and you need to quit hanging your head. Get out their and be aggressive!"

Our bench was directly in front of the opposing fans. I already had the fans attention with my shouting, but when I poked my point guard in the shoulder the fans reacted as though I had just landed a right uppercut to her jaw. I typically don't hear or notice the fans during a game, but their reaction in this case was impossible for me to ignore.

We rallied and won the game. Afterwards I thought nothing of what had transpired. As a football coach I had grabbed plenty of players' facemasks, so a poke in the shoulder to get the attention of a player that was hanging their head was of no consequence in my mind. The next morning I learned at least a dozen fans from the opposing team did not agree. Our AD forwarded me a few select e-mails that had come to him, our principal, and our superintendent that morning. One was characterizing me as a "monster that should never be allowed to work with kids ever again," another called me "satan's spawn," and a third suggested I yelled at each player and got in their face as though I was a drill sergeant and that I was "a notch below Hitler" in their estimation.

I was a first year teacher and coach in the district, and while on some level I was amused by the obviously exaggerated characterizations I also knew that if my administrators, who were still getting to know me, were to accept any of these comments as the truth I was toast. Unbeknownst to me, later that day our prinicipal called in a handful of my players to interview them about me and my coaching style. She asked the players if they ever felt physically threatened or in danger around me. Fortunately for me, the girls laughed at the question. I had a short meeting with the AD, the girl I poked in the shoulder and her parents, and after two days of e-mails and accusations we moved on. But this incident taught me a powerful lesson about how quickly an e-mail can do a great deal of damage to us as coaches.

Of course, it is even more damning when it is a parent or parents in your program that author an e-mail to detail what they perceive to be your many faults. At my current school, my administrators have become a bit numb to most of the e-mail complaints they now receive about coaches because they recognize that people tend to be far more inflammatory in an e-mail than they would ever be in a face to face conversation. They also understand the ease with which people can send a note and that people have a tendency to do it in the "heat of the moment" just as they arrive home from the game where little Billy only got to play two minutes.

Regardless of your administrator's attitude, e-mail's ability to do damage to us is undeniable. That is why it is all the more important that coaches encourage, if not implore, their parents to take up any and all issues with them, the coach, first. If the parents skip past you and go up the chain of command you can quickly lose control of the situation. Every new head coach or every coach that gets new administrators would be wise to discuss with them in advance how they typically respond to angry parent e-mails. Make sure your administration is aware that you would like to be in the loop on any negative e-mails that come their way. Good administrators will comply with this request. While reading scathing e-mails about ourselves can be uncomfortable, it is always best to know what kind of accusations are being made so you can do some damage control if necessary.

The Power of Old Fashioned Mail

As coaches, we have usually evolved and matured to a point where we no longer consider picking up the mail a fun thing. We are used to junk mail and bills and we sometimes forget the excitement we used to have as a kid when something in that big pile of mail to mom and dad was actually for us! Some of the best and most frequent positive feedback I have received as a coach has been in response to the personal notes I mail to the players in our program.

You cannot begin to imagine the mileage you can get from taking three minutes to write a note to a 7th grader that pitched a shutout to propel his team to first place in a weekend tournament. A simple gesture like that can create a loyalty from that player and their parents that lasts for years. And it costs so little in terms of time and money for a coach to do. I cannot recommend strongly enough that coaches take the time to write these notes, at least on occasion.

When I was young and single I would mail a note to every kid that participated in our summer program. It was not a generic note either, but a personal note that would comment on something specific I thought they got better at and something I would like to see them continue to work on and improve. I would write 40 or 50 of these notes in the couple of weeks between the end of the summer season and the start of the school year. Players got the strong impression that

I cared about them and that they were important enough for me to take the time to write this note. They also got the simple, unabashed excitement of getting that rare treat of something in the mail.

When the player is happy, the parents are happy. I would have parents tell me as their daughter was graduating that "she still has that note you sent her congratulating her on her game winning free throws when she was in ninth grade." A few minutes of our time can make a difference that lasts a lifetime to a kid. And the political mileage we can accrue from this simple gesture is nothing short of priceless.

Controlling the Message

By now every high school sports team should have, and quite frankly needs, its own website. I am no tech genius and I am as frugal as they come, but even our team has a website. There are free websites that cater to sports teams and they are designed to be dummy proof. I use a site that allows me to simply click on our team colors then it sets the background accordingly. When I want to input information I just type it in, click save, and it instantly appears on our website. There are simply no excuses for any varsity level sports program to lack its own website. And I would argue being without one is something a coach just cannot afford to do.

But it is not enough just to have your own website. You have to have direct control of the content. The value of the website is that it allows you to control the message being sent out to others about your team. Never turn the duty of updating or running a website over to a parent. That is recipe for disaster. The coach needs to be the one setting the tone for their program. To use a political term, the coach should be "spinning" the outcome of games. When you put a parent in charge of recapping a game, no matter how loyal you might consider them, you are still allowing the opinions and perspective of a parent to be projected to all the people in your program (and beyond). By delegating the duty of updating the website, you abandon a golden opportunity to impact the way your program is perceived. You also unwittingly provide a parent with the rope required to hang you.

I likely use our website to a far greater extent than many coaches do or would. After each game, I take about 15 minutes and type out a brief game story including stats and key information. Because I am the one that enters the information, I have the ability to highlight certain facts and statistics. This means I can impact how parents and the public perceive our win or our loss. Allow me to offer a few examples.

If we played a team that we should have crushed but players and parents in our program seem completely content with merely winning, I can start the game story by saying "The Rebels managed to overcome a lethargic start and less than inspired play to top a depleted Pirates team by just eight points on Friday night." Through that sentence I have sent a message to all the players and parents that visited the website that our performance was not adequate and that no one should be satisfied with the win.

Now let's imagine our team is merely average in its ability. Our parents and players think we are a lot better than we are and they are unhappy after squeaking out a three point win on the road. The game story might include a line like "though they don't have a stellar win/loss record, our opponents entered Friday night's game winning four of their last five and they are widely considered the most improved team in their section." With that line, I am spinning the facts in my favor. Sure we barely won, but I elected to highlight a fact that made it appear the win was far better than perhaps some initially felt as they left the game.

"Our Rebels faced their fourth straight ranked opponent on Tuesday, falling 65-49 to the Panthers."

What kind of spin am I implementing here? Clearly I am trying to buffer any disappointment our players and parents might feel and qwell any brewing rebellion by shifting the focus from our four losses in a row, instead highlighting the fact that we just played our fourth consecutive highly ranked opponent and we are in the midst of a brutal part of our schedule. No matter how effective your spin is, the unreasonable parents will still think that with any kind of coaching their band of misfits should have won all four games. A coach will never win over those parents no matter what their website says. You are not fighting to win over the nutjobs, but a wise choice of words can help a coach keep the support of the rationale parents.

Former Yankee manager Casey Stengal was once asked what he would describe as the key to successful managing. Stengal responded the key was "to keep the five players that hate you away from the four that haven't made up their mind yet." By crafting the message on your website to your benefit you are fighting to keep the five parents that hate you from influencing and corrupting the fifteen that haven't made up their minds yet.

I will offer one final example for you to consider in my push to emphasize the importance and value of a website. When we lose a game, I tend to highlight a crucial statistic to help parents do what they always want to do after a loss, and that is assign blame. I might offer something like "while both teams shot 40% from the floor, the Rebels were just 8 for 22 at the free throw line while the Cardinals were a blistering 17 for 20." Now those parents that want to assign blame can do it and they can assign it where it belongs. Yes, there will still be parents that say I am a terrible free throw coach, but the reasonable ones will recognize it was the players that failed to deliver, not the coach.

For those that have a website or will soon create one, if you do not update your website at least weekly, it will not serve the purpose you want as no one will ever visit it. You need to update the content on a semi-frequent basis to keep people coming. Also, I would advise against showering individual attention on players through your website. Avoid complimenting individual players in your game summary as much as you possibly can.

Historically, I have not listed players by name in my post game reports unless they did something exceptional like hit a game winning shot. I try to keep the focus on the team to avoid the famous "playing favorites" label parents love to slap on a coach. If I do list individuals by name it is to highlight a specific statistical category I would like to see all of our players put an emphasis on. I might say "Becky led the team in rebounding with nine boards. Alice was second with six rebounds." Everyone knows who scored the points. We all know parents focus on that stuff way too much anyway. If you are going to recognize individuals, do it in a manner that helps further what you are trying to get your players to accomplish.

At the very least, a website is a quick and easy way to spread information about your program. I would acknowledge that e-mail trumps the website as it goes directly to the people you want rather than relying on them to seek out your site, but a website offers options that e-mail does not. At its best, a website is nothing less than a perfect propaganda machine. It can help a coach control the message and the discussion about their program. Be advised that if the coach does not control the message, someone else certainly will.

The New Enemy: Online Fan Forums

Even if you have a team website and you are doing your best to spin the season the way you want it spun, those that would attempt to undermine you have a new weapon in their arsenal. In this digital age there are websites devoted to disseminating the latest news and information about every sport in every state. These sites are growing in popularity with each passing day and most of these sites have started to offer online fan forums. Forums are a place where fans can create an anonymous user name and post their thoughts and opinions, usually unedited. Increasingly these forums are being used by disgruntled fans, players, and parents as a means to trash coaches in a very public way.

Online forums pose a very difficult political dilemma for coaches; they offer anonymity so it is not always evident who is making the claims or directing criticism at the coach. This veil of secrecy inhibits a coach's ability to confront the critic or even question the credibility of the perpetrator. Further, if a coach responds directly to the criticism by posting a response or should the coach respond more indirectly by creating their own anonymous user name and posting in the forum, these actions only feed the fire and help to legitimize the critics' claims.

It can be exceedingly difficult for a coach to sit back and allow someone to criticize them publicly. It is even more difficult for some coaches to pretend they don't know or don't care what is being said about them. But the politics of the situation are such that coaches have got to stay away from participating in these online forums. It is crucial for coaches to recognize that posting on these forums will almost certainly do them more harm than good.

I recently saw an entire soap opera play out on one of these forums. It involved a coach I know well. The coach is outstanding and has a proven track record of success, but he had one crackpot parent trying to take him down. The coach played the politics of the situation perfectly. He did not take the bait and he avoided the temptation to retaliate or respond in the online arena. In the end it was the critical parent that was publicly humiliated.

The online drama began with two early season losses. This coach's team was ranked in the top 5 in all of the pre-season statewide polls. As he had always done, the coach elected to play the toughest non-conference schedule he could find in an attempt to prepare his team to win a conference title. After the two early losses, suddenly there were posts on a very popular state sports website breaking down all the "mistakes" the coach had made that had cost his abundantly talented team the games. The posts came from a person that called themselves simply "SWConferenceObserver" so as to imply that the poster was just a fan of the conference and watched various teams. The name was clearly an effort to disguise the fact that they were an outrageously biased parent from the team the posts specifically focused on. For the first week or so the responses to the "Obeserver's" negative posts were almost entirely skeptical. Others that had been at the games in question came to the defense of the coach. They pointed out specifics

in the games from an unbiased perspective and their posts helped
to dismantle the charges leveled by "SWConferenceObserver." The
"Observer" was silenced, but only temporarily. After the team's third
loss a few weeks later the "Observer" struck again!

After this new post focused intense criticism on the coach the
other visitors to the site caught on to the Observer's motives. Within a
week regular visitors to the site had deduced the post had come from
a parent connected to the team. Eventually they even nailed down
precisely which parent it was. Then the fun began as this parent was
blasted by name repeatedly in dozens of posts. After every subsequent
win the posters could not wait to ask the "Observer" if he was going
to give the coach credit for the win. Naturally, the "Observer" became
less vocal and essentially disappeared from the site for the rest of the
season.

The lesson learned here is that when someone makes an
accusation or offers a specific criticism of a coach online, their charge
will almost always be met with skepticism by the others that post in the
forum. People are smart enough to recognize when someone that is
supposedly "anonymous" has a specific agenda. It is for that reason that
coaches have to be above such nonsense and avoid posting a reply.
Regular visitors to the site will catch on to the coach's posts and agenda
too. When they realize the coach has a thin skin and will respond to
criticism they will almost certainly pile on. Those that post on the site
might also think that if the coach felt compelled to respond, something
about the original accusation struck a chord with the coach. If coaches
can avoid the temptation to participate in these forums, almost without
fail they will discover the negative post that was written about them
will be largely ignored. It will be ignored because it speaks to far too
narrow of a subject. Visitors to the site that respond will most often
dismantle the critical post with cogent arguments. It may be out of
character for many coaches to allow others to fight our battles for us
and come to our defense, but it is the politically shrewd move in this
situation.

I am not suggesting that coaches stay out of these forums; quite
the opposite. I think it is important to know any criticism that is being
directed at you. Sometimes the criticism is valid and we need to digest
it and let it help us to become a better coach. And whether it is valid or
completely insane, we need to be vigilant about what kind of a brush
others are trying to paint us with in these very public forums. As Sun
Tzu says in "The Art of War," we must know our enemy if we hope to
defeat them. There is virtually never a detriment to knowing what kind

of criticism you are being subjected to. The detriment comes when we internalize it and take it to heart. Pay attention to the criticism, consider its merit, then try to establish or determine where it is coming from and why. Typically criticism levied in these types of online forums is not worthy of much concern. The person writing the post clearly does not feel much support from others in your program because they are trying to drum up support in another manner. Their complaints have fallen on deaf ears and they have been forced to resort to an online forum in an attempt to validate their ridiculous viewpoint. But the fact remains, there is still someone trying to take you down. No matter how crazy you might consider them, it is always prudent to keep an eye on a person that is devoted to your downfall.

There could be the rare situation where someone starts a negative thread about you as a coach and others do not dismantle them, instead they pile on. If numerous negative posts are in agreement that you are incompetent and no one ever comes to your defense, it might be telling you one of the following things:

1. You need to do a major self examination and change some of your ways.
2. You need a change of scenery. It may be time to move on to a different coaching job in a different area.

OR

3. You may need to change professions!

Again, coaches should always take criticism from anonymous sources with several grains of salt, but if a coach is constantly subjected to criticism they need to seriously explore one of the three options outlined above.

New Forms of Communication: Facebook, Twitter, and Texting

Technology moves much faster than many coaches can keep up with, but coaches need to recognize that their athletes are immersed in these new technologies. If a coach hopes to stay connected with their players, they need to have at least a rudimentary knowledge of the newest forms of communication technology.

Facebook has rapidly developed into the communication tool of choice for many high school students. These students no longer check their e-mail, they simply log on to Facebook as it is a far more visual and interactive medium.

As a coach, I have been reluctant to join the Facebook community because I am acutely aware of the downside of doing so. When players can see the things posted on my page and I can see the things they post on theirs, it can remove the important boundaries that should exist in a professional player/coach relationship. I have also had parents ask to become my Facebook "friend." The whole idea of this seems like something that could lead to a lot of trouble down the road, so I have struck a compromise.

My students and then my players communicated that if I wanted to get messages out to the people involved in our program I would need to develop a Facebook page. Facebook now offers an avenue for organizations to create pages and post information without having all the same privileges that come from being a "friend." Players can join our page and when I post information like a change in the location of our practice, it will be posted on their page. I cannot access their page and because our team page is registered as an organization I obviously do not have personal pictures or friends posting things on the page. Coaches that want to stay current with their modes of communication should add Facebook to their arsenal. But don't get too attached. History suggests that Facebook will not be the outlet of choice for long in our rapidly evolving world of technology.

Some coaches take a very different approach to Facebook than I have. There are coaches that actually mandate that their players "friend" them on Facebook. Coaches do this to insure that their players are not posting anything inappropriate on their Facebook pages. Coaches that are requiring players to do this are certainly very pro-active in the policing of their players, but I also think these coaches could find themselves dealing with very legitimate legal challenges from players or parents that object to the mandate. The other thing these coaches will discover is if their players want to post pictures or material that could be considered inappropriate they will simply join a different social networking site. A coach that is constantly trying to stay ahead of their players in terms of technology is beyond ambitious. They are naïve to think they can corral their kids. Teenagers are always on the cutting edge of technology.

Twitter is another avenue that coaches now have available to communicate with their athletes. Coaches may even find that players on their team have Twitter accounts. Perhaps you have heard the stories of NBA players that send out "tweets" at halftime of games? I have yet to embrace Twitter because I have no evidence that more than a couple of members of my team use it, but it could be that half time or post game tweets complaining about a coach's strategy could be something even high school coaches need to confront in the near future.

While Twitter and Facebook have their place, my technological tool of choice has become text messaging. I find it to be abundantly reliable because teenagers seem to have their cell phone within reach 24 hours a day. Of course, while it is convenient and quick to convey information to athletes, as always, there are dangers that coaches should carefully consider.

The first thing every coach should know is that text messaging should only be used for official business. A coach cannot let texting become a way to casually converse with a player. Again, this type of interaction can blur the boundaries of the player/coach relationship.

Coaches must also examine any message they type before they hit "send" because a text message has all the gravity of an e-mail. It is a message in writing and once it is sent, it can't be taken back. If a coach is sending inappropriate text messages to a player, they are providing that player and/or the players' parents with all the evidence that is required to end their coaching career. Texting must be reserved for strictly professional matters. To take it beyond that is creating a real risk that no coach should be willing to incur.

Another potential issue emanating from sending text messages to players is that doing so means the players have your cell phone number. Years ago, when I was a young, single coach, I would get calls in the middle of the night from students that got my number by looking through a player's cell phone. These calls were certainly inappropriate, but they were the byproduct of my desire to have access to instant communication with my players. Text messaging can be a remarkably efficient and convenient way to communicate with your team but coaches must be cautious to keep thing professional at all times.

A separate issue coaches are encountering is their players' almost obsessive need to read and send text messages. There are more and more stories about players texting during water breaks at practices or during timeouts of games. The conduct of students at my current high school demonstrates the gravity of this growing addiction.

Champlin Park High School bans all cell phones from the start of the school day to the end. If a teacher sees one, they are instructed to confiscate it. The first time a phone is confiscated the administration keeps it overnight. The second offense means the phone is kept for a week. On the third offense, the school keeps the phone for a month. The students hate this policy and it has even been met with some resistance by parents that think they have the right to contact their student directly all day with no regard for how cell phone calls in class can disrupt the learning process. The end result of all of this is that our teaching staff has become the "cell phone police."

Despite the harsh penalties, I catch at least one student a day with their cell phone out in the hall or in class and many of the students I catch are repeat offenders. Confiscation continues because the kids have nothing short of a compulsion to check their cell phone. It has developed into a legitimate addiction and it is getting to a point where coaches have to create policies to address this cell phone/texting epidemic.

I have heard stories about players who have their cell phone in their bag on the bench. When they are subbed out, they grab their phone and check their text messages! While I think most coaches would agree this kind of behavior is out of line, a story I heard from a football coaching friend completely showed just how far the cell phone issue can go.

It was the second quarter of a playoff football game and the coach's team had just surrendered a touchdown. Their kick return unit was taking the field. The special teams coach was counting players. He counted once and then a second time. Both times he counted only ten. The coach frantically consulted his kick return chart to determine which player was missing. As the special teams coach did this, another coach scanned the sideline and spotted the missing player hammering out a text message on his cell phone! The coach hollered at the player to get out on the field. The player, caught off guard, quickly slid the cell phone into his sock and ran out on to the field just before the ball was kicked.

As fate would have it, the ball ended up coming right to the texting player! He returned the kick about ten yards before being tackled. As the defenders rolled off him, the coach said the player flipped the ball to the official and immediately felt his sock to find out if his cell phone had been damaged.

I heard this story and knew that if I had still been coaching football and witnessed such an event, it would have been my last game as a football coach because I would have killed that kid!

I think this story helps convey just how prevalent text messaging and cell phone addiction is becoming with our athletes. Coaches would be well served to develop a clear and consistent policy to prevent situations similar to the one just described from happening with their team and their players.

The Coach's Lifeline:
Constant Communication with your AD

For the last few years I have had the immense benefit of having lunch with my AD nearly every school day. There are a number of teachers and school employees that gather in the staff cafeteria at 11:20 daily and it just so happens that the AD and one of our assistant principals decide to make that their time to dine as well. On the vast majority of our days the conversation is about anything but high school sports, but there are days when we talk about the Friday football game or what happened to the hockey team in the section playoffs.

And there are days that someone at the table brings up the latest with my team giving me a chance to pontificate about our prospects of winning the next game. Lunch has been a great time to build relationships but there is no doubt the greatest value derived from this constant communication is that it has allowed me to weather some storms. I have had this ability because through our daily discussions my AD knows exactly what is going on in my program at all times. Even better, he knows what is going on through the prism that I provide.

If I get the sense that a mother is on a mission to get rid of me, I can bring that to his attention before he gets a voice mail from the mom. If I know we have major match up problems with a team that on paper, it appears we should beat, I can buffer expectations with him and the staff I dine with that "this will be a tougher matchup than most might think because they have three players over six feet tall in their starting lineup and we don't have a six footer on our entire team."

Being afforded the opportunity to have that constant line of communication with my direct supervisor has helped immensely in diffusing what could have otherwise been very dicey situations. I will present two specific examples:

As I referenced previously, the fall of '08 was the season of carnage when we had to cut over 20 upper classmen from our basketball team. The group of juniors that year had parents that were particularly opinionated and I knew there would be, as I described it to our AD, a "giant shitstorm" when the cuts came down. The mere fact that I communicated this to him was a huge help for both he and I. He was informed of the numbers we had trying out, the number we had returning, and the caliber of parent that would likely be calling him. All of this information helped prepare him to take whatever heat the parents wanted to give and it allowed him to defend my decisions throughout.

He told me about one meeting he had with a parent that was just insistent that it "wasn't fair" that 12 seniors got to make the team and only two juniors were on the team. He responded "and it won't be fair next year when there are 12 open spots created by graduation and your daughter makes the team because she happened to be a senior in a year when there were so many open spots."

Another example came recently when we had a headcase player on our team (you will get the full story of her exploits in chapter 5) that we suspended. The suspension eventually led her to quit the team. Shortly after quitting the team this players' mother sent me a strongly worded e-mail outlining how her daughter had been treated unfairly. She closed the e-mail by insinuating that she had some dirt on me that she didn't want to have to use, but that if I didn't see things her way she may be forced to go to the AD.

Of course, I called the mother as soon as I could and while we spent much of the conversation discussing her daughter and the myriad reasons she was suspended, I also probed the mother to find out what her "secret weapon" might be. She told me that her daughter had shared something I had said about an official at halftime of a game. The mother thought my comment was out of line and that our school's administration should probably be alerted. I can tell you that she was absolutely right. My comment was completely out of line and I admitted as much to my team about two minutes after I made the remark.

While I used to cuss like a sailor, I decided early on that my once profuse profanity would not be welcome at my current place of employment. I had worked hard for four years to limit my cussing to my conversations with the coaching staff. On the night in question I was particularly fired up at an official who seemed to have a personal vendetta against me. Five minutes into the game, before I had said a word to any of the officials and completely unprovoked, this official came over to the sideline and threatened to give me a technical foul. I asked why they only became more belligerent. I determined the best course of action would be to take the high road and not say a word so I could report the behavior to the state official's association. I was surprisingly successful at keeping my mouth shut the rest of the half but all of the anger and frustration I had fought to keep inside came boiling over during my halftime comments to the team. I strung together a series of words to describe this official that would make most anyone blush. Within seconds of my outburst I knew I'd made a mistake. It was a mistake because I lost my cool and said some things that high school students should not have to hear from an educator. It was also a mistake because I knew the dynamics of my team that season were such that I had a couple of kids and parents that were just looking for any ammunition they could find to take me down. With my halftime tirade, I had just put a bullet in their gun.

I quickly recognized my words could haunt me so I tried to diffuse the situation almost immediately. Moments after the words left my mouth I told the team that I had lost my cool and I apologized. I added that I did not really have anything personal against the official. The next day I followed up by having a conversation with our captains. I expressed again that I was sorry for what I said and I asked them if I should address my mistake a second time with the team. In their words "it was no big deal and some of the girls even thought it was funny. We think it helped humanize you to a lot of them." With that I thought the potential crisis may have been averted. Of course two weeks later when the player I had just suspended quit, her mom decided to load my comments into the chamber of her "get 'em gun."

In retrospect, I should have told the AD about my poor choice of words the day after it happened. But the truth is the outburst was so bad, even by my standards, that I was not sure how I could present the incident with anything resembling a good spin. But after the phone conversation with the suspended players' mother, I knew I had to tell him before the mother did and present the information on my terms. I did it at our daily lunch session.

I explained to him that I had a conversation with a mother that morning that was concerned about some comments I had made about an official. I told him she was right to be concerned and that I was out of line. I explained that I apologized to the team seconds after the words left my mouth and that after talking with the captains, it seemed the team was fine with my comments and subsequent apology.

A former coach himself, he got a grin and said, "can I ask what you said?" I did not remember everything I had said, but I knew the more inflammatory words and I elected to leave those out in my re-enactment. He chuckled and said, "We've all lost our cool as coaches. Thanks for giving me a heads up."

Though the suspended player decided to quit the team, it seemed her mother's threat to "alert the administration" had been a bluff. We played out the final six weeks of the season and I was confident that I had dodged another bullet.

Then, within days of the end of the season, as I was checking my school mailbox a few minutes after the final bell I saw our principal. She asked me to come into her office. Her request for me to do this was unusual enough, so I was already a bit concerned. Then when she explained that she received a phone call from the parent of one of our former players sharing a concern about comments I had made about an official, my heart started to pound hard in my chest. I thought to myself, "This is it. There is no way I am getting out of this one."

Our principal was an Ivy League educated, brilliant woman who was also extremely politically correct. Off color comments were not OK in her book and I could not think of any way to tactfully suggest my words were somehow taken out of context. When she finished the mother's description of what happened, she said "I just have to ask, is this true?"

I said, "Yes it is, every word of it." I then went on to explain why it was I lost my cool and that I recognized my mistake within seconds of its commission. I told her I apologized to the team. She said the mother claimed that I never apologized. I countered that I approached our captains the next day, before practice, to offer another apology and that she could call them in to verify my claim. I also informed her that I had told our AD about the mistake I had made. I added that I consider this mother's or any other parent's concern over this incident valid. I admitted as much in my phone conversation with this mother a few weeks earlier. To this, the principal replied "So you have visited with this mother?"

I explained that I had and during my conversation with the mother I admitted my mistake and apologized to her. My principal said that she wanted to visit with the AD about where to go from here and our meeting was adjourned. I went home sick to my stomach and certain that there would be some sort of disciplinary action taken. I was not mad at the mother (though I was confused by her choice of timing), rather I was frustrated with myself for arming this mother with the ammunition I knew she was looking for. My current crisis was an entirely self inflicted injury. I would not find out my fate until the next morning. It was a sleepless night.

I was at my desk about a half hour before the start of school when my AD came and found me. He had a smile on his face and shared that his conversation with our principal went well. By the end, he had her laughing about my comments and how ridiculous I can get when I get mad. I had dodged a major bullet, but just barely. And there is no doubt that the thing that diffused the situation most was my communication ahead of time with the AD. It allowed him to go into our principal and say I had been upfront with him, that I acknowledged my mistake to the team, and that I used the incident as a learning experience for the players. I demonstrated that we can all make mistakes but that the important thing is to take responsibility for them and learn from them.

Had I failed to communicate with the athletic director it is certain this mother's call would have triggered an investigation that would have led players to be interviewed causing a much larger controversy. The investigation and the interviews would have made the entire incident very public in nature and that would have almost certainly forced administration to impose some sort of disciplinary action.

While honesty was absolutely an important aspect of how I handled this situation, there is no question my consistent communication with the AD made this situation turn out very differently than it would have if I would have continued to keep this information from him.

There is no such thing as communicating too much with your administrators. Keeping them informed can prevent many problems. For those problems that are not prevented, consistent communication will make your administration feel far more comfortable about defending your decisions and actions. Administrators hate surprises and in a conflict, they gravitate toward the side that offers the most information. Coaches need to make a conscious effort to communicate openly, honestly, and frequently with their administrators. Constant communication is one of the best ways to keep these important decision makers in your corner.

Crazy Parents: Label Them Before They Label You

Study after study has demonstrated that the side that runs the first negative advertisement in an election wins a great percentage of the time. Despite polls consistently indicating that people despise negative advertising, we continue to be inundated with negative ads each election season for one simple reason; they work.

The reason they are so effective is because when a candidate launches a negative attack on their opponent, the opponent now is forced to spend most of their time and energy responding to the attacks rather than communicating their own message to voters. The opponent is put on the defensive and they tend to be stuck in that position for the balance of the campaign. The other reason negative ads are effective is because they allow the side running them to characterize their opponent in the manner of their choosing. They can paint the opponent as a "nut job left wing liberal" or as a "kooky conservative" and once that label is attached it is a very difficult thing for the labeled candidate to shed.

Coaches can learn much from this particular realm of politics.

In particular, this technique of labeling and characterizing can be especially beneficial in our constant battle against the proverbial "crazy parent." Please do not get caught up in my use of the term crazy parent. That is merely a label I have elected to affix onto a possible or perceived opponent. Allow me to explain.

Before each season I always get a pretty good gauge on which parents could create problems for me. I can gather this based on the kids that I know will not get much playing time and the level of involvement these particular players' parents have demonstrated in the past. Once I determine who is most likely to contact our athletic director with complaints I make sure to visit with my AD about each of these parents.

In our conversation I will give him a heads up about this parent and that parent and tell him that they can be "kind of crazy" or that they "have a history of griping about coaches screwing over their kid and playing favorites." In many cases the information I am sharing with my AD is true, but that is not the most important thing. The key is that I am going negative first. I am attaching a label to these parents in the mind of my AD so when the phone rings a few weeks later and the parent starts griping, my AD already has it in his head that this parent is "crazy." You see, I have already undermined the complaining parent's credibility by taking pre-emptive action. When the parent calls, my AD is less inclined to listen attentively and trust that what they are saying is the truth. The AD responds this way because I have already damaged the parent's credibility. My pre-emptive action of characterizing them in a negative light influences the way my administration considers the parent's complaint. Attaching the "crazy parent" label has been a yearly necessity at my current place of employment and it has prevented a number of possible problems.

For those that are reading this and thinking "I am not sure I could do that. It just doesn't seem right," I will share with you why it is bordering on a necessity that you do it.

If you do not label them first the upset parent will be able to attach a label to you that will stick in the mind of your administrators. Remember, the side that goes negative first wins. When an angry parent calls six weeks into your season and goes on a rant about how you have done this and that and they insist that you are treating their child unfairly, they have now effectively labeled <u>you</u>. You have become the tyrannical coach that lacks any compassion and does not reward kids for their hard work and commitment. When they get the first word in to the administrators you become whatever the parents make you. Now

<u>you</u> are the one on the defensive, answering questions from your AD like "why are you playing this person instead of so and so" or "I got a call from Mr. Johnson. Did you really say this to his son?"

I cannot emphasize enough the importance of landing the first blow in this inevitable battle. If you think you are above it and that you can survive by taking the high road, you will find that road gets rough and bumpy after a while and it can eventually fall off in the form of a cliff. Parents have one agenda and that is to do whatever is necessary to help their kid. If that means they have to embark on a campaign to eliminate the coach, many of them are willing and able to do just that. In the introduction of this book I suggested that coaches that do not play the political game are destined to become victims of it. This statement is particularly true when it comes to the "name game" and attaching labels. Remember, the side that goes negative first wins. Label them. Undermine <u>their</u> credibility and put <u>them</u> on the defensive. Doing so puts you in a position of strength and insulates you to a great degree from a parent's frivolous complaints and accusations.

Political Correctness: The Power of Words

We all know that modern American society has become a bastion for politically correct language. We can no longer use terms that were quite common when many of us were growing up. We must instead use language that is softer and less abrasive. In many cases I don't have any major objection to this trend in our society. In fact, I often consider it a demonstration of our progress. However, coaches must come to recognize that every time we open our mouth our comments can, and often will, be analyzed and scrutinized. We must be constantly vigilant about the words we choose to use or the decisions we make, even when we might not consider them a big deal. What we think our words mean and how we intend them to be interpreted are not nearly as important as how they are perceived by the players and parents that hear them.

A few seasons ago I had a team that was skilled but not very big. They had a tendency to get pushed around and in a physical game they were often left on the wrong side of the score. One team in particular had a huge mental edge on my squad. The seniors on my team had never beaten this opponent whenever they had faced them from fifth grade through varsity. The opposing team was not more skilled, but they were far more physical. My team needed to overcome the intimidation factor against this opponent and I thought I had the answer.

We had two days to prepare for the matchup. At our first practice I explained that in the past two seasons this opponent had exploded on us during the first four minutes of every game. They always seemed to make nine of their first ten shots and we were always getting smoked before we had even broke a sweat. I declared defiantly that this "will not happen again!"

"On Friday night, I want the first player on their team that takes a shot to get knocked on her ass. I'm not talking about a cheap shot here. I'm talking about a legit hard foul. They are too damn comfortable every time they play us. Hell, they can't wait to play us. We are going to set the tone and send a message in the first minute that nothing is going to come easy against us this night!"

I went on to explain the virtue of my plan, how a shooter that takes a hard foul is typically less comfortable when taking their next shot because that hard foul is never too far from their thoughts. The strategy I was suggesting was one that was used very effectively by my old high school coach against an exceptional player many years ago. I was sure that it would work for us this night.

Friday night finally arrived. I reviewed the game plan with the team one more time before the game and when the ball was tipped our opponent got possession. They came down, set up a play, and the first shot they attempted was a very pedestrian 15 foot jump shot. Not only did the shooter not get fouled, we didn't have a player come within three feet of her! Naturally she made the shot.

On our opponents' next possession one of their players strolled in for an uncontested layup. I was beside myself. I wondered if I had been speaking a foreign language the past few days. By their third shot attempt, a three pointer which they also made, we were down seven to nothing and we had not laid a finger on an opposing player.

I called timeout and in a rather animated fashion I asked my players if they had heard a single word I had said the previous few days. I then pointed out that their decision to keep on playing the same way they had always played against this team was not working out. I implored them to please execute the game plan. Foul the next shooter hard. Send a message. After that time out our opponent when on a twelve to two run and it took a full three minutes before we committed our first foul. The foul was remarkably polite reach in foul on a dribble out near half court. I don't know if I had ever been more frustrated with a team than I was at that moment. I can recall saying to my coaching staff that I had never had a team that seemed to deliberately do the opposite of what I had instructed them to do, but that is what I appeared to be seeing on that night.

We lost the game by 20. Over the weekend I was very distraught. I had begun to wonder if I had lost my team. We were in the midst of an excellent season, but to completely disregard my instructions to the degree with which they did that night was certainly a sign that something was wrong. I called my captains and asked them to meet with me at the school on Sunday night.

I asked them point blank why the team failed to execute my orders. They hemmed and hawed for a minute or two and then finally one of them explained that the girls on the team did not feel what I was asking them to do demonstrated good sportsmanship. They felt it wasn't right.

I immediately offered that it would have been nice for someone to communicate this <u>before</u> the game so I could have addressed their concerns. I asked what specifically I said that made them feel that way. The captains explained that one of the girls on the team expressed with the players that she was not comfortable with the game plan and she would not commit a foul if her player was the first to shoot. The player rationalized that she already got in foul trouble a lot and she did not feel she could afford to commit a foul in the first minute of the game. Then other players started to talk and they agreed that to foul a player on purpose would be cheap. By game time, there was an unspoken pact that no one was going to execute the game plan.

I thought what I had said was pretty clear. Hard fouls happen multiple times in the course of every basketball game. When a player is driving in for a layup, it is common to foul them hard to insure they have to make two shots from the free throw line rather than one easy shot from one foot away. Players are fouled on purpose at the end of games routinely in an effort to stop the clock. I never dreamed my players could interpret my orders as something sinister. Especially after I had said specifically I was not asking them to cheap shot or hurt anyone. That was not the goal. The goal was to convey a message to our opponent and to ourselves that they could not come into our gym and feel comfortable anymore. I thought it was symbolic, not sinister. But that was not how my players perceived it. What we mean to convey and what others interpret our words to mean are not always the same thing.

Incidentally, we had a major team meeting the Monday after that game. It was our only team meeting of an otherwise wonderful season. Much was covered and discussed but in the end the air was cleared and we emerged from the meeting understanding each other. I continue to wish there had been an understanding prior to the game and if there were, I am convinced it would have created a different outcome.

But it is not only words that matter, our actions are equally important.

It was the practice before our senior night and I had intended to visit with some of our underclassmen about how they wanted the evening to go. Sometimes players like to make comments about the seniors to the crowd. In other years the players will defer to me to make the comments. I had forgotten to ask our underclassmen what their preference was during practice. We had wrapped things up for the day and half of our team was out of the gym. Suddenly I remembered that I wanted to ask underclassmen what they wanted done for senior night so I hollered out the names of three underclassmen still in the gym and asked them to come see me.

"Do you guys want to say a few words about each senior tomorrow night, or do you want me to do it?" I asked. The three of them looked at each other for a moment and then said, almost in unison, "you do it." I thanked them for their input and our exchange came to a close.

Never did I anticipate an angry e-mail from a parent over this brief meeting, but again, perception is the important thing. The next morning I received this message from a players' mother:

> *Coach,*
> *Maria and I would like to know why she was the only underclassmen on the Varsity team to not be included in the discussions after practice for tomorrow's senior night. We would like to know if this was just an oversight on your part or if it is an indication of where she fits in the team and program for the next two years.*

I was floored at what I had just read. In my mind this was a meaningless 10 second exchange. I would never imagine a player or parent could somehow extrapolate this perceived slight as a possible indication of how they might be treated for the rest of their varsity career! Admittedly, this player and parent completely over-reacted to the situation and the situation was essentially resolved with a five minute phone call. However, it does demonstrate how things that are of little or no consequence to us as coaches can be viewed as having profound importance in the eyes of our players and parents.

Another area that demands our strict attention and prudence in the words we use is our individual meetings with players. When I talk to a player about their role on the team I am always careful to include a caveat like "this is where you fit in now. It is not necessarily where you will be in two weeks." By phrasing it this way I cannot be accused of having my mind made up and never giving the kid a chance. In our end of season meetings I will often offer what role I anticipate for the player in the future. Almost immediately after offering my assessment, I will follow it with the disclaimer "but a lot can change between now and the start of next season." Coaches have to be extremely careful about making promises or issuing statements that could possibly be perceived as promises because players and their parents will remember those comments and cling to them. Suddenly the coach finds themselves labeled a liar and the player becomes a betrayed and sympathetic figure. Always include a caveat.

One last area to consider is how to forcefully convey your intended message while staying within the confines of political correctness.

Nearly every summer I encounter conflicts with my players struggling to choose whether to attend our team events or the events of their club team. I found this particularly troubling when my players were electing to go play with an AAU basketball team rather than with our high school team. State rules prohibit coaches from exerting "undue influence." We cannot in any way make a player feel obligated to participate in our offseason activities. Because of that rule, this area was always delicate territory and a potentially dangerous conversation.

When I would visit with players about their decision to choose our team or another, I would always begin by saying that what team they choose is entirely up to them. I would follow that up with what I considered an honest statement, and that was to say that when the season arrived if I had seen player "X" on numerous occasions all summer and I had seen player "Z" only a couple of times, it is human nature that I would be inclined to go with the player I was most familiar with. Especially if the competition for playing time between the two players was close, the kid that was around and working with their high school team was likely going to have a huge edge.

Occasionally I had players suggest that I was pressuring them to choose our team over their other team. I would quickly reply that I was doing no such thing. I was merely presenting them with all the information so they could make the most informed decision possible. I would also tell them that I want to win as much as anyone and I was going to put our best players on the floor. If they were clearly one of the best players, it would not matter if they spent a single second of the offseason with us. But if there were a number of people that were good players and capable of playing a certain position, I would likely give way to human nature and play the athlete I was most familiar with.

I made a conscious effort to make sure all of my comments were within the confines of what I could legally say as a coach. I also communicated the message loud and clear to the player I was visiting with that while the decision was theirs on whether to play with us in the offseason or not, the decision was ultimately mine on who would play <u>during</u> the season.

While we may all feel handcuffed at times by the necessity to choose our words wisely, ignoring this reality is exceedingly dangerous. As I alluded to earlier, the comments I made about an official at halftime of a game were anything but politically correct and as a result, I supplied a disgruntled parent with the ammunition that could have been enough to end my coaching career. As coaches we must always be aware that there could be someone out there that would use our words or actions against us. We must endeavor to conduct ourselves in such a way that we do not provide these opponents with the tools they need to make their goal of damaging or destroying us a reality.

Do not arm your opponents with the ammunition they need to assassinate you and end your career. Try to choose your words in advance whenever possible. Analyze the language you intend to use then dissect the comments that could somehow be misconstrued or that an angry parent could take out of context. It is not a fun way to operate, especially for those of us that pride ourselves on "speaking from the heart," but speaking in that manner is now something that could provide parents with the tools to rip our heart out.

THREE
✳✳✳

Public Relations

"Some are born great, some achieve greatness,
and some hire public relations firms."
– Daniel J. Boorstin

While much that we have covered to this point could fall under the umbrella of public relations, this chapter focuses on very specific actions coaches can take to enhance their standing with the people in their program, in their school, and in their community. Some of the things shared here may not be at the top of your "to do" list but when things go south (and for most coaches they will at least on occasion) engaging in these activities can give you the coaching capital you need to weather the storm and keep your job.

Every community has different expectations of its head coach. I will offer two extremes and hope that you can determine where on the spectrum your community falls. We begin with what I will characterize as the "Small Town Drinking Buddy" community.

I have a friend that coached in a small rural town. Shortly after he was hired, he called me and shared one of the specific expectations he encountered in his new community. It was expected that after the game, home or away, he would make an appearance at the local bar to debrief and discuss the game with the home town fans. If he was absent even one night he would hear about it from community members the next day. If he made it a habit to skip this rural version of a post game press conference he knew that he would soon be looking for another job.

This example may be somewhat surprising and unusual to many readers. Their community might be the type that is appalled at the idea of the coach of their kids tipping back booze and shooting the breeze in a very public way after games. But depending on the community a coach lives in and the traditions that exist there, this could be a very real expectation. In several small towns across this nation the head coach of the local team is nothing short of a celebrity. Just as celebrities have to make public appearances to appease the masses, that may be part of your job description as well. Those that ignore this expectation or believe that they won't really be fired for a failure to cozy up to the locals demonstrate a callous disregard for small town politics.

While it is accurate that you may not be fired specifically for failing to show up for happy hour, in a small town the fans are every bit as influential as the parents because the community is one big extended family. If the locals consider you arrogant or aloof they will be the first in line at the AD's office saying that the coach has got to go. However, if you show up after games, win or lose, and commiserate about the bad officiating or the great defense that was played that night you can rest assured that many people will have your back when times get tough. Reaching out to community members in a small town, be it at a bar or the local bowling alley, is of major importance if you want to have the support of the community and if you want to maintain your employment.

The other end of the spectrum would be the puritanical community that considers it scandalous to see a coach within 30 yards of a liquor store or bar. In a town like this, you can bet that your sport is still a topic of discussion and that you are still going to be expected to give your version of a post game press conference with the locals, but instead of a bar the most likely venue is a church. While some communities consider their head coach a celebrity others expect their coach to be nothing short of a saint. Some communities count on their coach to be an exemplary role model to the young people in the area. If you find yourself coaching in a town like this you would be well advised to do any drinking or carousing a good lengthy drive from the city limits so as not to generate rumors or create a groundswell of sentiment that you are not the right person to lead their kids.

I have known coaches that have said "I'm an adult and there's nothing illegal about me going to a bar and having a beer." They are right of course, but this isn't about what's legal or illegal, this is about public perception. If your community condemns a behavior it may as well be illegal to you because you are going to pay a penalty for disregarding the expectations of the town.

How does a coach diagnose just what the expectations are in their community? I would suggest two avenues. First, error on the side of caution and don't make any public appearances in a bar or other establishment of ill repute until you receive a formal invitation from other coaches or teachers on staff. Staff members that have been around for a few years will have an excellent gauge on what the community's expectations are.

The other thing I would do is find out as much as you can about not only the current coaching staff at the school, but some of the prior coaches too. Find out why they moved on. If they were let go, dig around and discover why. While those that give you information may first claim a coach was dismissed because of wins or losses, if you probe a bit further you will find there was usually something about the coach that didn't click well with the community. Perhaps the previous coach was a booze hound and the community had enough? That would speak clearly to how you had better conduct yourself if you hope to win over the people of the town. Maybe the prior coach was cold and unfriendly. If that was the case you need to make an effort to be more visible and social. Whether that visibility occurs at church or at Charlie's Tavern is the thing a coach needs to determine.

The heart of effective public relations for coaches is an acute understanding of their constituency. I have coached in a blue collar, middle income town and I currently find myself coaching in a more affluent metropolitan suburb. The constituencies I have served are quite different. And by constituencies I don't just mean my players, but their parents and the community as a whole.

In Red Wing I cussed constantly as a football, basketball, and baseball coach. While I never cussed at a kid, I was never shy about throwing in colorful words to describe the other team or the officials. I might use profanity to paint a picture of how our team was doing as a whole, but I never cussed at an individual player. Regardless of the community you live in that behavior is nearly always a no-no. But in five years of coaching three sports in that community, not once did I have an administrator, parent, or community member approach me about my cussing. It was understood that I was very competitive and passionate about the game and that my passion frequently led me to express myself in a colorful way. In fact, I would suggest my profanity wasn't just accepted, at times it was even celebrated. Players and parents would give me good natured ribbing about my run-ins with officials. They considered it great entertainment and they did not see it as the least bit harmful or damaging to their kids.

Shortly after I accepted my current coaching position I recognized that such language and behavior would not endear me in the least to the administration or the community. As a result, I have been a recovering swear-a-holic for five years now. It doesn't suit me as a coach and I really don't feel like I am being myself much of the time, but it's what I must do to survive in my current environment. Just as we tell our players to adapt to the officiating during a game, we too need to adapt to the expectations of the community we coach in.

The coaching community is littered with the resignations of coaches that thought they could come into a community and conduct themselves the way they wanted, without regard for community expectations. Make a conscious effort to learn about your community and your constituency. When you do, you will find that in most circumstances your coaching career will end only on your terms and at a time of your choosing. Ignore your constituency and you become subject to the mobs toting pitchforks and torches albeit in the more modern mode of angry phone calls and e-mails.

Media Relations

There tend to be two distinctly different situations head coaches find themselves in when it comes to their relationship with the media. If a coach is in a community with a local newspaper and/or local radio station, they will find themselves dealing with the media on a regular basis. A coach in a very small, remote rural community or a coach in a major metropolitan area will find their interaction with print and broadcast media to be considerably more limited, but no less important.

The coach in the community with various media outlets must be forever cautious and conscientious about their comments. People throughout the community, especially players and parents, will listen to the coach's comments on the radio or read what they have said in the paper. If a coach's words can be construed as harsh or critical either towards their team or towards a player, these comments can create a storm of controversy that can be hard to contain.

When being interviewed, coaches should be particularly prudent in their choice of words. Here are a few rules of thumb to follow, regardless of the kind of questions a coach may be asked:

Speak in general terms about your team and their previous performance or their preparation for the next contest.

In my hometown we had a daily newspaper and two local radio stations that broadcast every football and basketball game as well as several baseball games. Growing up in this environment, I became accustomed to hearing high school coaches interviewed on the radio and reading their comments in the paper. When I coached in Red Wing, it was a similar community with the same type of media outlets. During the season I was interviewed by the sports director at the radio station at least once a week about a previous game or an upcoming opponent. In these interviews I made sure to address things in broad, non-specific terms. When he asked about our preparation for an upcoming opponent I would highlight how hard our players were working in practice to improve our defense or something to that effect. Speaking to specifics like "we are going to employ a full court press and alter our starting lineup" would only open the door for possible criticism from the community. There are always people out there that think they know more than the coach or that the coach is implementing the wrong system, but it is hard for anyone reading an interview to object to your team "improving on fundamentals" or "becoming more intense defensively." Keep comments broad or generic and you will do a great deal to diminish public criticism.

When I was asked about a game where we performed particularly poorly I was always sure to give credit to the opposing team. I would explain how well they executed or that we had just become the latest in a long line of victims to come up short against them. If questioned about a stellar performance by our team, I would attempt to be humble and comment about how we had things clicking on that particular night. Or I might reference how hard the team has been working in practice and offer that it is nice to see them rewarded for their extraordinary efforts.

By keeping things non-specific you make it difficult for others to criticize or mis-construe your comments.

Be as positive as possible when responding to questions.

This is particularly true when a coach is questioned after a poor performance or after a loss. You may have just read your team the riot act in the locker room, but if you share those same thoughts with the local media the backlash from the community will be immediate and harsh. If you criticize your team or a specific player in the media, not only are you going to aggravate and embarrass families in your program, you could also incite the ire of otherwise uninterested people in the community. Sure, there might be a few that listen to the interview or read the comments and think "it's good there is a coach out there that gives kids a swift kick in the pants" but those people won't be the ones contacting your school's administrators. There will be far more people that sympathize with the players and consider your comments out of line because, after all, "they are just high school kids." And the fact of the matter is, in this situation those critics would be right.

When a professional athlete gets called out in the media for dropping a pass or missing a shot it is entirely acceptable because they are getting paid a handsome salary to perform. High school coaches can sometimes consider their games as important as professional games (largely because they often invest so much of themselves into the outcome) but the fact is, coaches cannot subject high school players to the same level of public criticism as professional athletes. Coaches that commit this cardinal sin quickly find the community coming to the defense of the kids and the coach becomes the subject of criticism.

The other thing a coach must recognize is that when they levy public criticism at their players it is only a matter of time before someone in the community feels compelled to suggest that perhaps the players are not the issue. Parents have an intrinsic compulsion to defend their child, but you will find anonymous members of the community share the same feeling when it appears an adult is criticizing a group of kids. No matter how frustrated a coach finds themselves, expressing that frustration in the media is never appropriate. In addition, a coach that loses their composure and becomes critical in an interview is actually creating a public relations crisis that could eventually consume them.

I am not a particularly good liar and I hate the idea of being insincere, but when I was interviewed after a bad loss I always understood that the political reality demanded that I put the best face I could on what just transpired. I could criticize my team in private, but publicly I had better put on a positive spin or else I was going to create a controversy I could not control.

So after a tough loss, when I was genuinely frustrated and angry with my team, what would I tell the media? I would say something like "we are certainly disappointed with the outcome tonight, but we have to credit the other team. They played well. We learned some things tonight and identified some areas we need improve on. If we can learn from these mistakes and get better at the weaknesses our opponents helped expose, this loss can be one of the best things that ever happened to us."

I might have said that with my teeth and fists clenched, but when John Q. Public reads that in the paper the next morning, there is certainly nothing he can take away from it that could be construed as negative or an attack on my team.

Never provide parents or opposing teams with ammunition.

Nearly all coaches are familiar with what is commonly referred to as "bulletin board material." For the few that haven't heard the phrase, it describes what happens when you encounter a comment made by an opposing player or coach that can be posted in the locker room to motivate your team. When you have local media outlets covering you on a regular basis, you had better respond to interview questions as though your opponent will know exactly what you are saying, because often they will.

Years ago I began to bookmark the websites of our opponents' hometown newspapers. A week or two before or after we played a team, I would comb through the sports stories looking for a comment I could post or even one I could take out of context, to help my team get fired up and focused for the game. Most of the time my search came up empty, but every now and then an opposing coach or player would offer a nice little nugget that would anger my team just enough to give them a little more of an edge entering the game.

As a coach, you need to consider your comments and attempt to be respectful of your opponents at all times. If you allow your players to be interviewed by the media, it would be wise to remind them to be considerate with their comments as well. I have helped my players understand why their comments must be measured by telling them "The other team already wants to beat us. We don't have to give them another reason."

Coaches can also be certain the disgruntled parents on their team are combing through their comments on a regular basis. The parents are looking for any phrase that could reinforce their conspiracy theory that you favor a certain player over their child. The parent's dream come true would be to have a coach say something that could be considered even mildly controversial because that enables the parent to take the comment to administration and insist that the coach be suspended or fired.

Professional players and coaches are masters of tempering their comments to the media. Their responses are usually bland and cliché, but it would be wise for high school coaches to follow that example. Dealing with the media can be like driving a car. A car can get you where you want to go and can dramatically improve the quality of your life. But if you aren't focused and attentive while driving, the car can become a death trap.

The media can be an exceptional outlet for promoting your players and your program. Like the car in our analogy, it too can make a coach's life better. But if a coach does not deal with the media in a prudent manner, the media can make a coach's life miserable or even end a coach's career just as quickly as it enhanced it.

If you are going to mention players by name, be sure to mention as many names as you can.

I have always done my best to avoid mentioning specific names in interviews because while it might brighten the day of the player that gets mentioned, inevitably there are at least a few players on your team that are disheartened when they don't also read their name or hear themselves mentioned on the radio.

Whenever I was asked about a specific player's excellent performance, I would immediately shift gears and point out that it was a true team effort. If the individual had a particularly stellar performance and truly carried our team, I wouldn't try to deny their excellence. Instead I would acknowledge the player and then quickly incorporate the names of several other players that may not have had eye popping statistics but did things to help us win.

I have even gone into media interviews with a list of names in front of me and told the media member in advance that I was going to try to work in the names of certain kids because I thought they needed some ink or attention. Usually, your local media members can accommodate this request. When I would make it a point to acknowledge some of the unsung heroes on my team, I didn't just do it because I thought they deserved the attention. I did it because I understood it was excellent politics and outstanding public relations. When some of my bench players got recognized on the radio that would often appease their mom and dad enough to keep them at bay for a few more weeks.

Smart coaches don't just use the media to provide information or to promote their program, they also use it to enhance their own circumstance. If you can please some parents by integrating several kids' names into an interview, by all means take advantage.

Be careful about speaking "off the record"

When a coach has developed what they consider to be a good relationship with local media members the coach can sometimes fall victim to comments they thought were made in confidence. While it is perfectly fine to be friendly with the media, coaches need to be ever vigilant that they do not say something they would not want reported or repeated. There are media members that deliberately want to create a comfort level with the coach in the hopes that they will get better fodder for their stories by bringing the coach's defenses down or getting the coach to open up. This can be nothing short of catastrophic for a coach from a public relations perspective if the media member betrays the coach's trust and reports something that was supposed to be said off the record.

No matter how friendly a media member seems to be with you, remember that their job is to sell papers or report interesting facts. A coach's job, as it pertains to the media, is to promote their program and project a positive image to the community. Be careful about losing sight of the primary responsibility of both parties. Do not say anything to a reporter that you would not be comfortable having broadcast publicly.

While there are certainly risks when a coach is expected to deal with the local media on a regular basis, coaches with a local media presence also have a luxury that other coaches do not. Wise coaches will use the media to enhance the image of their program to a large audience, but coaches can also use the media to promote their camps and other activities.

In every community I have lived in that had a local newspaper or radio station, these outlets advertised our summer youth camps free of charge. A simple phone call or e-mail was all it took, and we got free publicity promoting our camp to thousands of listeners and readers. If a coach has the benefit of a local media outlet they are foolish if they do not use it to increase participants in camps or to improve the bottom line for fundraisers.

Coaches far removed from the media in rural areas, or coaches in the midst of a major metropolitan region do not have to deal with the day to day risks of making regular comments to the media. However, these coaches also miss out on the benefit of having their program promoted to their community en masse. Coaches in either of these two settings, rural or metropolitan, must become their own "sports information director" if they hope to get their team any degree of media attention.

When I came to Champlin Park, a suburb of the Twin Cities, we had a local paper that was published once a week. The primary news source for people in our community and throughout the metro area was the Minneapolis Star Tribune. The "Trib" (as it is called by the locals) does a laudable job of covering high school sports, especially when measured against other major metropolitan newspapers. But the Trib has one hundred high schools within 35 miles of any direction from its headquarters. On their best day, they can devote a paragraph sized game summary to the contest between a dozen different schools. Our school would get a paragraph sized story once a season, or maybe three or four mentions in a season where we were ranked highly in the state. No coach is going to change the way a major newspaper covers high school sports or their particular team. But a coach can do a few things to improve the likelihood that their team gains the spotlight from time to time.

At the stop I made previous to Champlin Park, the sports reporter for the local paper asked me to e-mail him a game summary with stats and quotes. I was quite happy to do so because it would ensure the story that appeared in the paper would be the story I wanted told. Further, I knew I would never be misquoted. I continued to provide this "service" for the sports reporters when I got to Champlin Park and needless to say, they loved the fact that I did most of the work for them. During my first season we received enormously more publicity than any other sport at the school. The lesson here is that a coach that lacks a media outlet anxious or able to cover their team needs to take on the task of promoting their program to the media. Send them stats, story ideas, quotes, and even pictures and while your team may not get media attention every week, you will find that your team gets far more attention than it would have if you waited for the media to come to you.

In terms of dealing with a major market newspaper like the Chicago Tribune or San Francisco Chronicle, a coach cannot expect regular coverage no matter how persistent they are in sending these outlets information. The best a coach can aspire to achieve with these media outlets is one feature story every year or two. The major broadcast networks and newspapers respond best to interesting or off beat ideas. Perhaps you have a player on your team that donated a kidney to a teammate, or your team annually skips a practice to go visit with elderly people at a retirement home. These outlets are looking for heartfelt human interest stories. If you can come up with an angle like that, you can sometimes get your team some valuable exposure from a media giant.

Coaches that lack the local news outlets have to be considerably more creative and pro-active, but it is still possible, and I would even suggest still important, for a coach to get their team positive publicity if they hope to maximize the political benefit available via the media.

The Best Public Relations Moves You Will Ever Make

If you have any intention of building a top flight program that consistently contends for championships, you are likely already working with your youth programs. Regardless of the sport, coaches have a vested interest in involving themselves with whatever youth programs their community has established. If your community does not have a youth program, you have an opportunity to generate even more positive publicity by taking the lead and spearheading the creation of a youth program for your sport.

While we all recognize the value of being "hands on" with the youth program for the way it produces more talented and skilled players, of equal importance is the positive public relations image this conjures up for a coach in their community. And to be clear, when I suggest getting involved with your youth program I am not talking about running a week long summer camp where you make a couple thousand dollars. That does little to enhance your image with the public. What I am talking about is the head varsity coach attending youth practices and games. When a coach is visible at these events, the youth players and their parents take notice. They see the coach is genuinely interested in them and their progress. This builds a degree of loyalty that cannot be generated any other way. When they see you at their practice or at their game, they see a coach that cares a great deal about the program. A beneficial byproduct of your presence is that the youth players and parents will become more committed to improving and working at your sport, due largely to the fact that they now know they are on the head coach's radar.

If you make a genuine effort to get to the know the kids and their coaches, you will find they become another group of important political allies, supporting you and advocating for you even when some of your varsity parents may have turned against you. The relationship between a varsity coach and a youth program is nearly always "lovey-dovey." The coach feels that way because they can see the potential in the younger kids and the coach gets excited about what they could become some day. The kids and the parents love the coach because the coach has taken the time to get to know them and support them. The varsity coach hasn't benched the youth player or cut the youth player (yet) so in the parent's mind the coach is a terrific person. When the inevitable coup begins to form amongst your disillusioned varsity parents, the bond you will have created by making an effort to get to know, on a personal level, the people that comprise your youth program will prevent this important constituency from being polluted and influenced by the malcontent varsity parents in your program.

As coaches, we can sometimes go long periods of time without any positive comments or thank-yous from our players or parents. That is to be expected because on a daily basis we are making difficult decisions that one player is better than another player and deserves more playing time. That said, I can't tell you how many positive notes and comments I have received from the parents of my youth players simply for taking the time to attend a game. The sixty minutes you sacrifice from your day is more than worth it in the coaching capital you accrue. Granted, some of these thank you notes come because the parent is in a position to want to kiss ass to help further their own kids' career, but I would characterize the vast majority of the contacts I have had as genuine and sincere.

Beyond attending a practice or game, here are a couple of other ideas you can incorporate to help build that bond between your youth players and your high school program:

Youth appreciation night

If you are in a school district that charges kids or youth players to attend your games, arrange with your AD for one game a season where all youth players and parents are admitted for free. It is great for all involved to see a couple hundred (or dozen depending on the size of your community) kids in the stands, cheering for the team they dream of playing for someday. Get some door prizes from the local restaurants or businesses to award at halftime or during your game. If your program produces a team poster, make sure you order enough to give away to all the kids at youth night, then have your players sign autographs for the kids after the game.

I always make sure we schedule youth night on an evening we play a team we are certain to beat, just to make sure everyone goes home feeling good. A youth night is one of those rare events where everyone benefits. The youth programs, coaches, and parents get recognition and your team gets a big, enthusiastic crowd to play for. If you aren't already doing this, make it a high priority to implement.

Future insert your mastcot here of the Game

This is perhaps the single most successful youth initiative I have ever run. The program is typically targeted at younger kids (we have used 3rd and 4th graders). I get a list of names and phone numbers from the local youth program and a week or so before each home game I contact two kids or more specifically their parents, to offer them the chance to be the "Future Rebel of the Game." As our future Rebel, they join the team for pre-game warm-ups. The little kids throw passes to players and other simple things that keep them out of harms way. The kids also get announced with the starting lineups and they receive a t-shirt touting their selection as "Future Rebel of the Game." Parents are almost always taking pictures or video of this event as their little star gets to rub elbows with our varsity players and hear their name announced over the public address system. The whole thing takes no longer than your pre-game warm up time is and it doesn't cost you more than a t-shirt but again, the public relations mileage gained from something as simple as this is priceless.

Free youth clinic

Every fall, a couple of weeks before our season starts, we host a free youth clinic for kids in grades 3 through 8. Our players lead stations for the two hour clinic, but the overwhelming emphasis is on making sure the kids have fun.

The kids get a few helpful hints as they prepare for their tryouts or their youth season and our varsity players have some fun with the younger kids. The best thing about the night though is how it offers an opportunity for the younger players to bond with our varsity players. This pays dividends during the season in terms of attendance at our games. When these youth players get to know a varsity player by name, they are more inclined to want to come cheer for that player on a Friday night. Hosting a free youth clinic is always a great public relations move.

Youth teams play at half time of your varsity game

Another way to get butts in the seats and generate some good will towards you and your program is to invite your youth teams to come play at halftime of your games. Even if it's just 10 minutes, the kids get a thrill playing on the "varsity field" and in front of a crowd much larger than they ever experience otherwise. Mom and Dad come and they bring the camera, take a ton of pictures, and everyone leaves with a good feeling, very appreciative that you, as the head coach, extended this invitation.

Getting involved with your youth teams does more than build a winning team for you in the future. It builds relationships and allies that will be important should you go through a difficult season or get confronted by a powerful opponent.

The Other Best Public Relations Move
You Will Ever Make

The other activity you can engage in that has to be considered public relations "gold" is supporting your players in their other sports or activities. If you are a fall sports coach and you have got a kid that plays a winter sport, make it a point to attend a game. If you don't tell the player in advance that you are coming, make sure you write them a note afterwards commenting on some specific aspect of the game so they know you were there and paying attention. To most players and parents, the gesture of you being there and supporting them means more than words can say.

Your attendance sends the message to the player and the parents that you care about the kid not just when they are a player on your team, but you actually care about them every day of the year. You care about them as a person.

And don't limit yourself to athletic activities. I have been to my players' band concerts, theatre performances, etc. Your attendance at any of these functions builds that precious coaching capital we have talked about previously. It helps you cultivate loyal allies that are necessary when times are tough, and it helps engender loyalty and dedication to you and your program. In nearly two decades of supporting my players outside of our season, I have never encountered a downside or a negative to publicly demonstrating support for my players in their other activities.

One more quick idea to help build loyalty in your program and to help you build a positive public image is to send birthday cards to the players on your team. One tends to get a bit more mileage out of this if they coach girls, but it is usually well received regardless of gender. I got the idea from my high school football coach. He sent a little birthday card he printed off on his home computer with a sentence or two scribbled in it to every player on their birthday. I was among the kids that could give a crap as I rarely remembered my own birthday until someone told me. But when I started making birthday cards for my girls' basketball players during my first year as a varsity coach, I instantly saw how much it meant to many of my players and I have continued to do so ever since.

Know Your Constituents

While every player and parent is different, general trends can be found within the group that you work with. These trends can help you understand what you can and can't do as a coach. When I tell you to "know your constituents" I am advising you to get a feel for the general type of parents and players you are working with.

I have encountered several types of groups in my years of coaching. Let us examine a few.

Competitive, driven, win at all costs

Working with a group of players and parents like this is a blessing and a curse. It is great because they will work their tail off. They will be very dedicated in and out of season. You don't have to work too hard to motivate them.

But the downside is if you lose a game or two, things can start to turn ugly pretty quickly. Their expectations are so high and their tolerance for losing so low, that anything short of excellence can create major drama and numerous headaches.

If you identify the majority of your program as being populated with this kind of people, know that you can push them hard. In fact, if you don't, they will probably be all over you for being too soft or lacking dedication. But also know that if you are not winning a lot more than you lose, this group will turn on you so fast it will make your head spin.

Kids are here to have fun/make friends

This is my least favorite group to work with. Players and parents see your sport as a nice recreational activity where they can spend time with friends and have fun. They will complain if you do drills that are too demanding or if you schedule conditioning in as part of your practice.

Players on teams with this identity are less likely to complain about more playing time for themselves than they are to lobby for increased playing time for a friend or more "equal" playing time so no one has their feelings hurt.

You will have marginal involvement in the offseason from a group like this. If you have one or two ultra competitive kids, the lack of dedication demonstrated by the rest of their teammates can really frustrate and alienate them. Coaches will find themselves counseling the competitive kids because they are upset that their teammates don't care. The coach finds themselves trying to motivate the group to work at something most players don't consider that important in their lives.

It is often said that a team takes on the personality of its coach. While this is often true, I have learned it is not always the case. The handful of times I have had a team with the recreational mentality I have found that I had to adapt to them rather than expect them to adapt to me. If I coached them the same way I coached the competitive, driven groups, I would start a season with 20 players and finish it with five. I am not suggesting you take the team out for ice cream after every game win or lose, but you may have to alter your coaching style. Integrate a bit more fun into practice, put a little less emphasis on wins and losses, and you might find you actually get more out of a group like this. They respond more to "rah-rah" than to "roar-roar." Adapt for the time being and cross your fingers that a competitive group is coming up through the ranks.

My kid is the best and the rest are garbage

I have coached teams that were teams in name only, largely because of an individualistic attitude that permeated from the parents on down. The parents poison their kids with the belief that they are the only good player on the team and that the rest of the team is holding them back. These parents will constantly praise their own child and just as consistently criticize the actions of everyone else.

These are very challenging teams to coach because you are competing for the psyche of your players and you only get two hours a day with them. Mom and Dad have the rest of the day to brainwash their kid into believing they play with a bunch of bums.

I have actually had a situation where parents told their kids never to talk to a player on our team. This was not an isolated incident. Two sets of parents both gave their daughter the same direction. They were not to talk to a certain player in or out of practice. The parents gave this order to kids that were sophomores in high school. What do you do as a coach when the parents are more immature than the players?!?

I elected to have the four parents join me for a meeting. I explained that if this is how they were going to insist that their daughters operate, then their daughters could sit in their mandated silent protest on the bench together. I can't tell you how uncomfortable it is to have that kind of a conversation with parents that clearly have the mentality of an eight year old. But the message got through, the players started to work together, and against the odds we went on to have a pretty good season.

We expect to win but don't think we have to work for it

You tend to see this attitude exhibited by players and parents in wealthy, upper class communities. Billy has always been a starter on his team growing up because mom and dad put up the money to make sure he was on a team where he could shine. They also have hired personal coaches because they are certain that a personal one on one coach they pay 50 to 100 dollars an hour must know more than some stupid social studies teacher that also happens to be a high school coach.

When you have a group of kids on your team that come from

this kind of a culture it can make for a long season. They think that because of who they are, things are just going to go well for them automatically. What you as a coach might consider a half ass effort the player considers working hard. And heaven forbid you push them. Their personal trainer didn't expect that much out of them, so how in the world could a high school coach expect them to do these things?

In this situation a coach needs to outline specific reasons why the team should work harder and the benefits that will come about as a result. It can be helpful to cite the in and out of season activities of other successful programs. This provides your otherwise unmotivated group with a concrete example of the path other teams have taken to greatness. It provides your players with a road map and it lends credibility to the expectations you put forth for your team.

One final word of caution about dealing with the high class crowd; when working with this type of team coaches really have to choose their words wisely because these people are just as likely to hire a lawyer as they are to e-mail your athletic director. Watch your back and cover your rear. While there are ways to win the political battles, even a win in a legal battle ends up losing a coach thousands of dollars.

The Expectations Game: Control Them Before They Control You

I have seen more coaches lose their job over a failure to meet expectations than for any other reason. Whether coaches create lofty expectations for their team that can't be met, or the people in the program generate unrealistic expectations, falling short of someone's projected performance is what brings a pre-mature end to many coaching careers.

If you hope to stay employed for an extended period of time, one of the keys to controlling your own fate is controlling expectations. This does not require any particular skill, but it does require persistence.

There are a few general scenarios that all coaches face. I will present these scenarios as well as the optimum way for you to shape expectations for your team amongst parents, administration, and the community.

Scenario 1: *You have inherited a team with a terrible track record or you have a team that just graduated a ton of seniors. Expectations within the program and in the community couldn't be lower. In fact, expectations are so low that you are starting to lose participants in your program because kids don't want to play for a team they know is going to lose all of the time.*

Many first time head coaches find themselves in this position, because quite frankly, it is the experienced, proven coaches that get the jobs with the strong, established programs. Walking in to a position with low expectations is usually an excellent situation for new coaches. It is low risk and high reward. No one expects your team to be any good so if you are just a notch above awful, you are hailed as a great coach!

But when your program is down so much that virtually no one believes it can be successful or it has gotten to the point you are hemorrhaging players, it is imperative that you elevate expectations. Players and parents in a program so severely distressed are just begging for any sign of hope or a reason to be inspired. The coach needs to be that hope and inspiration. Yes, there is some risk (which we will cover in a moment) but the greater risk is going along with the conventional wisdom and agreeing that the program is in the toilet. You will never get the program turned around if that is the attitude you project in public.

When I got the head job in Red Wing they had won a total of five games in the previous three seasons. They were routinely losing by 40 plus points and they were losing players at all levels of their program. I had the benefit of being completely cocky and naïve when I took the reigns. To that point I had never experienced a losing season as a player or coach and I didn't have any plans to start. I told anyone that would listen that my new team had talent and that we were going to work harder and be more dedicated than the team had ever been before. I proclaimed that those two facts were certain to make us a winning team and soon.

The enthusiasm that pulsed through the program that first season was palpable. Even when we lost a game, I could point to things that we were doing better than we had before and they realized that instead of losing by 40 they had only lost by 10. There were good vibes all around. We had begun to turn the program around and it all started with an injection of positive attitude and elevated expectations.

To further demonstrate how serious I was about expecting to win, I remember a game late in my first season where we blew a lead to a quality team in the final minutes, eventually losing by 10. As I entered the locker room after the game the girls were damn near having a party. It was high fives and smiles all around. I came unglued. I announced that we absolutely should have won the game and beat that team. In a rather colorful way I conveyed that our opponent didn't beat us, rather we beat ourselves. We pissed the game away and here they were having a freakin' party?!? I barked about how we had better hurt when we lose a game and if we don't hurt emotionally after a loss, I will make darn sure we feel a physical hurt at practice the next day.

We were going to learn to invest ourselves emotionally into every game and "when we do, we'll find that no one has any desire to high five after a loss!"

I left the locker room and as I walked down the hall to our coach's office I encountered one of my players' fathers. He was a middle school teacher and had done some coaching. I stopped and told him about the atmosphere I had just walked into in the locker room and how disgusted I was. He heard me out, then said "but coach, you have to realize….they lost to that team by 50 last season. To have a lead late in the game was as good as a win to these girls." I told him, and the next day I told the team, that we need to move away from that "hooray we came close" mentality and take the next step to where we actually expect to win. The players and the parents were more than willing to come along, but they needed someone to lead the way.

Again, for the most part people will appreciate the fact that you are pushing them. They also respond because you are showing confidence in them when no one else has. But elevating expectations, even in a situation that desperately calls for it, can have a down side.

The risk coaches run in elevating expectations is that eventually they have to meet them. In my experience at Red Wing we finished sub .500 that first year but we won more games than anyone thought we could and far more than they had in previous seasons. We were playing young players, so everyone was still on board the "we're gonna win" bandwagon. In year two we were only two wins better than year one. But we had four teams in our conference ranked in the top 10 in the state and we still had a core of our players returning for a senior season. While people weren't as fired up as they were before, they were still on board.

I really felt that in year three we had to post a winning record or people would start to feel like I had fed them a line of bull. I felt a lot of pressure that season and it was largely self imposed. We were hovering around the .500 mark most of the season. Of our final few games, three were against top flight teams, so I knew we would have to win all the other games if we were to end the season with a winning record. I didn't tell the team these other games were must win games, but I sure was telling myself that. In one of these late season games, we nursed a 4 point lead with two minutes to play when the opponent nailed a three pointer. We turned the ball over on the next possession and quickly committed an ill advised foul. They made two free throws to take the lead and our opponent held on to win the game. I didn't display my dismay to the team in the locker room after the game, but when I went into the coach's office I tore it up pretty good. I was throwing anything I could find and cussing so loud it may have gone through the 4 brick walls that separated my office from the players' locker room. I was telling my JV coach that we had screwed ourselves out of the chance to post the first winning record the program had seen in years. That would have been a major milestone to mark our progress as a program, and we threw it away by not taking care of business against an inferior opponent.

Unfortunately my analysis of our remaining schedule was dead on and we finished the season a game below .500. As it turned out, budget cuts and the subsequent teaching staff reductions that followed did not allow me to coach a fourth season, but I am reasonably sure we would have taken a step back that year if only because for three years I had failed to deliver on my very public promises. Yes, we were light years ahead of where the program had been three years prior, but I hadn't promised we would be competitive and respectable. I was promising winning records and state tournament appearances.

The lesson here is when working with a program or team that has no confidence in itself, you have to be the purveyor of that confidence. Allowing the program to wallow in self pity will end your coaching career faster than elevating expectations because with low expectations you won't just lose games, you'll lose players. Losing numbers in your program is the more immediate risk, so it is necessary to stick your neck out and guarantee a winner. While demonstrating confidence in the kids and elevating expectations is really your only move, realize there is a long term risk in making it. You have to put your credibility as a coach on the line and at some point, you will be expected to deliver on your promises.

The first scenario we have covered is one that rarely costs a coach their job, and if it does, it is only after several years of coming up short of expectations. In general, people like to be told they can be great. It can take several years for the axe to fall when you are blowing sunshine up their butt. There are considerably more dangerous scenarios to consider.

Scenario 2: *You have a team that hasn't been particularly great in past years, but they have everyone back and players and parents think that because they are all going to be seniors and they have varsity experience, they are going to win a conference or state title.*

As coaches, we want our kids to be confident. But if that confidence is unwarranted and people's expectations are completely out of whack we must be diligent about altering expectations. In the scenario I have just offered, if your team was about a .500 team the season before and your players think that just because the letters "Sr" are now next to their name on the roster that they are magically going to win a bunch of games, you as a coach, are getting set up to take an enormous amount of blame when the team doesn't make it to state.

When I have had groups that were decent teams, but not great teams, that have much of their roster returning, I always point out months before the season begins that our team is not going to go from middle of the pack to state champions just because we are a few months older. I make sure that they understand they are going to have to improve a great deal in those months and that they can't just coast in thinking that because they are seniors opponents will lay down.

The times I have found myself in a situation where players and parents were clinging to unrealistic expectations based solely on being seniors, I have shared with them the following story. My junior year of high school, of our 22 starters in football, 18 were juniors. We had a nice 5 and 3 season and made a little run in the playoffs. As a result, the belief throughout the program and the community was that the next season we would be a state championship caliber team. It was a reasonable expectation, but collectively our team did not do much of anything to improve that offseason. We just counted the days until our senior season began.

When the regular season of our senior year came to a close we were sitting at a woeful 2 and 6. We had been ranked in the top 5 in the state pre-season and we had finished well below .500. Do you think our head coach took a lot of heat that year? The poor guy had to walk around in fireman's gear!

He ended up resigning at the end of that season. There could have been any number of reasons that led to his decision to hang up the whistle, but I would be willing to wager that the way he got swallowed up by the expectations contributed to the decision.

In a similar situation, I have a close friend that coached a team of primarily juniors to a modest winning season. He knew that they had probably over achieved a bit as juniors and that they would be hard pressed to repeat the success of the previous season. But he shared that belief only with his closest confidants. He never disparaged the team's chances for a strong senior season publicly.

As it was, to a certain extent the players, and to a greater extent the parents on his team made it known to anyone that would listen how great the team was going to be the following year. It turns out, everyone from school administration to the guys at the local coffee shop were listening, and the parents' message of pie in the sky expectations was the only message the community got to hear.

As seniors, the team finished two games below .500, or about 3 games worse than they had the year before. The parents were up in arms. They were adamant that the coach must be what cost the team so many games because they were so certain heading into the season that winning was a foregone conclusion.

In both examples just offered, neither coach did anything to quell or control expectations in the community and they eventually became the victim of those expectations. A coach that doesn't do all they can to control or shape the expectations for their team is forever putting themselves at the mercy of those that do. Someone is going to paint a picture of what your season should be. It had better be you.

The scenario above, where you have got a marginal team that has unrealistic expectations, does not call for you being publicly discouraging or disparaging. And of course the worst thing you could do is go along with the prevailing opinion that the team will be awesome. All a coach in this situation needs to do is be brutally honest.

Communicate to the parents and the administration that while there is reason to be hopeful and optimistic, a state championship is far from a lead pipe lock. There are a number of ways to build your case. You can point out that many of the teams in your conference had rosters full of underclassmen as well, so they will all be as good or better next year. You can point out that of your 15 wins, 9 of them came by a slim margin. A bad bounce here or there and the team could have finished well below .500.

As you share this type of information, make it a point to convey that you are not saying this to criticize, but rather to communicate just how fine a line exists between winning and losing. Tell your players and parents that you are sharing this information so everyone is aware of the work that will be required if the team hopes to take the "next step" and become a top flight team. In my experience, everyone can respect that message and it can go light years towards providing a coach with a nice cushion to fall back on should things not work out the way they and everyone else hoped they would.

Scenario 3: *You have a team that is loaded. Your team is ranked in the top 10 in the state pre-season and you know that it should be. Anything short of a conference or state title will be a disappointment.*

Coaches in this position have got to work their tail off to control expectations because it is not just parents or community members spouting off about how good your team is. If you are ranked, your team is recognized as a powerhouse state wide. You are not likely to convince the community that your team is really over rated and that you will be lucky to win a game, but you can communicate the message of how tough it is going to be to live up to those lofty expectations.

Before I offer my advice on how you should go about controlling the expectations in this scenario, I have got to tell you about the all time master of the expectations game. I will change his name to attempt to protect his anonymity, but "Coach Johnson" was the ultimate B.S. machine and a master at manipulating public expectations.

Almost every year Coach Johnson had a team loaded with talent. Annually his team was ranked among the top in the state. And every year if you asked him what kind of a season they were going to have he would go to great lengths to convince you that they would just be lucky to win a game. He would outline why every team in the conference had an edge over his team. He would explain that his players, while good athletes, lacked the mental edge or the intangibles required to truly be a top flight team. For as long as you could listen, Coach Johnson could conjure up reasons why his team was not deserving of their top 10 ranking.

The ultimate example of his "sandbagging" was when his highly ranked team opened the season against a team that had been 2 and 21 the prior season. In the pre-game radio interview, Coach Johnson actually said the following about his teams' opponent: "They played a brutal schedule last season and they lost about 15 games by a bucket or two. I'll tell you, they could easily have been 21 and 2. We're going to have our hands full tonight." I laughed out loud as I listened on the radio. Coach Johnson's team got "lucky" that night and went on to win by 40.

The amazing thing about Coach Johnson is he could recite all of the reasons his team was over rated with a straight face. Perhaps even more amazing, there was a huge chunk of the community that bought his B.S. season after season. For this reason, there were two signs of spring in Coach Johnson's community; the robins migrating back from their winter vacation and the community praising Coach Johnson for somehow cobbling together another 20 win season when he had nothing to work with and he was playing against the best teams in the state on a nightly basis. Granted, Coach Johnson went so far to impact expectations that he eventually lost credibility with many people, but he never lost the expectations game. Every year the people in his community marveled at the job he did rather than wonder why in the world his highly ranked team fell short of the state championship. That disillusion at the teams' failure to win a title is precisely what the talk around town would have been if Coach Johnson did not wisely and effectively manipulate expectations.

Coach Johnson offers us a road map to navigate our way safely through a season with lofty expectations. Coaches have to go out of their way to praise their opponents and make them sound far better than they are. Coaches also need to tactfully downplay their own team's abilities. When a coach is leading a talented team, there is virtually no upside for the coach from a public relations perspective. If the team wins a championship and lives up to expectations, in the mind of the public that is what should have happened. The coach doesn't get much credit. But if the team doesn't match expectations it is much easier to pin the blame on the coach than it is to vilify a group of kids. Because of this harsh reality, coaches need to do whatever they can to diminish expectations.

I know when I have had great teams and we headed into a game against an opponent we were much better than, when asked about that night's game I would often be honest and say "if we win by less than 20 I'll be disappointed." I never go as far as Coach Johnson to lower expectations, because I think if you do that all the time you can lose credibility and people will stop believing you. However, if we are playing a team that is average but one we should still throttle, I might tell whoever asked about that night's game "well, they have won 5 in a row and they're playing great of late" or I might share that "they just beat a very good team on Tuesday so we need to be ready to play." Neither one of those comments runs my team down but they adequately elevate the status of our opponent.

Depending on my audience, I might say "we sure haven't been very sharp in practice lately" or "if we shoot like we did last game we are in big trouble." Both comments serve to inform the questioner that our team is not invincible. Neither could be construed as such harsh or direct criticism of my team that it could lead anyone to question my faith in them, but comments like that help control public expectations.

In fact, I have even warned my teams at times that I may publicly proclaim a few things like those just mentioned. I explain that I do it in an effort to take some of the pressure off them. I might say certain things publicly, but I want my team to know that I have total faith in them and their abilities, so I share my strategy with them privately.

One more effective comment to circulate in your community is that as a highly ranked team your group is wearing a "target" on its back. Because of your ranking you are going to get every opponents' best effort because you are their "Super Bowl." Again, this helps to demonstrate that even a highly talented, highly ranked team has challenges it must overcome.

As coaches, we have to play the expectations game and we must endeavor to control expectations to the extent that we are able. We either control expectations or we become a victim of them. It is really that simple.

Dealing with Public Confrontations

No coach wants to have to deal with a confrontation involving an angry parent or fan in public. There are very few scenarios where the coach comes out the "winner" in such a confrontation.

If the coach doesn't acknowledge the person creating the scene or if the coach just walks away, there are those (especially the person calling them out) that will perceive it as the coach backing down or being weak. If the coach addresses the heckler and responds to them, it could be construed as validating the heckler's comments. It could also be perceived as the coach showing weakness because the heckler or the angry parent got under the coach's skin.

Clearly the best way to win these confrontations is to work to prevent them from happening in the first place. A coach can do this by following the recommendations in chapter two. That is, have open lines of communication with any that might question or criticize. Giving critics an avenue to voice their concerns will make them less likely to share their criticism or complaints in a public manner. Of course, even given that open communication policy there could still be the occasional incident where a parent or spectator is so caught up in the moment that they exercise poor judgment and they voice their criticism of you in a very public way.

Should that occur the first and most important ground rule to follow is that the coach should never acknowledge public criticism or commentary during a game. If you hear a fan or a parent hollering at you and you react to them either through gestures, eye contact, or verbally, you will only make things considerably worse for yourself and your team. Acknowledging the comments of an idiot during a game empowers the heckler far too much. Part of the reason they hollered out their remark is because they were already clearly comfortable becoming the center of attention. Getting a reaction from the target of their tirade only enables the heckler to become the star of the show. It also further fuels their confidence and their ego to continue making comments because they know you have heard them and that their words have affected you.

I am as emotional a coach as you will find, but I have managed to discipline myself when hecklers have directed comments toward me or my team. I do this because I understand that giving them a reaction is letting them "win" and I am too damn competitive to let a heckler beat me in a battle of wills.

However, depending on the situation and who was doing the heckling, I have confronted certain hecklers after the game in relative private. That is largely what this section is about, helping you recognize situations that demand confrontation and then outlining how to go about such a confrontation to have the best possible effect.

Let's begin with heckling that you should never confront under any circumstances. Heckling from opposing parents or fans should never be acknowledged publicly. There is literally nothing to be gained by doing this. Yes, you might like nothing more than to win the game and to give them the double barreled middle finger salute on the way off the field but the brief moment of satisfaction you might derive from doing that will quickly be overcome by the avalanche of problems that would be certain to bury you in the immediate aftermath of that action.

I am not suggesting you ignore the opposing fans and their comments. Feel free to use their words to motivate yourself or your team. But keep your comments about the fans' actions confined to your teams' huddle. Let it be something that unites or rallies your team, but let it go no further.

If you are really rattled or angered at the comments of an opposing fan, do your best to remember the words uttered by hall of fame player and long time baseball "villain" Reggie Jackson. "They don't boo nobodies" is what Reggie said when asked about being heckled. Take the heckling for what it is, a compliment. The opponent feels so threatened and frustrated by you and your team that they are reduced to ripping on you. When it is clear they can't beat you in the athletic competition, they attempt to win the mental game. Don't give them the satisfaction.

When the hollering is coming from your own fans that typically calls for a different course of action. If it is students chanting something like "put in so and so" that is harmless enough. You may not like it, but it is another situation that you are much better off ignoring. If students are hollering personal insults or attacks towards you or your players and if your on site administrators aren't doing anything to discontinue or discourage it, that may merit you tracking a couple of the kids down the next day at school. When you visit with them, the best approach to take is to let them know how much their words hurt you or your players. Don't yell at the kid or try to intimidate them. Instead, appeal to them on a personal level. The student will usually be surprised that you are visiting with them in such a calm and reasonable way and typically if you treat them with respect, they will reciprocate. If it is a large group of students chanting or hollering inappropriate comments or criticism, you or your assistant coaches would be well served to identify the ring leaders. Rather than try to talk to a hundred plus kids, talk to the two or three that spearheaded the chants. Let them know how valuable they can be to your team and communicate how detrimental their actions were to the team's success. If you give these students a sense of ownership and let them know that they have an impact on the outcome of the game, they will be far more vigorous in their support for your team and considerably less likely to criticize.

When the loud hollering is coming from a parent or a group of parents, this often calls for a direct confrontation. The timing and nature of the confrontation very much depends on the situation, but I will offer a few real life examples to help you understand how and when to handle such situations.

I'll begin with a personal story of a situation that insisted on me directly confronting a parent within minutes of the end of a game.

In my first year at Champlin Park we had an excellent team and we started the season 16 and 0. I had been told that I had inherited a group of parents that were very involved, very intense, and very opinionated. While historically I had set a tone with parents that made them feel included and valued as a part of our program, the scouting report I was given about the new group of parents I was working with led me to take a very different approach.

Shortly after accepting the job I learned that the parents had made many of the key decisions involving the program and the previous coaching staff was apparently comfortable with that. For example, I was informed by a parent that youth night would be on a certain evening and that they would be doing various events during the game and at half time. I quickly made it clear to the parent that youth night would be when I decided to hold it, and if they wanted to assist in the implementation of my agenda for that night they would be welcome to do so. I needed to convey to the parents that I called the shots now and that if I wanted their input, I would ask for it.

This approach worked well for the first 16 games of the season. I suspected that when we lost a game or two though, I would be tested. In our 17th game we lost a close contest to a top 10 team on a Tuesday night. The test I anticipated came during our next game, just a few days later.

We were playing a good team on the road. We were better than them, but they were a well coached, talented team. Our calling card to that point in the season had been a strong full court pressing defense. We were very quick and the faster the game went, the more it favored us. So we opened this game as we had every game to that point, with a full court press. Within five minutes, we found ourselves trailing 20 to 4. The opposing team was on fire to start the game and obviously we were struggling offensively. After about five minutes of play, I heard a voice yelling from the bleachers opposite our bench.

"Take off the press!"

There weren't more than 200 people in the entire gym so it was not hard to hear this person screaming at the top of their lungs. And they didn't just yell it once. They yelled it every few seconds for about two minutes.

It didn't take long for me to discern which dad was telling me how to coach. I can't adequately describe how pissed off I was. I looked at my assistants and said "can you believe this bleeping guy? He thinks he's gonna tell me how to coach? Blank him! We're gonna press the whole bleeping game!"

Never mind the fact that what he was hollering was ignorant. After all, we had only made two shots and because we only pressed on a made basket, clearly it was not our press that was allowing our opponent to light up the scoreboard. I knew that the first five minutes were an anomaly. Our opponent would not continue to shoot as well as they had and we would heat up. I knew that speeding up the game and creating more possessions via our full court pressure was going to benefit us in the long run. So we stuck with the game plan, and by halftime we had rallied to cut the lead to four. We played well enough in the second half to pull away and win by 12.

I knew the way I responded to this public challenge by a parent was going to be particularly important considering the way parents seemingly steam rolled the previous coaching staff. So after visiting briefly with my team, I knew I had to seek out this dad and let him know that what he did was not going to fly. Several of the parents waited outside of the locker room for their daughter's after every game, so I knew I would find this dad and I also knew I would have enough

of an audience that word would spread to all of the parents about how
I had handled the heckling.

I left the locker room and headed straight for this father. He
reached out his hand to congratulate me on the win and started to tell
me how our competition for the conference title had done that night. I
didn't shake his hand and I cut him off mid-sentence.

"We need to get something straight right now," I said. "There can
be no confusion about who coaches this team. When you're up there
yelling to take off the press, I want you to know that just like you, I am
a stubborn son of a bitch and that means I am going to do the exact
opposite of whatever you are screaming. I'm going to do the opposite
even if it's to the detriment of this team. If you or anyone else in the
stands thinks they are going to tell me how to coach this team, they are
sorely mistaken.

"And I hope you realize that even if I think the thing you are
yelling makes sense, if I incorporate your less than subtle suggestion,
suddenly all of these parents think they can coach the team from the
stands. There can be no confusion about who calls the shots for this
team. I make the decisions."

This father was a proud, competitive, stubborn man. He wasn't
going to let me get away with a one sided confrontation in front of
these other parents. He said "I have the right to express my opinion!"
And to that I replied "You're darn right you do. And the next time you
decide to offer your opinion by yelling orders at me, I'm going exercise
my right to plant your daughter's butt at the end of the bench. I call the
shots!"

I think that comment stunned him as his daughter was our leading
scorer and a terrific player. Our conversation ended there, and for the
next several seasons we had no more issues with parents thinking they
could run the team from the stands.

My decision to confront the parent in this manner was a calculated
risk. It was a risk because it could have escalated into something ugly.
It was a risk because he could have called me on my threat and I
would have been forced to bench our best player. It was a risk because
by threatening to punish his daughter for his stupidity, he could have
argued to our school's administration that I was being unfair to his
daughter. I had not visited with my AD about this action ahead of
time. I had no way of knowing if they would have my back. But I fully
understood the situation before I walked out to confront this father.

I understood that while this father was competitive, he was not
stupid. I knew that a physical confrontation was extremely unlikely. I

knew that he cared deeply about his daughter and about her statistics and that he wouldn't risk her losing playing time for his actions. And I knew that with a 17 and 1 record and a #2 ranking in the state, I was very likely to get the support of my administration for nearly any decision I made at that point.

It is only fair for me to reveal this as well though; as we walked out for the 2nd half of the game I told my coaching staff that I wanted desperately to win so I could confront that father afterwards. Had we lost, it would have been next to impossible to have that kind of encounter because the dad would have been completely convinced that he was right about the full court press and that my decision to continue to press had cost us the game. He would have still been very fired up. After the win he had a positive vibe going so when I confronted him, he was not mentally prepared for a confrontation. I had the upper hand in that situation.

Had we lost, he would have been in the position of strength and I would have had to wait until the following day to address the situation with the father one on one, thereby losing the impact of getting the message across to the other parents as well. The situation had to be just right for the public confrontation to work. All the pieces fell into place on this occasion, but that is not always the case.

One of my coaching colleagues had an incident a few years ago where a parent, who also happened to be a fellow teacher in his building, came out to confront him on the team bus. This parent was upset that his daughter hadn't played enough. The dad made a comment to the coach then said "you're an asshole" and walked off the bus. The coach admitted to me that there was nothing calculated about how he responded. He reacted purely on emotion. He jumped off the bus and chased down this dad.

In full view of his team, he yelled at the dad saying "that's real professional of you to do that. Very professional" and then he proceeded to get in the father's face even to the point of bumping him chest to chest. The confrontation did not escalate to fisticuffs, but this verbal and somewhat physical confrontation happened with the entire team watching including this father's daughter.

The coach told me that in retrospect he gained nothing from that confrontation and in fact he lost a great deal. While administration supported the coach and suspended the father from attending the next two games, the coach was also scolded by administration for how he conducted himself. The coach received a threat from his players' older brother, a young man that the coach had once taught that was now a college student. This brother said that if the coach ever threatened one of his family members again he "would drive back and kick his ass." And of course this confrontation severely and irreparably damaged the coach's relationship with the player. She was already upset about playing time, but when the coach went after her dad it just gave her another reason to hate the coach.

This same coach shared with me another scenario where he elected not to engage in confrontation and he almost surely should have. During a game late in the season, the coach had removed a player from the game that had been performing particularly poorly. Within a minute of her being subbed out a group of team parents started chanting "Put in Becky! Put in Becky!"

When you have a group of parents publicly and openly question your coaching that is a major red flag and it is something that must be addressed. As much as you might like to, the time to address it is not in the midst of the game. And it may not even be wise to do it immediately after the game because rather than confronting one person, you would be facing a "mob" of sorts. The time to address it is likely the next day or certainly before your next game, but an action like that cannot be ignored.

Had I known about this when it happened, I would have recommended to the coach that he call a parent only meeting after practice and prior to the next game. In this meeting he would need to address in a very direct manner the inappropriate and frankly juvenile behavior of the parents. He would also have to ask them to reflect on how their chant made the player that just subbed into the game feel. Finally, he should remind them that if they have an issue with his decision making, there is a proper forum to voice those concerns, but during a game is never the proper place.

Some of you reading this might be thinking "why have all the parents at the meeting if it's only five or six that were the problem?" The answer is because if you only address the offending parents, the parents that witnessed the open display of insubordination might not know about your meeting and they may be left with the impression that the behavior they witnessed is acceptable and goes unaddressed. Further, it would be wise to have any parents that are your advocates in the same room with the parents that were so publicly disrespectful. It is entirely likely that these allies may speak up on your behalf in such a setting and further put the idiot parents in their place.

What if some of the key culprits don't show up for the meeting? The way I would prevent that is by making the meeting mandatory and saying that at least one parent has to be present or their child doesn't play in the next game. That would practically insure perfect attendance.

I wish I had been able to offer these ideas to this coach shortly after the incident transpired. As it turns out, he did not address the incident at all and within a couple weeks of his season coming to a close he was released from his coaching position. I would never suggest that this one act alone decided his fate, but it certainly empowered those that opposed him to think they could get away with things and that he wouldn't challenge them. As coaches we must always be careful not to embolden our enemies.

Confrontation is absolutely a necessity in coaching. If you don't like confrontation or if you do whatever you can to avoid it, you won't last long as the head of a program. While we have established that confrontation is sometimes necessary, the timing and the tone of the confrontation are of the greatest importance. Coaches must engage in confrontation only after careful consideration and calculation. Confrontation that comes entirely from emotion is typically going to turn out badly for the coach and will be a win for the critic that instigated the situation in the first place. I will close this chapter with a few basic rules coaches should endeavor to follow when it comes to confrontation.

1. **Confront on your terms.**
   Do it at a time and place of your choosing and in a manner that is in your best interest.

2. **Confront with a plan.**
   Don't speak from your heart or your gut. Go in with an idea of the points you intend to make and stick to the plan.

3. **Confront from a position of strength.**
   Give your AD a heads up about who you will be meeting with, why you are meeting, and what you will be saying. The coach establishes the ground rules for the meeting, not the person being confronted.

4. **Whenever possible, confront in private.**
   Public confrontations are a huge gamble. You put the person you are confronting in a position where they feel they have to "save face" and they can be far more likely to lash out. As we covered, there are rare occasions public confrontation can work to your benefit, but most of the time, confronting in private is in everyone's best interest.

FOUR
✴✴✴

Special Interest Groups

"When you buy a vase cheap,
look for the flaw;
when a man offers a favor, look for the motive."
— Japanese Proverb

pecial interest groups impact politics on a grand scale. Whether it is the National Rifle Association, the AARP, or any of the other hundreds of interest groups that are so pervasive in our state and national government, these powerful organizations always pick sides in a political fight and they are rarely reluctant about using their power to influence elected officials.

Coaches have to contend with their own version of special interest groups. Be they powerful parents or booster clubs, there are people that will use their power in an attempt to intimidate and mandate that certain things happen. How a coach responds to the pressure applied by these various groups often determines how long a coach lasts.

The Powerful Parent

Whether you coach in a small town or a major city there are rich, prominent, powerful people that will attempt to exert influence over your program. These powerful people can be excellent allies or they can be dangerous enemies. The frightening thing is that they can be both in the span of a short amount of time depending on various developments. As coaches, we can sometimes get overwhelmed by these people. In this section we will offer advice about how to manage the special interest group that is the powerful parent.

During my first season coaching baseball I was confronted with what has continued to this day to be the most difficult decision I have ever had to make as a coach. How and why I was forced to make this most difficult choice is the rest of the story.

I was coaching a group of 14 year olds in a JV level program. We were a feeder team to our outstanding VFW team that had won several

state championships in the previous few seasons. I had 18 players on
my roster. We played doubleheaders two or three times a week so
we went on a pretty straight platoon system nearly all summer. For
example, we had two second baseman. One would play the first game
of a double header and the other would play the second game. This
was how we did things at nearly every position on the field, every
game day. At the outset I had expressed to players and parents that
at the JV level the emphasis was on player development so we would
make sure that everyone got a chance to play.

But I had also communicated that as the season wound down,
we would start to identify the best player at each position and those
players would begin to get more playing time in preparation for our
end of season tournament. We would play to win that tournament and
we would play our best players more in those games. Essentially the
first 40 games of the year were an extended tryout for everyone and the
final 10 games we would roll out our best lineup.

As we approached the end of the season my two shortstops
were deadlocked in a tight battle for the top spot. Both were solid
defensively and both were doing decent at the plate. Then in the final
week they began to separate. Kevin went on a tear getting 12 hits in his
final 14 at bats. Our other shortstop, Jimmy, went in the tank. He struck
out more in that stretch than he had all season and he was taking his
offensive struggles out into the field. He started to launch balls past our
first baseman at an alarming rate. In crunch time one kid stepped up
and the other fell apart. It made my decision easy...or so I thought.

In the final double header before we hit the road for our end of
season tournament, my top lineup played most of both games. When
we built a comfortable lead in game two, newly christened backup
shortstop Jimmy got an at bat and got to pitch an inning. It was clear
he was not content with that.

The next afternoon I got a call from the President of our baseball
association. He asked me to come to his place of business and to do
so as soon as I could. This was very unusual. I had only been to see
him at his office one other time and that was to collect my paycheck. I
was a bit nervous. On the drive there I was racking my brain, trying to
figure out what I could be in trouble for.

After arriving at his business, he walked me back to his office and
shut the door. "Carl, I got a letter delivered to me at lunch today that I
want you to see." Then he reached across his desk and handed me a
two page, hand written letter. He sat there silently as I read it.

The letter was from Jimmy's mother. It began with a few

paragraphs explaining that when the season began Jimmy thought the world of me. He considered me the best coach he ever had. As a mother, she was elated that her son had found someone he could look up to and emulate.

Then the mood of the letter changed abruptly. The mother went on to say that her son is now a shell of his former self. His love for the game has been drained away. His dreams of playing professional baseball have been crushed and it is all because of Coach Pierson. By the end of the note she had attempted to suggest that I had damaged her son for life.

As I concluded reading, the association President asked me what I thought. I said "I think this mom is nuts. Her son choked during the final week or so of the season. Our other short stop played his best ball of the season. Jimmy is frustrated so Mom is coming to his defense, but this is a bit dramatic. In fact, it's a complete over reaction."

The President replied, "that may be, but I'm gonna tell you something. Jimmy's grandfather donates a hell of a lot of money to our program. If Jimmy and his mom are pissed off, guess who stops writing us checks?"

I could gather by his expression and his tone that he was not joking around as he told me this. "I don't care how you do it, but you need to make this right. This mom can't stay mad or we're out a ton of money." He didn't have to say the rest. I could figure out that the baseball program being out a ton of money also meant I would be out of a job.

I called Jimmy's mother as soon as I left the President's office. I asked her if we could meet. She agreed to meet me at a city park not far from her house under a picnic shelter. Though I was still a reasonably inexperienced coach, I arrived expecting a typical "my son should be playing more" kind of meeting. If only it had been that easy.

Within a minute of us sitting down face to face, the mother burst into tears. My first thought was "this is rather melodramatic for a situation where your boy isn't getting many at bats." But after her heavy sobbing subsided and she collected herself, she explained the real reason behind her letter.

"Jimmy's dad was at the game the other night." Jimmy's mother was re-married. I had never met his real dad. I could tell this was going to get complicated.

"He flew in from California to see Jimmy play. When he saw that Jimmy didn't play very much in those two games, my ex-husband saw his opportunity. After the games, he approached Jimmy and told him that if he moved to California with him that he would hire him a personal baseball coach and he would make sure that Jimmy was on a team where he would play all the time."

While I remained stone faced, inside I was reacting as though I had been punched in the stomach. This woman was telling me that if her son didn't play more she was going to lose him. I didn't think it could get any worse, but it did.

"I'm scared to death Coach. I'm scared because Jimmy's dad is an abusive alcoholic. That is why we got divorced. I was worried for my safety and the safety of my children. My ex-husband can be such a charmer when he's sober but he is a completely different person when he's drunk. Jimmy hasn't seen that side of his father in a decade. He may not even remember. I can't lose him!" and with that once again she began to cry so hard she couldn't speak. Her crying allowed me time to consider the full depth of the situation and the right way for me to respond.

Here I was, 20 years old, still somewhat new to coaching and I get this dropped in my lap? Play my kid or he moves a thousand miles away with an abusive alcoholic father. What the hell should I do? What would you do?

After hastily considering all the aspects of the situation, the pros and cons of granting her wish or ignoring it, I reached a conclusion.

"I certainly understand your angst." I said to Jimmy's mother. "I want to do what I can to keep your son safe and with you. But I feel like I also have to be fair to Kevin. Obviously I can't go to Kevin and say 'yeah you've been the best hitter on our team the last two weeks but I have to sit you down and I can't really get into the reasons why'. I want to do what's right for both players. So Kevin is going to continue to start but I promise you I will get Jimmy in as often as I can."

As you might guess, Jimmy's mother was not completely satisfied with my decision. But on some level I think she had already come to terms with the fact that her son was probably leaving her. We parted ways about as amicably as possible considering the circumstances.

Our team played five more games that season and in those five games Jeremy pitched two innings and got three at bats. Within a couple of weeks of the end of the season and before the school year started, Jimmy moved to California. I never heard a thing about him after that.

But the donations to our baseball program must have kept coming because I kept coaching for three more summers before moving to Minnesota. I have to believe the fact that I was willing to sit down and listen went a long way with this mother. I also think that upon further reflection she must have understood that what she was asking me to do just wasn't right. No more hate mail was sent to our board President. There were no more meetings. Simply by listening and by being straightforward and honest, the political ramifications resolved themselves. To this day it was the most difficult meeting I have ever had with a parent, simply because of the gravity of the situation. And to this day, I continue to hope that things worked out well for Jimmy, wherever he may be.

When the Powerful Parent Is Your Boss

A situation that seems so common it is almost cliché is the coach that encounters pressure from a school board member or administrator that has a child on the coach's team. As a coach, you really have just two options when confronted with such a circumstance:

1. Pretend the player does not have a powerful parent and play them as you would no matter what their last name would be.
2. Go into self preservation mode and compromise your morals by catering to the demands (said or unsaid) of the powerful parent.

Of course, there are variables to those two scenarios. The best case would be what happened to a colleague of mine. This gentleman supervised me as an assistant principal, but long before he became an administrator he started out as a social studies teacher and a three sport coach at a small school. He was an assistant football coach, head hockey coach, and head baseball coach. During his second season at the school he had the superintendent's son on his team. According to my colleague the kid was a total jerk. The boy routinely came late for practice, never hustled, and wasn't that talented. Early in the season this coach approached the superintendent and told him straight out "you're son is a pain in the ass!" He then listed off all the issues the boy had created for himself and the team. Fortunately, the superintendent was in total agreement with the coach.

The boy was suspended two different times during the season and ultimately didn't play very much. What a happy ending, huh? The coach was able to stand up and do the right thing and the powerful parent supported him. Of course, this situation took place in the 1970's. Back in those days if a teacher punched a student the parent might even side with the teacher and tell their kid to quit being such a knucklehead. Times have certainly changed.

When I asked this former coach and current administrator how he could muster the courage to have such a blunt and direct conversation with his boss he said, "I didn't care about coaching that much. My attitude was, 'I'm the coach and if you don't like the way I do things you can go find someone else." No doubt an admirable attitude, but many of us in the coaching profession don't share this man's lack of concern for our coaching future. That is why sometimes self preservation is actually the best move.

But before we go down that path, let us consider the politics of ignoring the powerful parent and playing the kid based on their merits. Of course, if the kid in question is a talented player then everything is easy. You can play the kid and while there will likely still be a few bitter parents suggesting the kid is just playing because of their name, in general you will have the support of the team and the rest of the parents because they recognize you are playing the best players. Your life is good!

If the kid in question is a middle of the road player, things could get a bit more complicated. My philosophy in this situation has been if the player with the powerful parent is equal in ability with another player, a coach should make life easier on themselves and play the powerful parent's kid more. I am not suggesting the coach crap on the other kid. But if neither kid gives the team a better chance to win, then why not play the kid that will prevent the most political problems for you? This might leave a bitter taste in the mouth of some readers, but remember what we say in the introduction; those that choose to ignore the politics of coaching become victims of the politics. In a coin toss kind of situation like the one just described, put the politics on your side!

Without question, the most precarious and difficult situation is when the kid of the powerful parent is a terrible player. In that situation a coach has much more to consider. First and foremost, the coach must evaluate the real power of the parent. If you play your best players and the team wins, will you still be in a position to continue coaching or could this one parent take you down? Or vice versa; if you play Johnny Rotten and the team loses, will the rest of the parents engage in a mutiny and will the one powerful parent be enough to preserve your position? Even then, with public opinion so strongly against you, is it a position worth preserving? Further, when the powerful parent's kid graduates, would they still advocate for you or would they lose interest and throw you to the wolves?

The fact is there are no easy answers in this situation. The key to the whole equation is how much power the parent in question wields. Will you be counting on them for a recommendation for your next job?

If so, you may lean towards playing their kid more just to set things up so you can move on to a new job in the future. If Johnny Rotten plays a lot but the team loses, will the powerful parent be just as pissed off as all the other parents about the losing? If that is the case, then you are probably toast either way and you may as well play to win.

The important thing to do when confronted with a crisis such as this is to consider all the pros and cons of your possible actions. If you just go with your gut, ignoring the politics, you lose control over your fate and your future. Maybe in the final analysis you decide you can't anticipate how things will play out if you play Johnny Rotten or if you bench him because you don't know the key people involved well enough. In that case, the default answer is always play to win. But if you know that doing one thing or another will help you preserve your coaching position, then you need to give careful consideration to the cost of doing that.

I would also warn you about confiding in other coaches when confronted with these tough calls. I warn you because nearly every coach you talk to is going to tell you to ignore the politics and play your best players. That is extremely easy for a coach to say when their ass isn't on the hot seat! You need to make this decision yourself. Just know that any advice you solicit is usually not going to have your personal best interest at heart, it is going to be a coach giving you the easiest answer of all, "play to win." As hard as it is to accept, sometimes playing to win is what costs a coach their career.

To be perfectly honest, just writing about this subject makes me uncomfortable. Like any coach, I would like to think that regardless of the situation I am going to do the thing that gives my team the best chance to win, regardless of who Johnny's parents are. I would like to advise my fellow coaches that playing to win is always their best move, but the politics involved with powerful parents means that is not always the case. Coaches with outstanding win/loss records have had their careers destroyed by pissed off, powerful parents.

That is why I suggest that if your team is going to be mediocre regardless of what lineup you field, then you may as well be mediocre and keep or create key allies. Mediocrity with no allies leads to a short coaching career as well.

Consider the politics, then make the best decision you can for yourself and then for your team.

Fundraising and Donations

Former President Ronald Reagan is famously quoted as saying

"They say that politics is the second oldest profession, but I've come to learn it bears a striking resemblance to the first."

For readers that are not familiar with what is commonly referred to as the "oldest profession," prostitution has been given that dubious title. Ronald Regan was right to equate politics with prostitution in the sense that in both cases, a person is taking money from someone that expects something in return. Politicians "prostitute" themselves to big donors and special interest groups in an effort to get elected. Then while in office, the elected official often does the bidding of the big donor.

Coaches have increasingly found themselves in a similar position, asking for donations to fund their program. In fact, in most places fundraising has become a major part of a head coach's job. With schools across the nation cutting teachers and other programs, coaches have found themselves raising money for even the most basic needs like uniforms or practice equipment. In the next few pages we will cover some creative ways coaches can generate revenue for their program without owing anyone favors. But the most important message in this section are the words of caution for coaches about how raising money could actually end up costing them.

Let's begin with a look at ways to generate funds from local businesses. In most cases, there is very little downside to this. I typically approach area businesses about sponsoring our summer camp. If they cover the cost of our camp t-shirts they get to put their logo and contact info on the back of the shirt. I tell the business our campers will be wearing that shirt on a regular basis for the next year and that they are essentially getting 100 walking billboards when they cover the cost of our camp shirts. In that sense, it is really advertising for the business and not a donation. In the very competitive world of fundraising, being able to offer the business something of value in return gives your program a huge edge. This is another reason a team website can be so helpful. I have approached businesses and said that in return for a donation, we will put their name and a link to their home page on our team website. I share with them that our site gets over 3,000 unique visitors a month. The business gets advertising and they get positive exposure by associating themselves with a local youth program.

Making the sales pitch to local businesses is not the reason any of us got into coaching, but getting your funding from businesses is best because it doesn't put you in a position to pay back any favors. Assuming they don't have any relatives in your program, the owner of the local bank or the pizza place down the street could care less who plays or how many wins you get. They want the tax write off and some positive publicity. That is where their agenda ends. When you get your money from local businesses, everyone wins.

Of course, as I alluded to earlier, doing this is getting to be more difficult. When a business gets bombarded with requests from the football, basketball, baseball, gymnastics, lacrosse, golf, tennis, softball team, etc. it becomes quite a drain on their advertising or donation dollars. That is why some schools are starting to combine their fundraising efforts. If you can manage to negotiate how the dollars will be divided amongst your respective programs that is a great option to explore.

Area businesses appreciate the idea that they can write one check and they have helped all of a school's teams at once. They also are comforted knowing they will not be solicited by a couple dozen different athletes during the course of the year.

Having a total school fundraising effort is good in theory but complex in practice. The football team with 90 players is not going to be willing to accept the same amount of funds as the tennis team with 12 players. But if you can work out the logistics in a way that everyone agrees to, the all sports fundraising really enhances your appeal to local businesses.

Parent Donations

I remember the first time I ever opened an envelope with a check written out to our program from a parent. I was immediately uncomfortable and questioned whether this was something we could accept. I went to my AD and asked if I dare deposit the check into our account. He acted as though I was crazy and he encouraged me to deposit it right away.

I then explained to him my cause for trepidation. With my background in politics, I recognize that rarely if ever, does a large donation to a candidate come without strings attached. The donor is usually going to expect something in return at a point down the road. I shared a possible scenario with my AD of the donor parent approaching me mid-season asking why their daughter isn't playing more and then reminding me of the generous donation they made to our team. As always, the AD said he had my back if something like that should happen, so I deposited the check.

But the scenario I suggested is something that every coach has to consider. If a parent is making a donation to your program what is the motivation for that move? If it is a simple 20 dollar donation I don't think you need to spend anytime considering the long term ramifications. But if they donate an unusually large amount you would be wise to wonder about it.

I have turned down a donation to our team that I sensed was for the express purpose of buying the parent some influence over me down the road. Their daughter was about to be a sophomore and was going to be competing for a spot on our varsity team. She was on the borderline in terms of whether she would make the varsity or not. These parents were quite wealthy, and the timing and amount of their donation just made it feel like they were trying to "break the tie" and buy her a spot on the team.

When I returned their check I explained that the team's finances were doing fine and I wouldn't feel right taking such a sizable donation, especially at a time where we had more money than we knew how to spend. They tried to insist that we accept the money but I was equally insistent that we would not. In the end, their daughter made the team and I could rest easy with the knowledge that there was nothing hanging over me, influencing that decision.

In the world of politics, special interest groups and corporations do not make sizable donations to candidates simply because they believe in the candidates' positions on issues. They make big donations so they can call that politician when a key vote comes up and count on the elected official returning a favor. In fact, many corporations make donations to both major party candidates involved in a campaign so no matter who wins, they can exert influence based on their contribution. A parent that makes a donation to your program is often going to expect that they are entitled to a favor if the time comes that they feel compelled to ask for one.

Before accepting a donation from a parent consider their motive, then decide if the donation could come back to bite you down the road. If you think it might, you have to weigh that risk with how much your program needs the funds or how much good it could do for your team. If you decide the definite benefits outweigh the possible risks, then by all means take the money. But keep this fact in mind; politicians that accept money from donors and then do the opposite of what the donor asks do not just lose that donation in the future. The group that made the donation typically makes it a point to take their donation elsewhere for the next election and they make it their mission to unseat the politician that crossed them. Don't expect a donating parent to behave any differently than a special interest group. They may very well make it their mission to take you down if you don't deliver on their request after accepting their donation.

Accepting Help from Parents

We know we have to raise money and most coaches consider it a terrible burden to be the sole organizer of the various activities required to raise funds. As a result, coaches often solicit or accept assistance from ambitious parents. This is fine to do, as long as the coach proceeds with caution.

Parents that approach the coach and seem eager to lead the fundraising charge don't always have an agenda beyond helping the program, but some certainly do. Identifying these parents can be tricky, so my advice is to avoid having parents lead your fundraising efforts as much as possible. The reason being that when it comes time for you to make decisions about who is going to play and who isn't, if you end up playing the fundraising parent's kid, there will be people in your program saying you are doing it only because the player's mom raised so much money for your program. And if the fundraising parent's kid does not play much, their parent is going to feel like they have a lot more leverage when lobbying you for playing time because you "owe them."

I had a parent that was very anxious to organize a big youth tournament to raise money for a team trip. The mother did an outstanding job, generating over ten thousand dollars for our program in just two days. We were all very grateful for her efforts. But a few months later when the season started and her daughter was only starting 2/3 of the games, this mother that had been very quiet and complacent suddenly felt empowered to blast me for "insulting and abusing" her daughter by not starting her every game. It is my overwhelming belief this parent felt that due to her efforts and her being so instrumental in the funding of our team trip that I should have gone out of my way to make sure her daughter started every game.

I didn't budge. While this mother was a thorn in my side off and on during the season, her daughter was a senior and I knew the mom would go away at the end of the year. There was little risk of her trying to mount a coup. Had the daughter and mother been around for another year or two, it almost certainly would have opened a huge can of worms that would have created issues that could have led to my untimely demise.

Booster Clubs

On the subject of booster clubs my best advice is simply "don't have one." Anyone I have visited with that has coached for any length of time has told me that their Booster Club does more harm than good.

I have never had a booster club for my team at any school I have coached at and when parents have approached me and asked if they should start one I am always quick to tell them that I am more than happy handling fundraising and that our team has all the money we need for the things we require. Despite my efforts, I did have a group of parents create a pseudo Booster Club, but any time they offered to pay for various items our program needed, I politely refused their offer.

Over and over again coaches tell me stories about how the panel of parents that makes up their booster club start off as allies and eventually erode into enemies. The booster club begins by offering to do all kinds of wonderful things for a coach's program. They offer to handle fundraising and make major purchases. But after a coach accepts these offers the booster club begins to feel entitled to make "suggestions" to the coach. What begin as suggestions evolve into requests, and eventually demands.

I had a discussion with a coach that had counted on their booster club for thousands of dollars each year, including funds for an assistant coaching position. With the appointment of a new booster club President came some new club policies. The booster club now requested that the coach meet with the board once a month during the season. It immediately became obvious to the coach that these meetings were intended to be an inquisition on why the coach was running a certain defense or why they took timeouts when they did. After a couple of meetings the coach decided to disregard the booster club's request and she stopped attending the meetings.

The next fall, the booster club President informed the coach that the boosters had decided they were not going to fund the assistant coaching position again that season unless the head coach hired a new assistant. This infuriated the head coach and the coach responded by having their players do a separate fundraiser to fund the assistant position and to spite the booster club.

In the scenario just described, the booster club went from an organization whose intent was to help the program to a group of people that began to consider themselves the team's "front office" or board of directors. When a coach counts on a booster club for funding the boosters have the ability to exert enormous influence. They may not start out abusing that power, but they can very well end up that way.

As much as possible, a head coach should do everything they can to avoid becoming beholden to a person or a group of people. When a coach accepts gifts or donations they must realize that they will often come with strings attached.

You may despise fundraising, but before you allow your booster club or a wealthy parent to purchase your new uniforms, you need to decide which you despise more; leading a fundraising effort or having a group of people feel like you owe them a favor?

Personally, I don't like owing anyone anything so I will do the fundraiser every time.

Control of Activity Accounts

Some coaches have activity accounts that they have sole control over. This is a wonderful luxury, but if it is not handled properly it can be another thing that ends a coach's career. In recent years there have been several examples of coaches that were accused of mismanaging their program's activity account or using money for personal items. In most of these cases the coaches have eventually lost their jobs over the accusation. A few have even gone to jail.

There are parents that use activity accounts like Elliot Ness used taxes. Ness couldn't convict infamous gangster Al Capone for any of the traditional crimes he committed so he eventually nailed him on tax evasion. The angry parent or parents that are not able to get rid of a coach for the traditional reasons will sometimes use the activity account to take them down.

If your activity account is run through your school, most of the time you should have little to worry about because your school will typically have policies in place that prevent or prohibit coaches from using funds in an improper manner. But also, be advised that if your account is through a school parents can request to see all the transactions from your account. Any account through a school is public information.

If you spend fifty bucks on some new team equipment and a disgruntled parent sees your son using that equipment at home during the summer, you may have given that parent all the ammunition they needed. They can now accuse you of abusing funds for personal use. You can never be too cautious with activity accounts. In my mind, getting in trouble for the abuse or misuse of an account is a dumb reason for a coach to lose their job because it is always entirely preventable.

While you may not want to make every purchase for your program public to all players and parents, it is wise to have a player and a school administrator sign off on every purchase you make. That way when an angry parent makes an accusation you can point to the approval of the player and the administrator of that purchase to prove you were not hiding anything, thereby exonerating yourself of any charges.

The best advice when it comes to activity accounts is to spend money on the players and only the players. Don't give parents any rope to hang you with.

There are some coaches that have control of an account outside of the school. Many of the same rules apply here. As I have one such account in my current position I have found it is impractical to have a player sign off on all purchases. There are times I buy something at the last minute like a ball pump the night before our summer camp begins. In the event a parent demands to see how funds have been appropriated I have done something to protect myself. I have kept every receipt from every purchase I have made since opening the account. I have kept every bank statement as well. Literally every penny that has come in or gone out is accounted for. The parent may not agree with how the money has been spent all the time, but they can never accuse me of any type of impropriety.

The main lesson here is to be aware that a parent on a mission will go to great lengths to take you down. Make sure you cover your rear end when it comes to your activity accounts.

The Allies Every Coach Must Have

Almost as important as having the support of your administration is having the school's custodians and secretaries on your side. Both have the ability to make your life wonderful or to make it miserable. There is no such thing as being too respectful or too nice to custodians and secretaries.

At every school I have been at, I have made sure that among the first staff I meet and get to know is the custodial staff. When I meet with them for the first time I don't explain how I would like things done. Instead, I ask them how they would like me to do things. I may explain that we would like to use the gym on these nights or at these times, then I follow up with "Does that work with your schedule?" If they say yes, I will ask "Could you show me where the brooms and the lights are so I can clean up and shut things down when we are done?"

I have always made it clear that I never want to do anything to inconvenience our custodians. I recognize they have a hard enough job as it is. I don't adopt this attitude because I am trying to get on their good side. I say it out of sincerity. It sure has helped me get on their good side though!

As coaches, if we ask rather than demand, we will find the

custodial staff will be far more receptive to our requests. In fact, what I have discovered is that they will often go above and beyond for our program when I make a request simply because they know that we appreciate and respect them.

In addition to always being respectful towards them, I always try to set aside a hundred bucks or so to give our custodial staff a gift card to a local pizza place or restaurant once a year. The good will that gift card generates is worth way more than the hundred bucks it costs. When we need the floor cleaned before a big game or need a rim fixed, they do it right away. You can be sure that if they weren't treated with respect and given that occasional gift, they would not be in near as much of a hurry to help us out. Take care of the people that take care of you!

Custodians often need to close down the high school gym for a week or more every year to refinish the floor. The timing of this task can be very damaging to a coach's program if they were counting on having a camp or some other activity when the custodians decide to work on the floor. I have been fortunate to avoid this issue every year I have coached by being pro-active and communicating with the custodial staff months in advance of when they typically do their work. I will ask them, not tell them, if they could wait until such and such day to begin the floor surfacing. If they say they really have to get in by a certain date, I will alter my schedule. One year I was not able to alter my schedule and because I had been flexible with them in the past, they altered their timeline for me. There has to be give and take.

A friend of mine made the error of getting into a power struggle with his school's head custodian. The coach thought he had more power and pull with administration than the custodian. The coach was wrong.

With two full weeks to go in the summer training program for his players, the coach came into the school one day to find the locks completely removed from the locker rooms and gym doors. There were signs up saying the gym was closed for floor refinishing for the next three weeks. That is two full weeks longer than the custodial staff ever needed previously.

The coach was irate and marched up to the superintendent's office. The superintendent confirmed that the custodial staff needed all three weeks to do their job. Despite the coach's arguments the Superintendent had no intention of going against the custodian's wishes. The gym could be seen from a balcony up above and for two full weeks the coach had to walk by and see nothing being done to the gym floor. He had angered the wrong person. Custodians can be among your greatest allies or they can become your worst enemy. Do everything in your power to keep them on your side and your tenure as coach will be considerably more pleasant.

Secretaries are another key allegiance to cultivate. While they may not be able to make your life less pleasant in such an obvious way as the custodial staff, they play a far more valuable role than most coaches realize.

Secretaries deal with more people on a daily basis than we might ever imagine. When someone calls the school, the secretary is the first person they talk to. As a result, secretaries are often the first filter of parent complaints or concerns. Before they direct the call to one place or another, the secretaries are often asked questions and they have an opportunity to either calm the caller down or pour gas on the proverbial fire. A secretary that feels you appreciate and respect them is very likely to advocate for you with a disgruntled parent, or at the very least, not make the situation worse. In fact, I have had secretaries support me simply by saying to the principal, "Wow you wouldn't believe how belligerent that parent was with me. They are wacko." This probably wasn't a conscious decision on their part to take my side over the parent, but because they know and like me, they are naturally more sympathetic when someone attacks me or complains about me.

Secretaries are also the ones that are most likely to bail you out of difficult situations. If a referee doesn't show up for your 9th grade game or your bus hasn't arrived yet, no one can save the day for you like a secretary. But they aren't going to be all that anxious to drop everything and save the day for you if you don't demonstrate the respect for them that they so very much deserve.

There are a couple things you should always try to do when dealing with your school's secretaries.

1. Never treat them like your personal secretary. Don't ask them to do menial tasks you could easily do yourself. If you rarely ask favors of them, they will be far more likely to help you when the time comes that you truly do need their assistance.

2. Make it a point to visit with them for a few minutes every week. Few people are as tapped in to the goings on of a school or a community as a secretary. They can offer you valuable info just through your casual conversations.

3. Make a grand gesture once a year. Send flowers to the secretarial staff at the start or end of your season to show them how important they are to you and to demonstrate how much you appreciate their help.

Following these three simple steps will score you big points with one of the most important public relations people a school has.

In summary, remember that no coach is "more important" than any other member of the support staff. In fact, without their support, our job as coaches can become considerably more difficult. Respect and appreciate your support staff and you will benefit in a number of ways.

FIVE

✱✱✱

Confronting a Cancer in Your Program

"What we don't condemn, we condone."
– Anonymous

Diagnosing Cancer

n the sporting world we often hear the analogy that a player is a "cancer" to their team. The analogy is often entirely appropriate. When such a player is removed from a team, the team tends to function at a higher level or in a much healthier way.

Given this fact, it can be astounding how slow coaches can be to recognize or "diagnose" a cancer on their team or in their program. This is particularly true if the cancerous player is talented. Before we explain how to properly treat a cancer in your program, let us first establish how to accurately diagnose the cancer.

Early Warning Signs

* Separates self from the team at every opportunity
* Plays in a selfish manner (or if a parent, promotes selfish play by their child)
* Overtly hostile towards players or coaches

When players or members of your program demonstrate any of these symptoms, they are in the early stages of becoming cancerous. It is certainly possible to treat them and make them a contributing, healthy member of your program again, but the treatment has to be immediate and aggressive.

Sometimes you might notice a player acting rather distant from their teammates. This can be for any number of reasons and the action, in and of itself, does not necessarily mean the player is in the early stages of becoming a cancer, but the behavior can certainly become problematic so it needs to be investigated.

For example, if you have team dinners before games and a player rarely or never comes, as a coach the first thing you should do is reach out the player and find out why this is happening. It could be something as innocent as they were not able to get a ride and they were embarrassed to ask a teammate for a lift. That is not a player being a cancer. That is a player being shy. But you have to ask the question to properly explain the behavior.

Maybe before your game, all the members of your team sit together in the bleachers but one player always goes off by themselves. Again, this action should not be ignored or written off as a player just wanting to get focused. It could very well be that is what it is, but as a coach you need to find out. Often the initial answer a player will give you will not be the real reason for their behavior. They will usually try to put the best possible face on things. In the event of the player sitting alone in the bleachers, they may suggest that the other players are talking about mundane topics and they would rather focus quietly on the game. If a coach probes them a bit further the player might reveal that they don't feel comfortable around the rest of the team or they don't feel accepted. This is a sure sign that there is a problem. And the problem might not even be the player that is separating themselves. But it is certain someone is driving a wedge between them and the rest of the team. When you recognize you have a problem, you now have a reason to examine the situation further.

Before I continue, I am compelled to say that I am not a coach that cares that much about team chemistry. I think chemistry is very over rated and a perceived "lack" of chemistry is used as an excuse by mediocre teams far too frequently.

I had a team that was scuffling along at .500 one season and we should have been better than that. After conducting meetings with some of our players about our under achieving I administered a team survey. The overwhelming reason for our mediocre performance was "bad chemistry." My response to the team was that their reason was a big pile of B.S.

You don't miss layups or free throws because you don't feel a close connection with a few players on the team. You don't swing at a pitch in the dirt because a teammate decided not to go to lunch with you. Using chemistry as an excuse for losing is ridiculous. I believe good team chemistry is a real thing and I think it can make an average team good and a good team great, but I don't believe it leads to losing. As I am telling you to try to find out why a player is separating themselves from the team, it is not so you can bring everyone together to hold hands and sing songs for team bonding. It is because their actions could be an early indication of a potentially larger problem.

After you visit with the player that is isolating themselves and encourage them to get out of their comfort zone a little and join team in various functions, it is also important to approach a couple of players on your team and encourage them to reach out to the loner player and make them feel included. If the attempts by one or both parties fall flat, it is just a matter of time before your team develops a full blown cancer. What you then need to determine is if the loner is the cancer or if they have become a loner because someone else on the team is the cancer and they have deliberately pushed the loner away from the team. What to do when that has been established is covered in the next section; "player cancer."

When a player is behaving in a selfish manner, the coach must confront this in rapid fashion. It must be made clear, in no uncertain terms, that by playing selfishly the player is not only hurting the team but hurting themselves as well. The coach should convey that continuing with that style of play will lead to less playing time for the player. There are coaches that are reluctant to have this conversation because the player in question is talented and they are afraid to upset or anger the player. But looking the other way or hoping the problem will go away on its own only allows the cancer to grow.

We all recognize there are some teams that have a true superstar caliber player that must carry their team. A look at statistics may suggest the player is selfish. I am not suggesting a clear cut superstar player is a cancer. I once had a team where I flat out told the players and the parents that Becky was going to take most of the shots because she was our best player. There is a difference between being a star player and being a selfish player. Selfish players force things and do things out of the context of what you intend for your team to do. They ignore better opportunities for teammates in an effort to give themselves more chances to shine. Your star player can be a cancer, but if they are that is usually the result of the way they carry themselves and how they relate to teammates.

If a player is playing outside the role you have established for them, it could be they don't fully understand their role but it is more likely they are playing to accommodate their own agenda. The quicker you confront this and condemn it, the quicker this player is on the road to recovery. Remember, what we don't condemn we condone. The player must be called on it.

Sometimes the player is just manifesting the wishes of their parent and the parent is the true cancer. I once had a father tell me that he instructed his daughter to take 20 shots a game if she hoped to earn a college scholarship. (Notice he made no mention of how many she had to make. Apparently he thought college coaches were just impressed by players that attempted a lot of shots!) This girl was a decent player, but we had a lot of good players on our team and the idea of her taking 30 or 40 percent of our team's shots every game was absolutely preposterous.

I attempted to explain to this father that the direction he was giving her was really not in her, or our best interest. I outlined what it is that college coaches are really looking for. He didn't seem to buy what I was selling. Much to my relief, his daughter decided to finish out her career at another school. Just like doctors are not going to be able to save every sick patient, a coach is not going to be able to prevent every player from becoming a full blown cancer. Don't beat yourself up over the ones that get away. Do your best, and if it doesn't work out, move on.

The other early sign of a growing cancer is a player that is openly hostile towards their teammates or their coaches. Sometimes this is simply immaturity or not knowing how to properly deal with difficult situations. But when a player acts in an inappropriate manner, again the prescription is swift acknowledgment by the coach that such behavior will not be tolerated.

This does not have to mean barking at the player or even benching them right away. In fact, if they are being verbally abusive it is probably best to visit with them in as private and calm a way as you can so you aren't role modeling back to them the very behavior you are condemning. But the soft spoken, non-confrontational approach doesn't work with some kids. In that case, you may have to get in their face and communicate that if anyone needs barked at on this team you, the coach, will do the barking. The player's job is to pick up their teammates with positive comments and encouragement.

In the event the confrontational approach doesn't remedy things, the bench is option three in your effort to help the player recognize their role. Often, this last resort will resonate with even the toughest customer. Riding the pine proves to be an excellent teacher for many hostile players. But on occasion even that doesn't work. Then the only treatment left is to remove the cancer completely.

It's time to remove the cancer when...

* a player is unhappy after a team victory
* a player is unphased or even downright happy after a team loss (because they personally played well)

* a player's (or parent's) comments or actions are polluting or infecting other players or people in the program
* a player, parent, or coach is doing things to deliberately undermine you or your program

Those of us that have coached for any length of time have occasionally noticed a player exhibiting an altogether opposite reaction after a game than we would anticipate. If a player is pouting or sullen after the team wins, you can be sure it is because they are focused on themselves and not on the success of the team. Often this attitude can be counseled and treated. Sometimes you encounter a kid that played poorly and when confronted they say they feel bad because they let their team down. That might be a genuine feeling. They may have their focus on the team and feel that they did not perform to the level the team needed them to. For those players, I have always been quick to point out that "if you're going to have a bad night, do it on a night we win. If you played bad and we lost a close game by all means feel bad, but if you play bad and we still win, you should be the happiest person in the locker room! Your team didn't need you tonight. You picked a good night to have a bad night!"

If a kid responds well to this discussion and you don't see the behavior again there is no more that needs to be said. But if after this exchange you continue to see the player pouting after wins, you can be certain they fed you a line about "letting the team down" and their focus is selfish in nature. Left to fester, their attitude becomes poisonous to your team.

Just as bad and dangerous to your team is a player that is jubilant after they personally played well but the team lost. This is an attitude the player cannot easily explain away. Regardless of their individual performance, no player should be pleased or happy after a team loss. When you see this, you can be sure you've got a "stat rat" on your team. Stat rats are players that are concerned only about their individual performance and statistics. The success of the team is secondary, at best. Teammates notice these players even more quickly than those that pout after a win. There is little counseling to be done when you have a player like this. If they are talented they might help you win a game here or there, but the impact they have on your program over the long haul will always be a net negative.

I had a player that exhibited both of the above behaviors and I learned the hard way how damaging an effect it can have on a team.

Player Cancer

Kelly was a talented player but somewhat troubled on a personal level. She was on varsity her sophomore season and was a top reserve on an outstanding team. We started five seniors and played three sophomores off the bench. There was no disputing who should be starting or playing the majority of the minutes on this top ranked team, or so I thought.

Late in the season, as our team was getting ready to make a run to the state tournament, I heard through the grapevine that Kelly had been complaining to people at school that she should be starting. This was nothing short of a ludicrous suggestion. The player starting over Kelly was a senior in a battle with another one of our seniors to be the school's all time leading scorer. The starter had already accepted a scholarship to play collegiately and she led our team in scoring. Did Kelly honestly believe she should be starting over this senior?

I couldn't believe what I was hearing was true and I wasn't too anxious to stir the pot with our team rolling along so I dismissed it as rumor. Even if it were true, I wrote it off as a sophomore being immature. She would grow out of it.

During the final few games of the season I saw Kelly exhibit some of the "early" warning signs of cancer. She was pouting after our team earned a 20 point win over a quality opponent. While everyone in the locker room was clearly excited about the win, Kelly was crying in a corner. I went over and talked with her after dismissing the team. She used the "I let the team down" line. I bought it, but the real reason for her moping would be revealed soon enough.

I again heard from kids at school that Kelly was complaining during lunch that she only got to play "X" number of minutes in our blowout win and she only scored 8 points. After hearing this I knew I had to confront her.

When I asked her about the comment she admitted she had said it. She went on to explain that she felt a great deal of pressure to score because her older sibling was a division one athlete and there seemed to be an expectation that she earn a basketball scholarship. I sympathized with her plight. I told her that while she might feel pressured that I was sure her family loved her and all they really wanted was to see her be as successful as possible. I offered to talk to them about how she was feeling. She insisted that I should not. I got the impression that she believed such a conversation would only make things worse.

We made it through the season, but during that season Kelly seemed to be close to only one player on the team and that player was a senior. I discussed with Kelly my concern about what she would do when this senior graduated. Would she finally feel compelled to integrate herself with the rest of the team? Kelly responded that there was some bad blood between her and her teammates from 6th and 7th grade; wounds that had not healed. I thought that sounded odd but again, I tried to counsel and support her. I talked to some of our team members and asked them to make a concerted effort to reach out to Kelly and make her feel a part of the team during offseason workouts. They complied and absolutely reached out to her, but she continued to push away.

During the spring when our entire team played together in various tournaments, Kelly was on a separate spring team. Her interaction with her high school teammates for the next few months was minimal. In the summer season, when she did join our team for games or tournaments, she usually traveled with her parents rather than piling into a van with a group of 4 or 5 of her teammates. She rarely ate with the team, always creating an excuse. It seemed like being with the team off the court, and even on, had become a huge burden to her.

About a month before the start of new season my JV coach came to me and said "Kelly told me something the other day you have to hear. She made me promise not to tell, but you have to hear this. She said that she plans on transferring after her junior season. She said that she should have her scholarship locked up by then so she will finally be able to go to whatever school she wants to for her senior season."

Again, I thought based on her attitude and behavior plus the pressure she was putting on herself to score a scholarship that this was just an example of her being immature. She would grow up a lot during her junior year. That is what I kept telling myself. But internally I knew that Kelly was becoming a major cancer to our team. Despite this gut feeling, a part of my brain kept telling me I could get through to her. In retrospect, the part of my brain that was only focused on winning games was probably the part I was listening to. Kelly was talented. Not an amazing player but talented, and she could help us win games. Instinctively I knew her baggage outweighed her talent, but my instincts weren't winning the argument with my head yet.

Finally, after watching her interact on and off the court with our team during fall league, it was clear that despite her talents she was going to be more of a hindrance than a help. A week or two before tryouts I asked my AD if I could simply cut her and save everyone a lot of headaches. He was not on board. He said that tryouts are supposed to be based on ability and that if there were problems during

the season we would address them then. I should have been more
insistent.

During Kelly's junior season we went 17 and 9. Not an awful
season by any means, especially with a team full of juniors. But
excluding our record the season was nothing short of a nightmare
for most of the players and coaches involved. We had three full team
meetings during the first six weeks of the season, one of them a very
emotional meeting with tears by several players. The amount of drama
created by Kelly was off the charts.

Though I fielded complaints on a regular basis about Kelly's
corrosive attitude, she had not done anything so noticeable or
egregious that it justified me benching or suspending her. When I
visited with our AD about the various issues she was causing for our
team he responded that we needed to document her infractions so
we could verify why we were taking action when the time came. The
trouble was none of her offenses were obvious or blatant. You can't
suspend a player for giving dirty looks or "forgetting" to high five their
teammates. At the time, I thought to myself "you can't bench a kid for
being a bitch."

Kelly never yelled at a teammate or directly disrespected a coach.
Everything she did was subtle. For example, when a player was subbed
in for her the player entering the game would extend their hand to high
five her and she would just blow by them. Admittedly I didn't ever see
this as my focus was elsewhere but it was one of many concerns my
players brought to me. I told the girls that complained about this that I
couldn't be the "high five police," but little things like this were adding
up and tearing our team apart. My team was a lot like a patient that
visits a doctor numerous times saying they don't feel right; adamant
that something is wrong. I was the doctor dismissing their symptoms
as a minor cold or virus that would eventually take care of itself. In
retrospect my diagnosis was so wrong I was guilty of malpractice.

In truth, it is not even fair to say Kelly was tearing our team apart.
The players were coalesced and united in their disdain for her. She was
actually bringing the players together. What Kelly was actually doing
was damaging <u>my</u> reputation with the team. The players saw all these
little jabs Kelly was taking at them and all they saw from me was that I
ignored Kelly's behavior and I continued to play her.

Kelly was our leading scorer. That shouldn't have mattered, but
to the weak part of my mind it did. She wasn't our best player. I never
believed she was our best or most important player. But she was good
and through all the turmoil I decided I would continue to council

her and try to help her mature and become a better teammate. I had
meetings involving her and our captains. I had meetings with other
players and parents complaining about her. We had more meetings than
games that season!

The meeting I remember most vividly was during a holiday
tournament. My JV coach and I spent a portion of halftime talking to
Kelly about her obviously selfish play. We did this after the rest of the
team had returned to the court. Kelly went out to start the second half
and forced a shot, completely out of the flow of our offense and I sat
her for the rest of the game. I told her she would not play again until
we had a sit down meeting with her and her father. My JV coach and I
met with Kelly and her dad the next morning.

I explained to the two of them what prompted Kelly being
benched and I outlined several other issues we had been having with
her throughout the season. I even made reference to issues from the
previous season. I explained that we had attempted to coach and
council but that none of our efforts seemed to be getting through. The
last learning tool we had left to use was the bench.

Her father's response floored me. He said that he felt like his
daughter was being treated differently than all the other girls on the
team and that I treated her unfairly. This comment completely set me
off.

"Unfairly?" I asked rhetorically. "She leads the team in scoring,
in shot attempts, and in minutes played and you are suggesting I
am somehow treating your daughter unfairly?" My face was growing
increasingly red with each passing word. "You are right about one
thing. I have treated your daughter differently than every other girl
on the team. I've put up with more crap from her than I have put up
with from any player I have ever coached in any sport! I have looked
the other way when she's been insubordinate to me, disrespectful to
teammates, opponents, and officials. I have bent over backwards to try
and help your daughter grow up. I've looked the other way more times
than I care to remember. Well I'll tell you something, I am done doing
that. If she so much as rolls her eyes between now and the end of the
season she is going to be suspended."

Kelly's dad was clearly angered by my comments but he seemed
to know better than to piss me off any further as I had the final say in
his daughter's playing time. I laid out very specific ground rules for her
to live by for the rest of the season and the meeting came to an abrupt
and uncomfortable end.

For the next month there were literally no issues with Kelly. I wouldn't characterize her as the model teammate, but all the subtle jabs she took at her teammates apparently evaporated. She was more of a team player on the court as well. I was hoping this final attempt at rehabilitation and this direct discussion with her father had put us on the right path.

Then in the final two weeks of the season things started to turn south again. Like before, Kelly never did anything so obvious that we could get administrative support to suspend her, but her behavior and attitude prompted her to be benched for extended periods. Finally during our section semi-final game, as we trailed by three with four minutes remaining, Kelly moped over to the huddle during a time out. I knew blowing up at her at that moment would do more damage to the team than good so I went about my business drawing up what it was we intended to execute. As the timeout was ending I caught her rolling her eyes and just giving a "you don't know what the hell you're talking about" look. I couldn't take it anymore. I hollered at her that she could sit and watch the rest of the game from the bench if she wants to pull that crap.

Now the cancer that was Kelly had even spread to me. I disregarded doing what was best for the team and I lost my focus. Because I reacted to her antics I created a distraction for our team with only minutes left in a playoff game, certainly a time when we could not afford it. It is no surprise we collapsed in the closing minutes and went on to lose the game by nine.

What looked like a good season on paper is actually remembered by most participants as an unpleasant four months. As a high school coach one of my goals is for my players to have a good experience and build great lifelong memories. By refusing to remove the cancer from our team that season I failed miserably at that goal and I failed my players.

The weekend of our playoff loss I got my coaching staff together and we lamented at what we were going to do with Kelly the next season. We had a lot of talent, but it was abundantly clear that she was a major cancer and our team would never reach its potential with her as a part of it. I also knew that her continuing to get playing time had severely damaged my credibility with the players and parents in my program. If I wanted to continue coaching at this school I had to take a stand and I could not continue to have Kelly on the team. Our coaching staff brainstormed all kinds of ideas that night but came to no conclusions. Fortunately we didn't have to. An opportunity presented itself a few days later.

One of our captains came to me and said that Kelly had been telling people at lunch that she was going to transfer. She had made these comments before and when players asked me how to respond I told them that Kelly was just trying to get attention. She wanted teammates to come up to her and tell her "you can't go, we need you!" I told the players that unless that is how they felt they shouldn't say anything to her about her comments. It was a cry for attention, nothing more.

Needless to say, not one of the 17 other players on our team told Kelly we had to have her. And Monday afternoon I decided to take a chance and see if I could make our problem go away. I texted Kelly and asked her to meet with me before school on Tuesday. I asked my 9th grade coach to be present so nothing I said could be twisted or taken out of context.

When Kelly sat down I got right to the point. "I've heard on more than one occasion, the most recent being yesterday, that you're not happy here and you're looking to transfer." I'm guessing that Kelly was expecting me to plead with her to stay. After all, she was an all conference player. It was obvious by the look on her face that what I said next was not what she expected. "I just want you to know that if you want to transfer I support your decision 100%. I want you to be happy and if playing somewhere else will make you happy, let's make it happen. If there is anything I can do to help you just let me know."

Kelly sat speechless for a moment. Then she asked if there was anything else I wanted to talk about. I said no and she left to go to her first hour class. By the end of the day I had players coming to me saying "Kelly says you told her she has to play somewhere else next season." I could honestly say that was not at all what I said. But I also knew that Kelly was going to twist things to make me the villain. I was more than content playing that role if it meant the cancer would remove itself from our team.

By the end of the week, Kelly had announced to everyone at school that her transfer was official and that she would finish out the school year and be on her way. I can't tell you how relieved I was. And the rest of our team was nothing short of giddy. In the days after the announcement several players approached me asking "have you heard Kelly is transferring?" and while asking they were completely incapable of keeping the smile off their face.

With the cancer gone, our team came together in a way that was far better than I anticipated. We started the next season 12 and 0 on our way to a 23 win season. How many times can a coach say they lost their leading scorer and they were going to be much better off as a result? This was certainly one of those times.

Incidentally, Kelly moved on to a prominent basketball program and became a role player on a 20 win team. I genuinely hoped things would work out for her because there was no doubt they worked out for us. And through the experience I learned a valuable lesson.

When the "cancer" on your team is also talented, it can be similar to a situation when a person is confronted with the awful choice of amputating a limb. When the doctor first tells them the limb needs to be removed to save the rest of their body they bargain. Even though the limb is a horrible hindrance, they remember when it worked just fine and they think that if they give it time or the right therapy, the limb will heal and it won't need to be removed. But eventually the patient understands the limb must be cut off to save the rest of their body from disease. The same is true of a coach dealing with a player that is a cancer. Regardless of how talented they are or if they used to be a functioning part of the team, in the end they must be removed in order to save the rest of your team.

I continue to regret not cutting out our cancer sooner. I will forever be sorry that our players had to endure such an unpleasant season because I was so enamored with a player's talent that I was willing to overlook all the negatives they brought to our team. It was a hard lesson learned, but it was learned well. And when a new cancer started to form on our team just two years later I treated it aggressively and effectively.

Annie was a short, quick, aggressive point guard that was an explosive player in every possible sense of the word. The first time I saw her play was in 7th grade and while she dominated the game with her talents, she also drummed up plenty of drama with her antics. When she got fouled she would hop up as though she was ready to throw down with the person dumb enough to hack her. When she thought she was fouled and the official didn't call it, she would make sure the ref and everyone watching the game knew that she had been wronged. Annie could say more with facial expressions and body language than most people can say with actual words in a lengthy conversation. But when she got really fired up she didn't leave it to her body language to express herself. Annie would blow up in a fit of foul language and yelling.

In between games of the first tournament I watched her play, I pulled Annie aside and explained to her that she had exactly two years to grow up and leave those antics behind. If she was going to yell at her coaches, at refs, and at teammates she was not going to play for us. She seemed to get the message and she made what appeared to be a concerted effort to reform. But despite her best efforts, she was a naturally spewing volcano of drama in the classroom and on the court.

Her freshman year Annie was likely talented enough to make our JV team, but we had just gotten rid of a cancer (Kelly) and I wasn't ready to put our varsity team through that misery again. My plan was to start Annie on the 9th grade team. If she exhibited the maturity and self restraint we had asked her to demonstrate, we would promote her by mid-season. I explained this plan to Annie's mother in advance of tryouts and while not totally thrilled with the move, the mother was mostly on board. She knew Annie had a long history of issues. "I told her that attitude would catch up to her someday. I guess that day has arrived," Annie's mother replied.

When we announced the teams after tryouts, Annie offered a prime example of why she didn't make our JV team. After seeing the list of players she went storming down the hallway screaming "I am better than Brandy. This is bullshit! I'm better than Brandy!"

In terms of sheer talent, Annie was right. Brandy was a senior that wasn't particularly skilled in too many areas of basketball, but Brandy was a great teammate. When I heard of Annie's outburst I pulled Brandy aside and said "Annie's tirade and attitude is exactly why she is not better than you. I'll take you on my team every time."

By mid-season Annie had served her time on the 9th grade team. She had created no major issues and collected no technical fouls. Our varsity team was undefeated so I was reluctant to rock the boat, but I decided to honor my end of the deal. After getting the blessing of our captains I promoted Annie to our JV/Varsity team.

She seemed to understand quite well that her attitude and antics would not be tolerated. We went most of a month without an issue. Then at a practice we had split into teams and Annie seemed to not understand which team she was on. One of our seniors called out "Annie, you're down here with us," to which Annie snapped back "I KNOW! Just back off!"

As promised, I immediately dismissed her from practice. I didn't yell or make a big scene. I just said matter of factly, "Annie, you need to go home." She started to protest but just before spewing words she knew would only make things worse, she went to the locker room. She came in after practice in tears and we talked. I asked if she understood why I did what I did. She said she understood and that she was trying really hard to change. I said I appreciated her efforts and that she was welcome back tomorrow. We would start fresh.

About a week later, Annie arrived late for practice. I have had a rule on every team I've coached that if you are late, you run. And it is not just a little running, it is "kick your ass so you never want to be late again" running. In the midst of this running Annie was getting her familiar "I'm going to kill you" look on her face. She was stomping and scowling as she ran. Hard to do, I know, but her physical vocabulary was really quite remarkable.

In the midst of her display I barked "who are you mad at Annie?" not looking for a reply. "Because if you're mad at me, you're mad at the wrong person. I didn't make you late. I didn't decide to spend time talking to friends or whatever it was you were doing. You made that decision. All this anger you are displaying better be directed at yourself because you are the person responsible for this. Not me."

Annie didn't utter a word and kept running, but it was apparent her venom was not self directed.

Her freshman season came to an end with no other issues. Like the preceding cancer Kelly, Annie was no where to be seen during the offseason. When our team did something, Annie wasn't there. She was off with her club team, chasing a scholarship she would never get. And I say she would never get a scholarship not because she was 5'2" (which was reason enough that she would never be paid to play basketball), I say it because with her attitude and body language there wasn't a college coach in the nation that would take her on their team. But soon her absence from our team wasn't just about her pursuing her own personal agenda, it was due to injury.

While playing with her AAU team she suffered an injury that required surgery. She would be out until just before our tryouts. As is my nature, I tried to look at the bright side. All offseason we would be developing other players, making them better. When or if Annie returned to the team healthy and ready to play it would be like signing a good free agent just before the season. But the bright side I conjured up was covered by dark clouds not long after tryouts were over.

Annie made it through tryouts, though she was clearly out of shape. This was to be expected as she wasn't able to do much strenuous activity the previous few months. While she was the most talented of our point guards, her inability to finish any conditioning drills led me to declare our senior point guard the starter as we had only 10 practices before our first game. I told Annie that when she got in shape and was able to fully participate in practice she would have a chance to start. Six weeks into the season she still wasn't able to finish conditioning drills. Any of the athletes that have played basketball for me would tell you we don't condition nearly as much as most teams. The reason for Annie's inability to finish conditioning drills and other drills was, in my estimation, largely mental. She just wasn't responding to any of the challenges she was being confronted with and she was actually creating some of her own challenges.

By January her frustration was starting to spill over into her actions at games and in practice. She was benched for a half here and there for various outbursts. We communicated with her mother every step of the way, but things just weren't improving.

Annie and I had a verbal confrontation on the bench during a game, and there were arguments after games. This time my AD completely had my back and he said whenever the time came to suspend her that I had done my due diligence in terms of documentation and communication with the mom. The time for suspension came on a cold January night during a road game.

We weren't a particularly good team that season but on this night we were playing a team that was hovering near the bottom of our conference standings. The game was a tooth and nail tussle for most of the first half, but we had built a narrow three point lead and we had the ball with 30 seconds left in the period. We called out a play to get one of our better players a shot, but the player traveled and we turned the ball over. Our opponent quickly came down and scored to cut the lead to one. We got the ball back in bounds and as Annie was bringing the ball up the floor she also turned the ball over. Now, with just a few seconds left, the opposing team was frantically trying to get the ball across half court to throw up a desperation shot. Of course I was hoping all of our players would just stay away as the opposing player threw up a prayer, but Annie was angry about her turnover and she went flying at the shooter just as the buzzer sounded. Subsequently she fouled a player that was shooting 30 feet from the basket. I was not happy, but I also knew I didn't have to make a scene as we would be heading to the locker room in a moment and we could address the major mental mistake there. As the opposing player was lining up for the first of her three free throws Annie came storming over to the bench. Amidst her stomping and yelling the "F" word protruded prominently from her mouth. I went over to Annie and rather than being accusatory or confronting her publicly (which I knew would only lead to more trouble) I simply asked her "Who are you mad at?" My hope was that she would accept responsibility and say she was mad at herself for committing such a stupid foul. But of course she didn't say that. "That wasn't a foul!" she shouted. "That girl jumped into me!"

I will advocate for my team vociferously with the officials when it is warranted and sometimes when it's not, but there was zero chance I could stick up for Annie in this situation. When she should have been running away from the opposing player like they had a disease, she went over and clobbered them.

I told Annie "the person you should be mad at is yourself. You shouldn't have come close to that girl." As I said this, the player sank her third straight free throw so instead of leading by 3 or more at halftime, we trailed by 2 because of one physical mistake and one mental mistake."

"And let's assume for a moment the ref made a bad call, what do we always tell you? Don't put yourself in a position where the ref can make a bad call because they probably will. You put yourself in a bad position." Annie was not the least bit receptive to this and she stormed off to the locker room.

In the locker room I decided to take a calm approach and make sure we learned from our two last minute mistakes in the hopes that we would execute better in the future. I addressed the first mistake, the travel, and talked about how advantageous it would have been to get the final shot like we had planned. Then I moved on to Annie's error. As soon as I started to discuss it she erupted "why are you always on me?!? You are always blaming me for stuff. Why do you always have to be on me?!?"

I did not handle this as well as I could have and I erupted back by saying "I am on you because you came storming off the floor screaming the F-word! Are you suggesting I should just ignore you saying the F-word?"

"I didn't even say it that loud" she countered.

"Oh, so now you're calling me a liar? You're saying that I'm making up how loud you screamed the F word? I think everyone on our team heard it not to mention the people in the stands!"

As Annie started to offer her rebuttal I said "STOP! That's it. Instead of talking about what we need to do as a team, I am arguing with you about the volume with which you said the F-word. You're done."

I went back to coaching the team as best as I could and the team did the best they could to forget about what had just transpired. We played a decent second half, but we found ourselves down one with 30 seconds to go and in a position where we had to foul the other team. They made their free throws and we lost by four. I still wonder how things might have turned out differently had we maintained our one point lead at the half instead of giving our opponent three free points, the lead, and all kinds of momentum at intermission.

On the bus ride home I called my AD and told him the time had come to suspend Annie. He gave me the green light and before she got off the bus I told her of my decision. She would be barred from practice the rest of the week and from our game that Friday. She would not be eligible to re-join the team until we had a meeting with her and her mother to lay out strict ground rules. I visited with her mother that night. Her mother had obviously got a very different story from her daughter, but after hearing my version of how everything transpired Annie's mom seemed to understand.

The decision to suspend her was one that my JV coach and I had suspected would ultimately end her affiliation with our team. We knew that based on her previous demonstration of mental toughness, or the lack thereof, if she were to be suspended she would likely quit. After she and her mother postponed the Monday re-instatement meeting, on Tuesday our prediction came to fruition. Annie decided to quit the team. Again, the feeling of relief on my end was immediate and overwhelming.

The game that prompted Annie's suspension marked the end of our first time through the conference schedule. We had won just three games and lost six. When she left the team, though we certainly weren't as talented, we were instantly better. The second time through the league we went six and three. I have no doubt our turnaround and subsequent late season success was almost entirely because we removed a cancer from our team.

Cutting a cancer from your team is not always easy, but living with the cancer is always more difficult, no matter how talented the cancer might be.

Parent Cancer

A different kind of cancer, but one that is just as dangerous is when a player or parent is making comments that pollute the minds of the people in your program. If you have players or parents openly questioning your decision making as a coach in a public way they have to be removed.

As I have mentioned previously, it is probably worth a sit down meeting with the offending parties first so they can get some things off their chest and so you can explain your way of thinking. Consider it a form of "chemotherapy" if you like. But if this treatment does not end the insubordinate actions you have no choice but to discontinue the player's relationship with the team. If you allow a player or their parent to publicly chastise you, other parents will eventually start to follow their lead. The other parents will see that there are no repercussions for such attacks and they will be encouraged to engage in similar behavior. Not all parents will of course, but it only takes one diseased parent to get the ball rolling. Then a few others will almost certainly follow.

All coaches have to be willing to take a certain degree of criticism, but if you feel it is becoming detrimental to what you are trying to do in your program you are well within your rights to remove that player/ parent from your program. If you don't, you could fall victim to the same situation one of my coaching colleagues did.

A long time coaching friend of mine lost his job to a parental cancer. Parent cancer can sometimes be difficult to diagnose because coaches don't interact with parents on a daily basis. My friend was unaware of the cancer that was eating away at him and his program. When he got called into the AD's office at the end of the season and was told they had decided to "go in another direction" it was like a doctor telling someone they have got cancer and when that person asks the doctor how long they have to live the doctor says "you've got 24 hours." My buddy was blindsided. But he was shocked by the developments largely because he didn't recognize the symptoms.

The parent that took him down was a prominent member of the community that had a reputation for being opinionated. But rather than sharing his opinions with my coaching colleague, this parent played the political game to perfection and took his complaints directly to school board members and the athletic director. While doing this, the parent asked those key decision makers to keep things quiet until the end of the season. He asked for this discretion "so as not to jeopardize his daughter's playing time on the team."

The cancerous parent's daughter was a senior that was having a very poor season. But due to the lack of other talented players on the team, by default she got a good deal of playing time. This senior had her father's charisma and was a leader on the team. As many coaches have learned, leadership does not always manifest itself in a positive manner. This player, no doubt due to the influence of her father, began leading players in a negative way. She was questioning coaching decisions after losses, not in the locker room or within earshot of the coaching staff, but to players later in the evening or the next day. While she was polluting the players, her father was planting seeds with the other parents, also second guessing various moves made by the coaching staff and painting the head coach's decisions with the most negative brush possible.

The entire time this campaign was underway, the coach was completely oblivious. When we visited a few weeks after he had been fired I asked him if, with the benefit of hindsight, he could pinpoint when things started to go south. After some reflection he decided it was after a particularly bad loss to a poor team. He said the next day at practice "it was like the team had just tuned me out." Nothing he was saying to his players seemed to register. This went on for the rest of the season and he said he felt like he was just banging his head against a wall.

What this coach was unable to identify was the reason for the team tuning him out. He didn't recognize that propaganda coming from this disgruntled parent and this parent's daughter was polluting the players and the parents on his team. Eventually the propaganda polluted the people in his program to the point that no one believed in or trusted the coach anymore.

As coaches, we may occasionally have practices where our players seem to tune us out. But if this happens for an extended period of time, say a week or more, you can be sure there is an issue you need to get to the bottom of. Should you find yourself in this situation you will need to do some subtle detective work. Hopefully there is a player or two on the team that you can trust and if you approach them the right way, you can get them to share why the team is behaving the way they are. With enough probing you can usually pin down who is responsible for public opinion turning against you. When you establish who the culprit is, the best thing to do is call the person out in a very public way. This forces your opponent to get their complaints out in the open. Ultimately this allows you to offer your own perspective in an equally public manner. It is difficult, if not impossible, to win a battle with an enemy that is always hidden or lurking in the shadows. Force your opponent into light of day.

Some coaches may be reading this wondering why it would be beneficial to compel a parent to state publicly the damaging things they have already been saying in private. The first thing to realize is that when this type of parent is pushed into a position where they can no longer whisper their criticism and they have the glare of the public spotlight on them, many will tone down their rhetoric considerably. When a parent that criticized with conviction and bravado behind the scenes is put in a position to air their concerns publicly and they back off, such an action immediately leads those that had been listening to the parent to question whether or not the previously powerful complaints carry any credibility. Most people are far more comfortable making critical comments about someone behind their back with the cover of anonymity. When forced to say the same thing to a person's face, most people will temper their words or rescind the criticism completely.

Of course, not all parents will become shrinking violets when exposed to the glare of the public arena. When the coach calls out a cancerous parent and the parent continues to be equally critical in public as they were in private, the coach still gains an advantage they did not have previously. It is easy to wage a campaign of criticism against a coach by whispering to one person at a time as the cancerous parent often does. It is impossible for a coach to respond to such criticism in an equally subtle manner. A coach can't expect to effectively rebut criticism one parent or player at a time, especially when the coach has been denied the ability to know precisely what criticism they have been subjected to. Think of dealing with parent cancer like preparing for a game. How hard is it to game plan for an opponent when you don't know what offense or defense they run? Would you be content merely asking a couple of people what they know about your opponent or would you prefer to scout the opponent with your own eyes? Obviously a coach can always collect more information and prepare a better game plan when they have seen an opponent first hand. It is no different when dealing with a cancerous parent. Rather than trying to respond to charges by using second hand information or hearsay, a coach has a far better chance of being successful if they can establish exactly what criticism their opponent has expressed. When you make your opponent visible you can be much more prepared to create an effective game plan to defeat them.

Parent cancer can be more complicated than player cancer. Simply cutting the cancer (the player and subsequently their parent) from your team can actually make things worse. People in your program were already being told that you are a terrible person and a terrible coach. By cutting the cancer it could actually serve to confirm what the cancerous parent has been suggesting. The people in your program could find themselves feeling sympathetic towards the cancerous player/parent.

When faced with this type of cancer a coach has to be more creative in their approach. Rather than attacking the messenger, attack the message. Refute ridiculous claims and call them just that, ridiculous. Whether the complaint is playing time, strategy decisions, etc. present your perspective to the people in your program and you will begin to win some back. Emphasize that you are always working to do what is right for the program and for each of the players in it. Then remind players and parents that you don't have the luxury of furthering the agenda of just one or two players, but that you have to do what you think is best for the entire team. Most people will respect that position when reminded of it. And if parents are piling on and blaming you for losses sometimes the best move is to accept responsibility, even if you don't feel it is your fault.

Shortly after becoming President, John F. Kennedy was contacted by the CIA about some plans that were already in the works to assist Cuban exiles in an attempted overthrow of communist dictator Fidel Castro. The CIA explained that these exiles would be parachuted onto the Cuban coast by US planes. After landing on a beach at the Bay of Pigs, the exiles would charge through the towns and people would empty out of their houses and join the rebellion and "take back" Cuba from the Castro regime. Kennedy was initially skeptical but when the CIA explained that former WWII allied commander and Presidential predecessor Dwight Eisenhower was fully supportive of the plan, Kennedy caved and allowed the plan to continue.

When the Bay of Pigs proved to be a major disaster, Kennedy could have gone in front of the cameras and said "One of the greatest military minds of all time, Dwight Eisenhower, championed this plan. Who am I to dispute the great General Eisenhower?" But instead of passing the buck, Kennedy shouldered the blame and his approval rating actually shot up. People admired the way he took responsibility. It was unexpected, brave, and it exhibited true character and leadership.

While accepting responsibility for your team's losses may not win you full approval amongst your players and parents, enough will admire your willingness to shoulder the burden that it will at least win a few more over to your side and buy you some time to rebuild your reputation.

Among the main reasons for the short duration of many coaching careers are the cancers as described in this chapter. Many coaches take the "tough guy" approach to their real life illnesses, saying to themselves, "I don't need to take any medicine. It will get better on its own" or "I can tough it out." That approach can lead to some major medical issues. The same approach towards a player or parent cancer can lead to a premature end to your coaching career. Recognize the symptoms of cancer early and determine the best course of action. Does it need to be removed or can it be "treated" with some wise public relations moves? That is for you to determine, but this much is certain, doing nothing or hoping it will heal on its own is a recipe for disaster.

Assistant Coach Cancer

We all want assistant coaches that are dedicated, knowledgeable, enthusiastic, and loyal. But from a political perspective the trait you should value most among those listed above is loyalty. In the NFL when the starting quarterback is doing poorly, regardless of the track record of the starter, fans begin calling for the backup quarterback to become the starter. Similarly, when things are going poorly for a high school team it is not uncommon for players and parents to start a push for one of the assistants to become the head coach. If you have a young, ambitious assistant whose loyalty is in question you have a cancer waiting to happen. I should know because I was that cancer many years ago.

After a couple of years as the JV baseball coach in my hometown, I had become quite popular with the players and parents. This could be attributed to primarily three things.

1. I was young and the players related to me much better than the program's head coach.
2. We won a lot of games.
3. The head varsity coach had been around for a while and had accumulated enough enemies that his reputation was becoming tarnished among many players and parents.

It was a bitterly cold January evening when a member of our baseball board of directors called me. He asked "if the position were to become available would you entertain the idea of becoming the head varsity coach?" I knew that if I said yes I could be starting a chain of events I wouldn't necessarily be able to stop, so while I my immediate internal response was to scream "yes!" I resisted.

"Why would the job be open? Is Coach Thomas stepping down?" I asked.

"Well, there are several of us on the board that have been talking and we just think the program would be better off if you were in charge," said the board member.

This comment led to an in depth conversation about just who on the board felt this way and how certain they were that they could accomplish this coup. After nearly an hour on the phone discussing all the variables, the board member had me convinced that if he could get a firm commitment from me that I would take the position, the board would take care of the rest. Without any regard or loyalty for the man that had given me my coaching job I agreed to attempt to take his job away from him.

When I hung up the phone I had zero regrets. In fact, I was very excited. I was already planning out who would be on my roster and what our pitching rotation and batting order would look like. The board member stayed in regular contact with me for the next several days, keeping me updated on all the developments while I was attending college in a community over two hours away.

About a week into the attempted coup I received a call from the head varsity coach. He called because he had been hearing rumors that some board members were trying to fire him. He asked if I knew anything about it. I admitted that I had received a call from a board member to discuss the possibility. Though he never asked directly, I gathered that the varsity coach was well aware that I was the likely successor and he almost certainly knew why the board member called me. Our rather uncomfortable conversation ended after about 15 minutes. When I hung up the phone I had my first inkling that maybe this attempted overthrow wasn't going to be the slam dunk I had been led to believe.

Over the next two weeks there was much controversy in my home town over the potential dismissal of the head baseball coach. There were certainly two camps forming; his supporters and mine. My focus and concern shifted. It no longer revolved around the excitement of getting the head job. For the first time I was focused on how much I had screwed myself if I didn't get the job. Why on earth would this coach continue to have such a turncoat backstabber on his staff? Though I didn't think it through at the time, when I agreed to accept the head coaching job I had also likely ensured my own firing if the coup was unsuccessful.

In the end, the head coach had just enough support to survive the board vote and retain his position. What happened next was surprising to me. The head coach reached out to me and asked me to continue as the JV coach. To this day, I don't know if it was a remarkable gesture of good will or if this coach just realized that firing a very popular JV coach would only put him back in hot water. Either way, I was grateful to keep my job. And I can say definitively I would not have extended the same courtesy to any assistant that tried to take my job.

Young, popular, ambitious assistant coaches can be a huge asset to your staff but you must insist on total loyalty. Address with them the exact situation described above. Tell them that it's very likely that at some point they will be approached by a parent or someone affiliated with your program and what might seem like an innocent enough question… "Do you ever aspire to be a head coach someday?" could be the first domino to fall and lead to a chain of events that could be damaging to their chances of eventually reaching that goal.

I have had a few assistant coaches that communicated to me that they would like to be head coaches. I have made it clear to them that I would assist them in any way I could in reaching that goal as long as they remained loyal to me. The best way to treat assistant coach cancer is to avoid developing it in the first place. Communicate openly with your assistant coaches. Genuinely listen when they have a difference of opinion with you. You may not incorporate every suggestion they offer but they will usually appreciate the fact that you respect their opinion enough to hear them out. If you don't demonstrate a willingness to listen to your assistants they will be far more inclined to jump on the criticism bandwagon when it arrives.

The other way to prevent assistant coach cancer from ever afflicting you is to hire assistants that have absolutely no ambition to become head coaches. This can give you a sense of security knowing that no one on your staff is after your job, but it can sometimes mean you have assistants that aren't as intensely committed to your program and its ultimate success. A coach content with being a lifelong assistant that is as committed and hard working as an aspiring head coach can be hard to find. As a result, you may be forced to decide which type of assistant is the best fit for you given the stage you are at in your coaching career. In general, I would recommend young or unproven coaches surround themselves with less ambitious assistants. Established or successful head coaches are usually better equipped to have the aspiring future head coach on their staff.

There are other strains of assistant coach cancer that head coaches might encounter. One type manifests itself in the form of an assistant coach that people in your program do not like or flat out despise. I have had colleagues that have lower level coaches that the parents and players consider a tyrant. These colleagues are often inclined to remain loyal to the assistant because the assistant coach is implementing their system and the assistant has been loyal to them.

The political ramifications of remaining loyal to a wildly unpopular assistant coach must be carefully considered. When parents come to you as a head coach, voicing concerns about someone on your staff, you must determine whether the concerns are valid or merely the usual complaints. In general, if the players or parents filing the complaint feel shorted on playing time or if you know this player will likely be cut from your program in the not too distant future, you can usually dismiss the complaint. If the concerns come from parents and players that will be prominent members of your program for years to come, that calls for a thorough examination of the charges. If it is something as simple as a complaint about the coach being too hard on players, a heart to heart conversation with the coach about altering their coaching style or offering more positive re-enforcement may be all that is needed. I had a coach like this a few years ago. He did a great job of teaching our system and he was a good X and O coach but he was extremely demanding and quite negative with his players. After his first season he and I discussed his demeanor informally. After season two I engaged in a more direct conversation explaining that he really needed to change the way he dealt with kids. Fortunately he elected to leave our staff after the following season because I was going to have to tell him we could not have him back. In that particular situation, I could afford to try to treat the "cancer." When the complaint is that the coach is too hard on players, that is a slow moving, rarely fatal affliction. However, there is an accusation that almost always calls for immediate amputation.

If you have an assistant coach that gets a reputation, deserved or undeserved, for behaving in an inappropriate manner around players, as a head coach you must act quickly and decisively. When I mention inappropriate behavior I am not necessarily talking about yelling or even cussing. In this circumstance, inappropriate means anything dealing with drugs, alcohol, or things of a sexual nature.

We have all heard stories about coaches that lose sight of the line separating them from their players. Perhaps they have supplied alcohol to players or they have made sexually suggestive comments. Any event related to something in this realm is politically radioactive. As a head coach, remaining loyal to an assistant that is caught up in these accusations means risking your own career.

I had an assistant coach a few years ago that was a terrific young guy. He was very enthusiastic and a good teacher of the game. He had a great relationship with most of the kids on his team. The parents of these players were just like jackals though. When their kids lost a game they could not pin the blame on the coach fast enough. All through the season, various parents were lodging complaints with me that my assistant didn't play the right defense or take timeouts at appropriate times. Through all of these complaints I never considered letting the coach go because I knew he had very limited talent to work with and that most of these parents were just insane.

By the end of the season, it must have become obvious to the parents that no matter how much they complained about game strategy I was not going to throw my assistant over board. As a result, they unleashed what I call the "nuclear option." Two parents wrote me notes outlining their concerns with my assistant because of his "inappropriate touching" of players. They claimed that he "touched their shoulders" and that he hugged players on occasion. Both of these things were true, but the parents were taking these things way out of context. I had not been witness to most of these "touching" incidents but I had done some investigating with other coaches and players and they all said it was run of the mill demonstrations in practice or, in the event of the hugs, comforting a kid that had missed a game winning shot or fouled out of a close game. There was nothing sexual about these encounters.

But the parents had made the charge and our administration became aware of it. Other people in the program began talking too. I knew if I were to keep this coach on staff, should any future player or parent have even the slightest concern I would be accused of ignoring the warnings. If I were to remain loyal I was going to be putting myself in a very precarious position.

I was forced to have a very disappointing conversation with this coach. He did an excellent job and he was being treated unfairly, but I also told him that if he were to stay on our staff his reputation in our program was already tarnished due entirely to these evil parents. He would be wearing a bull's eye on his back. The next disgruntled player or parent complaint could end his career, and quite frankly mine with it.

I would equate firing an assistant in a circumstance like the one just offered to the President firing their secretary of state. The President may like the cabinet member on a personal level, but sometimes the political reality demands that someone must be fired to appease the masses. There are countless examples of political underlings getting the axe during turbulent times. We also see this in the NFL or other professional sports. When the head coach is taking heat they will first fire the defensive coordinator or special teams coach. This action deflects the criticism and buys the coach some time, but such a move is often only a temporary fix.

In the case where I had to let my assistant go, I went home and told my wife "but for the grace of God go I." I knew that in a year or two when his players and their parents were of varsity age, I could easily become victim to the same heinous and baseless charges. With that in mind I made a calculated political move oriented at self preservation. Before any of those players (and therefore their parents) could attempt to take me down I cut them from our program. I recognized the parents were the carcinogen (the cancer causing agent) so I cut the parents. Yes I took some heat for a few days after their kids were cut, but it was a far better option than subjecting myself to the witch hunt that certainly would have ensued had I kept those kids and allowed the parents to engage in their trademark character assassination.

One other variety of assistant coach cancer is more difficult to diagnose because it will often show no symptoms. By the time a head coach realizes something is wrong, it is usually too late. The assistant coach cancer I am referring to occurs when the ambitious assistant coach that is after your job is on a different coaching staff.

I have a friend that was a head hockey coach. His career was a bit of a roller coaster in terms of wins and losses. A couple of mediocre seasons would be followed by a couple of strong seasons, then the cycle would repeat. The parents in his community were already calling for his head by the time his assistant coach cancer began to metastasize. I first became aware of my friend's predicament by reading the newspaper.

In the sports section there was a brief article about a young man that had been a successful head hockey coach at a small school. He had resigned to accept a teaching position in my friend's school district. This young coach had led his team to two straight state tournaments before resigning to take this new teaching job. There was no mention in the article of coaching duties in conjunction with this new teaching position. I saw red flags flying all over the place for my friend after reading the article and I called him that night. I asked my friend why this guy resigned a head hockey job at a successful program to merely take a teaching job in his town. My friend responded that the guy had a girlfriend in town and he wanted to move closer to her. I was still very suspicious.

I knew the vultures had already been circling around my friend for a couple of years so I recognized the arrival of this new guy as a major threat. "You need to get this guy on your staff" I said to my friend. "You've heard the saying keep your friends close and your enemies closer? I would want this guy where I could keep an eye on him," I added.

My friend was not in total agreement. By the time he bothered to visit with the new guy, this coach had already accepted an assistant job with the school's girls' hockey team. I was certain it wouldn't be long before this new coach would create additional issues for my already embattled friend.

Sure enough, at the end of the season my friend was informed that he would not be brought back as head coach. Later, it was revealed that a group of boys' hockey parents had approached the new assistant girls' hockey coach (the one that had been to two state tournaments) and asked him if he would ever consider switching back over to boys. His answer was yes. That was all it took. When the parents came to the administration and said they had someone more qualified than the current head coach that was willing to take over the boys program, it was the end for my friend. This story demonstrates that a head coach can't just look for assistant coach cancer from within their own program, they must be aware of what dangers lurk elsewhere.

In situations other than the one just described assistant coach cancer is among the most easily prevented forms of cancer. But as is the case with all cancers, it must be properly diagnosed and the earlier it is caught, the easier it is to cure.

SIX
***

The Politics of Youth Sports

"You are only young once,
but you can be immature forever."
— Former major league
baseball pitcher Larry Andersen

W hile high school sports are fraught with political intrigue, there may be no place where politics is as prevalent as in the world of youth sports. The primary reason for this is the people that stir the political pot most frequently (parents) are the people that act as the administrators of youth sporting organizations. Youth sports and politics are inextricably intertwined and if you hope to survive as a youth parent or coach, you had better be aware of how the political game is played.

In addition to examining the politics of being a youth sports coach/ parent, this chapter will also include items a high school head coach should consider when dealing with the youth sports organizations that act as the feeder system to their program. We will begin with the perspective of being a parent/coach in a youth sports program.

Coaching Your Own Kid

I have heard coaches extol the joys of coaching their own son or daughter in one breath only to disparage the notion of ever going through it again in the next breath. Coaching your kids' team can be a wonderful bonding experience between parent and child but it can also create hostility towards both the parent and the child from others on the team, fracturing longtime friendships.

In my years of observing, I have seen two main philosophies develop when parents coach their own children. In one situation, the parent becomes considerably more demanding of their child than they are of any other player on the team because the parent/coach is hyper- sensitive to the idea that someone might accuse them of demonstrating favoritism towards their own child. The other approach I have seen is the polar opposite where the parent volunteers to coach the team

primarily to insure that their kid will be the star and the parent can be
certain their child gets more playing time and more opportunities than
any other player on the team. Yes, there can be a happy medium, but I
can count on one hand the number of times I have witnessed it in over
40 seasons of coaching and playing sports.

When it comes to the relationship between you and your child, the
"demanding approach" can be very damaging. I can recall an example
from when I was an athlete. One of our baseball coaches also had a
son on our team. His son was an above average player, but this poor
kid's butt was planted on the bench an inordinate percentage of the
time. It was clear to all on the team that this player's father wasn't going
to allow anyone to accuse him of playing favorites so his son played
considerably less than anyone on the team thought he should. This
wasn't in the best interest of the son and frankly, it wasn't in the best
interest of our team to have one of our better players on the bench 70%
of the time. But it was how this father elected to balance his dual role
as coach and father.

My experience has taught me that situations like the one just
described are certainly in the minority though. The greatest percentage
of the time a parent tends to use their position as coach to put their
child in an advantageous position. And even if the parent/coach does
not abuse their position, they will almost certainly be accused of
favoritism by any parent whose child is not playing as much.

From a purely political point of view, it is really only advisable to
coach your child if:

1. your child is clearly one of the best players on the team or
2. there is no one else even kind of competent willing to coach
    and you genuinely feel allowing one of these other people to
    guide the team could be detrimental to your child's and the
    other kids' development.

Of course, even in the situation where others acknowledge that
your child is among the best or agree they are <u>the</u> best player on
the team, you almost certainly will still have to deal with disgruntled
parents. In recent years many coaches have found the percentage of
parents that consider their child a "star" is growing at an exponential
rate. It is becoming increasingly difficult to find parents that share a
coach's unbiased perspective and that can accurately evaluate their
child's ability. Understand that even if your child is the biggest, fastest,
strongest, smartest player on the team and this is abundantly clear to a
majority of observers, you will still have to deal with a parent or two
that are convinced their child is as good or better and is being denied

the chance to shine because the coach's child is stealing the spotlight. If you are thin skinned or can't handle such criticism, it is best to pass on a youth coaching position.

But let's imagine for a moment that you are emotionally equipped to handle these hecklers. The next question you have to ask yourself is "is my child equipped to deal with the criticism?" You can be sure that any comments or jabs people make will not be directed exclusively at you. Your child is going to hear it suggested that they are only playing or doing well because their parent is the coach. They are also likely to hear you criticized for specific decisions you make in terms of game strategy. If your child is not prepared to deal with these comments, it can lead them to lose their love for the sport. They may feel like they need to play less or not play at all to spare their parent from being harshly criticized. You cannot ignore the impact your coaching position could have on your child. It must be near the top of any prospective parent/coach's list of considerations.

In the second situation described at the open of this chapter, where a parent coaches a team with the express purpose of attempting to enhance opportunities for their child, obviously that parent is coaching the team for the wrong reasons. Even if you convince yourself that is not part of your agenda, if you find yourself drawing up plays for your child even though a strong consensus of players and parents on your team seem to consider other players better for that role, it is time to look in the mirror and realize that you are becoming a biased parent/coach. If you reach this conclusion, first pat yourself on the back because many parent/coaches don't evaluate themselves honestly enough to figure this out. But then you need to take a step back and recognize that as a coach, your primary responsibility is always to do what is best for the team first only catering to the best interest of each individual player second. If everyone else on the team seems to think Kelly is the best kicker but you always send your child out to kick, you are not serving your team and in the long run you are not serving your child because a strong resentment will grow towards them amongst their teammates.

Regardless of the reason you choose to pursue coaching your child and their team, another consequence you must be prepared to accept is the loss of long time friends. I have encountered numerous coaches that have talked about how coaching a youth soccer or football team created such hostility that people they had been friends with for years stopped talking to them completely. If a kid doesn't make a team, doesn't make the "right" team, or fails to get enough playing time, these

parents you have had a long standing relationship with can turn on you
incredibly quickly. It is an unfortunate by-product of the position, but
it goes with the territory and it is best to be aware of it before you dive
into coaching youth sports.

In visiting with high school coaches that have coached their own
kids, I have found that those who are most successful are the ones that
keep the role of parent and coach very compartmentalized. During
games and at practice their child calls them "coach" just like every other
player. Their child goes through all the same drills and they endeavor
to treat them and evaluate them no differently than every other athlete
they have coached over the years. When practice or the game is over
and they are on their way home, there is little to no discussion of the
sport unless it is initiated by the child. And if the discussion turns to
playing time, another player's role, etc. the lines between player and
coach become very blurred. I have had some coaches tell me they
don't talk to their child about those issues and the other parent has to
have those conversations with the kid. I have even had coaches tell
me their spouse was their biggest critic all season because they didn't
think they played their child enough. It is one thing to get griped at by
parents about playing time, but when you have to share a bed with the
parent that is griping at you that can get very complicated!

Again, there are some joys that go with coaching your child that
many parents never get to experience. Coaching your kid allows you
to spend more time with them than you otherwise would. It creates
shared experiences and memories that could help bond you together
for years to come. But when you are trying to decide whether to coach
your child or not, don't merely focus on all the positives that can come
from the experience. Ask yourself and your child if you are prepared
to handle all the negatives that can result as well. Prepare yourself and
your child for the criticism and the conflicts of interest that can crop
up. Addressing these things together doesn't ensure your experience
will be free of conflict or controversy, but it will allow you to deal with
these situations more effectively as you will have mentally prepared
yourselves for them.

Finally, if you coach your child in a youth sports activity, don't be
shocked if your coaching experience is cut short by your youth sports
board. Of the numerous youth sports coaches I have encountered in
my years of coaching, regardless of the win/loss record their team
posts or how positive the experience of most of the players was, there
will always be at least a couple of angry parents that complain to the
board and insist that you not be allowed to coach the following year.

Some boards disregard the complaints, others will fire a coach the first time there is a hint of unhappiness. Just recognize that this is part of the politics of the position. It goes with the territory. There are ways to hang on to your position by employing some of the techniques suggested elsewhere in this book, but for what is most often an unpaid position you really need to think long and hard about whether it is worth all the headaches.

Youth Tryouts

If you are going to coach your child's team and there is a tryout process, it is wise to recuse yourself from the initial evaluation that happens during tryouts. More and more youth sports organizations are hiring outside groups to come in and conduct their tryouts in an effort to create unbiased (or the illusion of unbiased) evaluations and to protect themselves from those that would suggest certain players made certain teams based solely on their last name.

If your organization has the means to do so, it is very wise to have an outside group conduct your tryouts. For youth baseball, I have seen youth associations hire amateur baseball teams to put the players through drills and to score the players on a scale of 1-5 on throwing, hitting, fielding, base running, etc. After the tryouts, the board or the youth coaches compile all the data and pick teams largely based on the evaluation of the neutral group. Of course there is a little jockeying that is done if Billy's dad is the only person that has volunteered to coach but Billy didn't score high enough to make the team. In order to keep a coach, some organizations may let the less skilled player bump a better player from the team. While this isn't necessarily fair, it is more practical than having a team with no one willing to coach them. It is simply a reality of youth sports.

I have seen youth basketball programs that have their 8th grade coaches observe and evaluate the 6th grade players while the 6th grade coaches pick the 8th grade teams and so on. This also prevents some of the conflicts of interest from occurring though there are certainly instances where nepotism is still involved.

There is no escaping the fact that youth tryouts will always be tainted by some degree of parental influence and politics, but the use of outside groups for evaluation is a better method than asking the coach to pick the team. When a coach is solely responsible for determining the roster it puts the coach in a horrific spot as they have to choose which of their child's classmates to cut and which to keep. It also means the coach is the lone lightning rod for angry parents to attack at the end of the tryout process.

Warning for head high school coaches: While it is at least somewhat advisable that you involve yourself with the selection of teams in your youth program you do not want to be seen as the driving force in selecting the teams in 6th, 7th, or 8th grades. Any influence you exert should be done in a very subtle, behind the scenes manner.

There are plenty of parents at the high school level that will be unhappy with you. You cannot afford to start creating enemies in the youth programs by picking the teams at those levels too!

I always attend our youth tryouts. I even put the kids through drills in most cases but I am never holding a clipboard or officially evaluating players. On occasion, I do visit with the evaluators afterwards or in private and find out who they have on which teams. If they have a tough decision I will offer my opinion. If they clearly have a player on the wrong team I will make that clear to them as well. But all of this is done in a very discreet manner. It would be very politically damaging if the head coach was perceived as picking teams as early as 6th grade. Stay above the fray on this one and in the style of old fashioned politics, exert your influence behind the scenes, not in public.

Every Parent Has an Agenda

Whether you are a parent/coach or just the parent of a youth sports athlete, it is important to recognize that every parent that serves on your youth sports board is there because they have their own personal agenda. Their agenda could be as harmless or altruistic as wanting to see the organization get more kids involved or improve its financial position. There are certainly parents that get on these boards for the right reasons. They may be in the minority much of the time, but it does happen.

The parents you must be wary of are those whose agenda is not intended to improve the program for all kids, but rather to enhance things for their kid specifically. I witnessed a classic example of this first hand just a few years ago.

Our youth basketball organization had a long standing policy that a player could only play at their age level. They could not "play up." This had led to a player or two leaving the program over the years because a parent was insistent that their child was too good to play with kids of their own age and their child needed to be challenged by older players. Finally, one of the parents hell bent on having their kid play with older players decided rather than have their child play in a program somewhere else they would just get on the board and change our youth program's policy.

This particular mother was adamant that her son, and eventually her younger daughter who was not yet old enough to be a part of the program, would need to play a grade or two above their age if they were to advance their skill level. She served on the youth basketball board for two years and every time she proposed her policy change it was shot down by the board. Undeterred, this mother maneuvered her way to becoming board president, a position where she would exert great influence about who was to serve on the board. Needless to say, there was some turnover in the board shortly after her rise to power and at her first official meeting as President the youth program altered its policy on kids playing at a higher grade level. This was a policy that had been in place for over 20 years. But one parent was able to push their personal agenda by playing the political game.

The example just presented is an obvious one. Many of the parents on youth sports boards have less obvious agendas, but make no mistake, they have an agenda. If you are a coach that serves one of these boards it would behoove you to ascertain just what it is that drives each person on the board, that is if you have any intention of coaching for more than a year. If you are merely a parent, it is still a good idea to attend these board meetings so you can get a feel for what direction the members are trying to take your child's youth program. Very few parents push for a position on a youth sports board because they love the way the board has been doing things and they want only to continue its current policies. Parents push for a position on the board because they are unhappy about something that is currently happening and they want to make sure it changes.

If you have a direct interest in the future of your youth sports program as a parent, parent/coach, or as a head high school coach, you need to get a gauge on the individual agenda each board member holds most dear to their heart. This puts you in a better position to advocate for it if you support it, or create a roadblock if you deem it a dastardly agenda that they are promoting.

Convincing Youth Coaches to Integrate Your System

Whether you coach a team sport or an individual sport, it is vitally important to have a strong working relationship with your youth coaches. While most team sport coaches already recognize the value in having their elementary or middle school coaches incorporate the same defensive and offensive systems they use at the varsity level, even track, golf, or tennis coaches can benefit by working with their youth coaches to create uniform terminology as well as insuring the technique taught at the varsity level is also being taught at the youth levels.

Something I learned a long time ago is that as a coach I am only as good as my youth coaches. If a player comes to me at the high school level unable to shoot a layup or dribble a ball they are so far behind the curve in terms of skill development that no matter how much time I spend on those skills the kid will not catch up to our competitors. Conversely, when I have had players come through that had outstanding youth coaches, people that really knew what skills to emphasize and how to teach them, I have looked like a coaching genius! I have reached the conclusion that I coach like I play poker. When I have good cards I'm a good poker player. When my cards aren't very strong it is a lot more hit and miss. When I have good players I appear to be a much better coach. Now of course, I am just as good a coach when I have players with a low skill level but it sure doesn't appear that way to the public. That is why I make it a point to get to know my youth coaches and I work very hard to guide them on what specific skills they need to develop and at what ages.

One of the ways I do this is by passing out what I call a "youth coach's resource guide." More accurately it is a youth coach's handbook, but I thought that sounded to condescending so I softened it up (an example of wise public relations) by calling it a "resource guide." In the opening pages of the guide I outline what skills I would like coaches to emphasize at each grade level. I also include an offensive or defensive concept I would like them to incorporate at that particular grade.

While this book includes nearly all of the offenses and defenses we run at the varsity level, I tell coaches not to feel overwhelmed or intimidated by the magnitude of the information offered in the handbook. They are not expected to teach and incorporate all of the things outlined in the guide. However, they are asked to focus on their respective part. I have created a skill progression that allows players to master a skill before graduating to the next skill. If integrated properly, by the time a player reaches 9th grade they are nearly fully integrated into the way we do things at the varsity level.

This is not only true in terms of offenses and defenses. It is also true when it comes to teaching technique and the use of terminology. I want and expect my youth coaches to be teaching the same footwork in 5th grade that I want the players to exhibit in high school. I don't want to have to start all over or re-teach a basic skill like that when those kids come to me. The primary purpose of the handbook is to get everyone, players and coaches, on the same page. If I call out "Fist" my 6th graders and my sophomores should both understand what that means. If we are running a drill I should see the same fundamentals from my seventh graders as I see from my seniors. There is no substitute for that kind of continuity. It is what builds programs that perennially contend for conference and state titles. If you haven't already created a handbook like this for your youth coaches, make it a major priority to get it done in the near future.

Another thing I have done to enhance my relationship with youth coaches my annual pre-season "Coaching Clinic." I have my players come in and demonstrate various drills or run through plays so the coaches can see, live and in person, all the things that are diagrammed in their "resource guide." I always distribute the resource guide a couple of weeks in advance of our clinic. I encourage the coaches to page through the guide and scribble down any drills they would like us to demonstrate. I also invite any questions they might have about how we teach certain skills. I bring a short agenda of things I feel are important enough to show to all the coaches, regardless of whether they have questions about them or not. My presentation takes 20 to 30 minutes. The rest of the time is reserved for the youth coach's questions.

The entire evening only takes about an hour but it is another great opportunity to ensure that our youth coaches are indeed teaching the concepts we espouse and it helps create a comfort level for them with the things we are asking them to implement.

The resource guide and the clinic are usually embraced enthusiastically by youth coaches that have minimal background in the sport or in coaching in general. The coaches that were successful athletes themselves or that have coached for a few years are often less willing to adopt or integrate the system. I will offer insight about how you can bring those coaches on board later in this chapter.

Another thing I have done in an attempt to create continuity between our youth and high school programs is my standing offer to attend youth practices. I have had a handful of coaches take me up on this offer over the years. I have come in and, at their request or with their permission, I have run parts of their practice to make sure the players (and the coach) know exactly what it is we are trying to get out of a drill or to help show some of the nuances of our offense or defense. Not only does this help our program in terms of on the court continuity, but it is a wonderful public relations move. When the parents on that youth team find out the head varsity coach was at their kids' practice that night they are often more excited about it than the kids. Making these appearances usually only takes an hour or two of your time but the benefit to your program and to your public image is immeasurable.

One last idea on how to cultivate a relationship with your youth coaches is an idea offered to me by a colleague. For each home game my colleague invites a youth coach to join the varsity team as an "honorary coach" for the evening. The guest youth coach congregates with the coaching staff before the game. The guest coach is in the locker room for pre-game comments, on the bench or the sideline during the game, and they huddle with the coaching staff at halftime. While I have never implemented this program myself I can see immense benefits to it. This opportunity allows the youth coach to get an inside and up close look at how things are done at the varsity level. They can then offer insight from the experience to their youth players. It also helps the youth coach feel like a valued member of the program. I have yet to incorporate this idea because while I don't cuss at or around players anymore, I still have a tendency to get a little loose with my language in the presence of my coaching staff. In my case, the risk that my language around the staff would offend a guest youth coach outweighs the possible benefits derived from having a new coach on our bench each game. This gets back to one of our earlier sections, "know your strengths and know your weaknesses." I know foul language is one of my weaknesses so I elect not to expose people to it and open myself up to criticism if I don't have to.

Sell Your System, Don't Mandate It

Especially as a new coach to a program, the way you ask your youth coaches to incorporate and integrate your system is of paramount importance. Unless you come in with numerous championships on your resume you had better not come across as mandating that your youth coaches do anything. This will lead to ill will and push them away more than it will bring them on board.

And even if you have an impressive resume and a case full of trophies somewhere, if you are new to a program it is still a better idea to come in with the intention of selling your system rather than imposing it on anyone. You sell your system to the youth coaches just as you do to your players. You need to explain what makes your plan as good, or better, than anything they are doing right now. You should be able to outline the long term benefits of them implementing your system and ideally you can cite examples of players or programs where the continuity you aspire to has translated to championships.

Even as you share the benefits of your system, be sure to emphasize that you are not asking them to run your stuff exclusively. You have to give your youth coaches at least a bit of freedom and flexibility to put their own mark on their team. While there are certain plays that our 7th graders should know as well as our seniors, I have one play in particular that we alter almost every year to suit our personnel in that particular season. I always offer to our youth coaches that if they have a favorite play from college or something they ran in high school that always works, by all means they can put it in and name it the same as the play we always alter from one year to the next. I tell them that when their child's team gets to high school, we can run that same play they have installed and it will be a smooth transition for everyone, right down to the terminology. Offering this option gives the youth coach some ownership in your program and it makes them considerably more inclined to comply with the other things you want them to install. Whether you actually run their play or not five years later is immaterial. The point is to get them to run your plays in the years leading up to their kids entering your program.

I can recall working with a 6th grade coach my first year as a head coach, trying to teach him the basics of our offense. He never seemed to get comfortable with it and by mid-season he was clearly exasperated. He said to me "My team just can't run it. We're getting mauled every game and the players are losing confidence in themselves. We have to revert back to our old offense."

I knew what their old offense was and it was a gimmick that would win you games in 6th grade and never again. Clearly, I needed to continue to sell my system to this guy so I gave him the following analogy.

"The offense you like to run is kind of like buying an old, beat up, used car. It's cheap, and it will get you where you need to go for a few months, but eventually it will break down and you're stuck. Our offense is like buying a Rolls Royce. It is expensive and it takes a long time to pay it off, but it's going to run great for years and years and you're gonna look damn good driving it!"

He seemed to get the message. His way would be good in the short term, my way would be better in the long term. And then I quickly added "I know everyone is competitive and everyone has an ego. I coached 5th and 6th grade basketball once too and I was as driven to win as anyone; too driven in fact. What I know now that I wish I knew then is this; no one is going to ask you ten years from now 'how many weekend tournament championships did your kid's team win in 6th grade?' but they might say 'Hey, wasn't your kid on that state tournament team? I think I saw them on TV!'"

This helped the dad to recognize that the best perspective to have as a youth coach is always the big picture. It can be hard to be a youth coach when there are parents barking at you and telling the youth board that you are awful and they need to fire you. If that situation comes up, that is where the head varsity coach has to step in and convey to those complaining that the youth coaches are doing what is best for the kids and for the program. Rarely, if ever, is the parent of a youth player going to challenge or confront the head varsity coach when they issue an endorsement such as that. Parents of youth players will almost always avoid angering or alienating the varsity coach. They wait until their kid is in high school to do that!

The highlight of the whole exchange with this 6th grade basketball coach came four years later. His daughter was a sophomore on a state tournament basketball team. The morning after the team qualified for the state tourney I happened to see him having breakfast at a local restaurant. I walked up to his table and said, "Hey, isn't your daughter on that state tournament team?" We shared a smile and he knew right away what I was referencing. Now I tell this story to all my youth coaches every fall at our clinic as part of my sales pitch to them to run our system.

When Selling Doesn't Work, Scare 'Em

At my most recent school I had been the head coach for three seasons when I decided I was tired of suggesting and politely asking youth coaches to run our system. Despite my best sales efforts there were still a couple of youth coaches completely ignoring our stuff and doing their own thing. As I watched the youth teams play one weekend it annoyed me that these coaches didn't even have the decency to implement any aspect of our system, not even a simple out of bounds play. I went to our youth board and explained my frustration and re-iterated that the unwillingness of some coaches to implement our system was going to have a negative long term impact on our program and the players those coaches were working with. I asked for the chance to visit with all the coaches collectively prior to the start of the next season. The board agreed to help me get all the coaches on board.

We had won a lot of games during my first three seasons at this school. I felt I was finally in a position where I didn't have to politely ask if they could run some of our stuff if it was convenient for them. When the night of the meeting arrived, I dug in my heels and talked in very clear and direct terms. No more sales pitch. This time I gave the youth coaches more of a lightly veiled threat.

I began my comments by saying that after three years of coaching here, "I'd like to think that I have demonstrated to everyone that I know my head from my ass. Clearly the stuff we're teaching and promoting has been successful." Then I went on to share my frustration at the failure of some of our youth coaches to implement even a single aspect of our system. Without naming names, I cited situations where I went to watch one of our teams and they didn't run a single play that we do or even use a single word of the same terminology. Then I played the card I knew would get the attention of even the most stubborn or skeptical parent/coach.

I outlined how the current 8th grade coaches had been running our stuff for the previous three years. I acknowledged that during the first year of incorporating the system they took some lumps, but that their teams improved dramatically in the years that followed. Then I presented a hypothetical scenario.

"Now let's imagine the 7th grade coaches have not implemented any of our stuff. Then fast forward two or three years" I said. "When the current 8th graders are juniors and the current 7th graders are sophomores, and one group has run our system and been doing things the way we want and expect at the varsity level for the better part of six years while the other group is in their second year of our system, which kids do you think will have the advantage at varsity tryouts?" I gave an extended pause to let that sink in with the uncooperative coaches.

"I hope you realize that when you don't run our stuff you are directly jeopardizing your players' chances of making our team someday, not to mention your own child's chances. I'm not saying they can't still make our team, but you are putting them at a distinct disadvantage when they are in direct competition with kids that <u>have</u> run our stuff. The 8th graders have developed a comfort level with our system and it has become second nature. There is no substitute for the familiarity of running our system. I can't force you to run our stuff, but if you want to do what's best for your players you <u>will</u> run our stuff." That winter, it was remarkable how even those that had not done so in the past suddenly embraced various aspects of our offense!

Again, a confrontation like this should not be had when you first take over a program and you should endeavor to never have such a confrontation at all. Do your best to be an effective salesman. But if the sales pitch falls on deaf ears you may need to play the "don't cost your own kid a chance at varsity" card.

Beware the Parent That Won the 6ᵗʰ Grade Championship

One of the leading candidates to develop into a parent "cancer" is the mom or dad that coached their child's youth team to some sort of championship. These parent/coaches collect all kinds of trophies with their 5ᵗʰ or 6ᵗʰ grade team because they do one or more of the following things:

They only play their best players.

Rather than playing all players and attempting to develop a number of good players through the youth program, some parent/ coaches play only their top players and leave the others to rot on the bench. As they do this, many of the opposing teams are doing things the right way and playing all kids. This usually equates to a stellar 6ᵗʰ grade win/loss record for the parent/coach but it does little to develop depth at that particular grade level and can cost the varsity coach dearly down the road.

They put their team in an inferior league.

A baseball coaching friend of mine took heat from parents every year. The parents would point out that their kids won their youth league championship in 6ᵗʰ, 7ᵗʰ, and 8ᵗʰ grade, but every group that got to the high school was only slightly above average. The reason these kids did so well in middle school is they played in a second tier league and never faced the same opponents they would eventually face in conference or section play in high school. The parents put their kids in this league because they knew their kids would win a lot and it made them feel good about themselves, but it did little to advance the players' skill level.

Winning against inferior opponents gave the players and the parents an inflated sense of their ability. At the high school level, when team after team turned out to be merely average against the elite competition in their conference the head high school coach was the one that got the blame.

They run a gimmick offense or defense.

This is found most frequently in youth football and basketball. I have seen 6ᵗʰ grade basketball teams sit in a 2-3 zone and win a ton of games because almost no players can shoot from the perimeter or penetrate effectively at that age. The team wins tons of meaningless 6ᵗʰ grade games and as they are winning, the players are developing terrible habits. By the time they get to high school they have no idea how to play defense. As the high school coach, you are losing games because your players are horribly out of position and have terrible footwork. While you are losing, the parent that coached the team to the 6th grade title is announcing to everyone in the stands that they can't understand why you are losing games. "We went 25 and 3 when I coached this group!" they proudly announce.

The thing that makes these parents so dangerous is not that they won a ton of games in 6th grade, it is that in their mind they have coached before and therefore they have all the answers. They frequently offer commentary throughout the game to other parents in the stands about how they would have done things differently. These youth coaches really burn you twice. They burned you by not developing players during their time coaching in the youth program, and then they burn you again by undermining your credibility as you try to coach the crappy kids they sent you.

It can be particularly difficult to confront these former parent/ coaches. If you try to tell them that the players can't execute the things you are asking them to because of their lack of fundamentals, the parent/coach can simply fire back "well if you would just have them run the system we used in sixth grade they would do just fine." You probably recognize that if you were to do that, your team would be in even worse shape. Any attempt to reason with them and explain that their "system" could not be effective at the varsity level because opposing players and coaches have more advanced skill sets than they did in middle school, the parent will inevitably disagree. This is one of those political fights that can be very difficult to win. The answer then is to not let the situation erode into a fight.

If you learn that a former parent/coach is publicly critical of your coaching, it would be wise to ask for a meeting with them. Any initial attempt to discuss things should be done as diplomatically as possible. Emphasize that the two of you want the same thing; for the team to be successful. Make it clear that you appreciate their service to the kids in the past, but that you need the parent/coach to be supportive now. If they fail to be supportive they will only make things worse as the players will develop divided loyalties.

If the diplomatic approach doesn't work, then consider the parent/coach a cancer and treat it as needed (i.e. amputation) in order to save the rest of the team.

The Residual Effect of Youth Sports Boards

As long as there have been high school sports, there have been parents clamoring for a coach to be fired. However, parents seem to be increasingly assertive in contacting school administrators to seek the ouster of high school coaches and this recent amplification of outcries from parents can be traced directly to youth sports boards.

Previously we pointed out that these boards are populated almost exclusively by parents. During the elementary and middle school years the parents on these boards have direct control of who coaches their childs' team. They do the hiring and firing. When little Billy moves on to the high school, many of these parents have a hard time relinquishing control over who coaches their kid. I have been at a school where over a half a dozen times, parent groups in various sports have approached the athletic director not only demanding their current coach be fired, but also insisting that the "parent's choice" be hired.

The parents' conversation with the athletic director usually goes something like this:

"The parents have talked it over and we have decided it is time for Coach So and So to go. The team just isn't responding to them. Coach So and So doesn't motivate them and the team isn't playing up to its potential. The kids' played for Coach Jackson a few years ago and they had a lot of success. All the players and parents really respect and like Coach Jackson. We are here to insist that you put the best interest of the players and the program first. You need to dismiss Coach So and So and hire Coach Jackson."

Having an athletic director that is tough and that can stand up to this kind of parent pressure has never been more important. We have generations of parents that have been intimately involved with every aspect of their child's athletic career for their entire life. These parents have handled budgets, scheduled games, and hired coaches. After calling the shots for years and years, they want and expect to continue to wield this same power and influence when their child is in high school. The only way they can typically do this though is through the athletic director. If you have an AD that will cave to the whims of parents you had better get an updated resume ready. If you are blessed to have an AD that knows how to tell these parents "thanks for the input" while simultaneously reminding them that as the athletic director they and they alone make those decisions, you stick with that AD as long as you can because they are worth their weight in gold.

SEVEN
***

Learning From and Dealing With Other Coaches

"I don't expect to win enough games to be put on NCAA probation. I just want to win enough to warrant an investigation."
— Bob Devaney

The coaching community is widely considered a sort of fraternity. There is a camaraderie that is created between fellow coaches. We can relate and commiserate with each other over the common challenges we all face. But as is the case in any profession, there are always a few coaches that stand out from the crowd, and sometimes not for any of the right reasons. From a distance, we might be inclined to look at these coaches that find themselves eternally embroiled in controversy and wonder how they can continue to coach. This can be particularly puzzling when we see so many apparently good coaches that are also good people get unceremoniously pushed out of the profession.

The key to all of this confusion in the coaching community is the perspective from which we view these fellow coaches. "From a distance" they appear forever on the hot seat and at the eye of the storm. But a closer examination usually reveals they have one of three traits that many other coaches do not.

The media dubbed Ronald Reagan the "Teflon President" because no matter what accusations were leveled against him, nothing seemed to stick. His popularity with the American people always stayed strong. While Reagan certainly had his critics, he was always able to maintain a strong base of support regardless of what he was accused of. There are coaches that are blessed in the same way.

These "teflon" coaches that never seem to have any of the negative stick to them usually have one or more of the following things going for them:

1. A collection of championships to insulate them from critics
2. A softer side that the public never sees but that endears them

to the people in their program or

3. An astute instinct for politics that always keeps them ahead of the curve

Trophies as Critic Repellent

One of my favorite people on the planet is my old high school basketball coach. He was demanding and intense on the court but could be a barrel of laughs and would do anything for you off the court. He was a polarizing kind of personality. Most players loved him, but those that didn't hated him. The same could be said of our community. He had many fervent fans, but his critics were as adamantly opposed to him as his admirers were in his favor.

My old coach had his vices. Among them, he used foul language frequently and with feeling. He was a bit of a booze hound and he was a regular at our local strip club. In most towns, gaining a reputation for engaging in any of those activities is reason enough to run you out, but among the things Coach Munsen always had on his side was he won games. In fact, he won a lot of games, and he did it all the time. And the majority of people in my hometown put winning at the top of the priority list. They didn't need a coach to be a role model and raise their kids. The people of my hometown could raise their kids just fine on their own. They needed a coach to get their kids to the state tournament and Coach Munsen was as good at doing that as anyone has ever been.

It took him nearly a decade at the helm as head coach before he claimed his first state championship, but in the nearly 30 years since that first state title there have been over a dozen more to decorate the trophy case. Hanging a state championship banner in your gym every couple years has a way of helping people overlook some of your less attractive attributes. What follows are two situations from when I was in high school that 99% of coaches in America would have been canned for. Coach Munsen survived these situations and others for reasons we'll get into shortly.

We were gathered at the school on a Saturday morning to watch game film of that evening's opponent. We had won a big home game the night before and apparently coach had gone out to celebrate at a local watering hole. We would not have known about his actions of the previous evening were it not for the fact that coach strolled in to the next morning's film session wearing dark sunglasses. Even the sunglasses didn't necessarily mean we would be able to decipher his actions from the night before, but when coach removed his sunglasses to reveal a big black eye, that was going to create some questions!

Coach explained that he ran into a former player at the bar. This former player had graduated about five years ago and he was still pissed off about his perceived lack of playing time. Coach went on to say that he could handle this former player saying all kinds of negative things about him. But things got physical when this guy started to bad mouth the program. Coach, who at the time was 50, went after a kid in his early 20's. While coach didn't walk away unscathed, apparently this kid took his share of a beating too.

Anyway, coach got it all out on the table and then promptly got down to the business of breaking down the game tape. What would have been a monumental scandal in many towns was just another day at the office for Coach Munsen. As was typically the case, over half the community took the side of the coach while the usual suspects griped and whined that he should be stripped of his coaching duties.

The other incident is the only one I know of where our coach really got disciplined in some way. In addition to his coaching duties, coach was a driver's ed instructor. As a result, he had access to the school's driver's ed vehicles. These cars were clearly marked and were of course only to be used for school business. In a fit of poor judgment, somehow coach managed to drive a driver's ed vehicle to the strip club just outside of town. In a bit of good judgment (I'm assuming after a few drinks), he didn't drive the car home. Of course, the bad part of that good decision was that the car was left in the parking lot for people to see as they were driving in to church the next morning. It didn't take much detective work for people to determine who drove the driver's ed car to the strip club and left it there to pick up the next day. This happened out of season, so coach was suspended from teaching for a couple of days and then returned to his duties.

Again, unless you have built up an incredible amount of coaching capital, this is the kind of thing that would get nearly any one of us fired. But when you see a coach managing to dodge what seems like certain death, take a moment to consider how much hardware they have delivered to their school and it may offer a bit of an explanation.

That being said, in our increasingly politically correct society even winning cannot insulate everyone from the lynch mobs, but winning championships usually doesn't hurt a coach's cause either.

The Softer Side

Coaches that may seem tyrannical when viewing their behavior from the stands can sometimes be beloved by their players and parents. I have come to know at least a handful of coaches that appear to breathe fire on the sidelines only to be as timid and polite as Mr. Rogers away from the arena.

These coaches can get away with hollering and yelling because their players and parents know and believe that the coach really has their best interest at heart. If you truly care about your players and demonstrate that on a regular basis, no matter the volume at which you bark your directions, players will know that you are only so animated because you want so badly for them to do well.

Coach Munsen was one that opposing players would say they could never play for. But most of us that played for him would take a bullet for the man. As a coach, I have encountered others that stomp and holler at officials and players, but they are absolutely supported by parents and administration.

The lesson here is if you are going to be a yeller, you better have a softer side and you had better show it often, otherwise the yelling and stomping will not be well received.

Old Fashioned Political Acumen

The coaches that seem like they just shouldn't continue to be hired or keep their coaching jobs are likely just very astute political minds, and at the heart of that is a keen understanding of people. While I think I have got a bit of the first two areas we have just covered going for me, I know the thing that has allowed me to dodge some very bad bullets in my coaching career is my intuitive response to crisis type situations as they unfold.

I could cite four specific times when my coaching career could have come to a premature end based on my words or my actions. Each time the immediacy and nature of my response is a huge part of what saved me. While I am certain this book will already cause a stir, I am not interested in it creating any lawsuits, so in the name of self preservation I will offer just one example of a time my coaching career could have ended.

I first started coaching at the age of 16. I coached 5th and 6th grade basketball at one of the elementary schools in my hometown. I also coached two years of what is commonly referred to as "traveling" basketball. But my first experience coaching football didn't come until I was 20. Still a college student, I noticed postings on campus that the local middle schools needed football coaches. While I didn't really aspire to coach football, I thought this might be a good way to get my foot in the door to coach basketball in the school district. (It turns out it did just that.)

I was assigned the defensive coordinator position for a 7th grade football team at one of the middle schools. It was a fun fall but there was one incident that could have brought my burgeoning coaching career to a screeching halt.

There was a boy on the team named Ricky. He was a stocky lineman that, like most middle school boys, just wasn't very emotionally mature. For much of the first few weeks of practice as the team would run around the field to take a warm up lap before stretching, Ricky would steal my hat off my head. He thought it was hilarious. The first few times I found some humor in it as well, but by the 15th time I was beyond annoyed. I had told him clearly and firmly that he had better not steal my hat anymore. Apparently my message didn't make it through to his adolescent brain.

After a few more days of stern warnings, again Ricky ran by and swiped my hat. I responded by picking him up and shaking him in a rather playful fashion, telling him to put my hat down. Ricky thought this was even more hilarious and he was giggling like a kid at a carnival. After my shaking didn't do the trick, in a moment of frustration I dropped him, hoping that would lead him to fumble the hat. My plan worked, but when Ricky hit the turf his giggle changed abruptly into a whimper. He was starting to cry.

Instantly my brain fast forwarded through my firing, the trial, and to what college major I would have to switch to now because I would never get a teaching or coaching job. This literally all went through my head in about two seconds. Then I quickly surmised the best way to deal with the situation in an attempt to make sure nothing would come of it.

I knew that if I became scared and overly apologetic Ricky might realize I had screwed up big time. He would almost certainly tell his mother that his coach body slammed him at practice and the cops would be by to pick me up shortly after that. So I decided the best way to approach this was to appeal to Ricky's "tough guy side" that all middle school boys have.

"Get up Ricky," I said with a touch of gruffness. "I can't, my hip hurts!" he moaned from the ground.

"Get up and get your warm up lap in or you're not playing tomorrow. Quit being a pansy. You're a football player aren't you? You take hits a lot harder than that in every drill we do. Get up Ricky."

Ricky hobbled to his feet and started to take his lap with a very pronounced limp. As he made his way very slowly around the field I was becoming even more certain I was screwed. All it would take is for mom or dad to ask him "why are you limping?" and I was toast. But I treated Ricky just as I normally would have for the rest of practice. I didn't offer him ice or an apology. I might have even thrown in a line like "I bet you're not going to take my hat again," just to really play the tough guy card. Ricky must not have uttered a word at home about how he hurt his hip because the lawsuit never came. And incidentally, he never did swipe my hat again.

Reading people and responding in the proper way to a given situation is what keeps coaches like me alive in this business. I had a friend get fired not too long ago and a mutual friend of ours called and said to me "No offense, but I told my wife if anyone deserves to be fired it's you!" Oddly enough, I did not take offense to that comment because I was in complete agreement. Our friend that got fired was a straight arrow. He never did anything to rock the boat or ruffle feathers. I, on the other hand, have a tendency to do both of those things semi-frequently. But I also have studied politics and people my entire life. Our friend just loved coaching. I enjoy coaching and I love politics. I guess that is why I have written this book. To help people like my friend survive in this increasingly difficult profession.

Dealing With Coaches in Other Sports

Many coaches find themselves in competition for athletes with the other coaches at their school. Even if you are at a very large school, every program wants the top athletes. As a result, some coaches connive, recruit, and maneuver to help their program even at the hindrance of others. In this section we will take a look at positive ways to work with your fellow coaches as well as some ways that will cultivate enemies on your school's coaching staff. Which path you choose is up to you.

I will begin by sharing what I consider to be some of the best programs to create camaraderie on a school's coaching staff. Incorporating these concepts can help to build a sense of community across the various sports at your school.

At one of my previous schools, our AD would host a lunch once every four to six weeks for all head coaches. Usually held on the day of a teacher workshop, the coaches of the various sports would gather together for lunch and our AD would have an agenda of some high school league policies we needed to cover, budget issues, etc. But beyond that, it was really just a chance for us as coaches to share our concerns and celebrate each other's successes. This helped create a climate of open communication amongst a group of coaches that otherwise rarely saw each other.

Another thing that helped create a sense of "team" amongst the coaches of the various sports came courtesy of our local radio station. They aired a "coach's corner" program on Saturday mornings all fall, winter, and spring. The coaches would congregate at a local restaurant, get treated to a free breakfast, and take 10 or 15 minutes to recap their week and mention some of their players names on the air. But it was off the air that relationships really formed. I would sit across from the hockey coaches and find out how they did the night before. Our gymnastics coach would chime in about some drama she was dealing with on her team. We all listened to each other and laughed with each other. It was one of the healthiest coaching climates I have ever had the privilege to be a part of.

This feeling of community helped lead to another program I felt was fantastic. The offseason can be a particularly tense time as coaches are all vying for their athletes' attention during the short window that is the summer season. At other schools my athletes had to choose between going to the soccer team workouts, lifting for track, or coming to our open gym, but at Red Wing we had a daily training session for all athletes in all sports called "strength and agility training." Head coaches from nearly every sport embraced this program and attended. Each coach ran a station and we put kids through drills that were not sport specific, but rather designed to make all of them better, more explosive athletes. We had well over 100 boys and girls attend this morning workout session on a daily basis all summer long and every sport benefitted from it. Each coach still had their sport specific camps and training, but rather than forcing a kid to decide if they were going to lift weights with the football team this summer or the basketball team, the kid could just lift weights. We were all doing it together.

I realize facility availability and the willingness of coaches to participate in such a program could limit your ability to create something similar at your school, but there is no doubt it enhanced the team spirit amongst our athletes and our coaches and it made all of our programs better for our respective seasons.

On the flipside of this, we sometimes encounter coaches that advocate strongly for their players to specialize exclusively in their sport and abandon all others. We also find coaches that recruit athletes away from sports to have them join their team. The most egregious example I have seen of the latter came from a track coach that seemingly cared only about his program. He did not hesitate to recruit athletes away from the baseball, softball, and other spring sport programs at his school.

I heard my fellow coaches complain that the track coach was writing notes to kids as young as third grade, telling them that they would be on varsity in middle school and that they would be able to pay for their college if they ran track for him. The coach made it a point to identify the top athletes at each elementary school. He started recruiting kids to compete for his program before they had even learned their multiplication tables!

I was coaching 9th grade baseball during the height of the track coach's pillaging of other programs. A young man that would have been my star player came to me a week before practice started to inform me he would not be playing. When I asked him why he said he was going to run track. That prompted me to ask one more time "why?" He responded that the coach had promised to give him a varsity letter, even if he didn't run varsity.

I grew up in a place where no one ever wore a letter jacket so I didn't understand why anyone would care about earning a varsity letter. But in the community I was coaching in it was a very big deal, especially for a freshman to walk around in a varsity letter jacket. This track coach was doing everything he could to take the top talent for his program, even if it meant taking a big steaming dump on another coach's team. Obviously, this rather unethical behavior was not well received by the other coaches on our staff. After years of successfully dodging any reprimand for his recruiting from other teams there was a happy ending for this coach and all the others at my school. The coach moved on to a place where recruiting is encouraged, a college track team.

You don't have to be best buddies with every coach of every sport at your school, but you also don't want to go out of your way to anger them by blindly doing whatever you can to make your own program the best it can possibly be, in particular when it comes at another coach's expense.

The other thing we have all witnessed (and frankly it is something some of us have done) is pressure being applied to athletes to play a particular sport year round. The era of the three sport athlete has passed. Many parents and players are deciding as early as elementary school that they are going to focus on only one sport with the hopes that specialization will help them earn a much coveted athletic scholarship. Many head coaches do nothing to discourage this practice. Coaches that encourage specialization had better understand the politics of their school. If you have administrators that are supportive of the practice it is certainly easier to push your players towards specialization. However, there are several other factors a coach must consider.

At one of the schools I coached at, volleyball was far and away the most popular sport for girls. If I came in as the new head basketball coach and proclaimed that I expected our players to play basketball year round I would have lost eight of my top twelve players immediately because volleyball was their first love. Even when I have been at a school where I have had enough numbers to issue such an ultimatum, I have never seriously considered mandating specialization because I never want to alienate the stellar athlete that may also be a soccer, track, or volleyball star from having a positive impact on my program.

While I didn't advocate for specialization, the volleyball coach at my former school basically did. He didn't do it publicly, but let's just say he didn't do anything to discourage girls that seemed to be leaning towards playing volleyball year round. When it became clear our programs weren't often going to share athletes I tried to tell him that if he wanted to get into recruiting wars that we could do that. Some years I would win the war and I would have a good team while his team would be awful and vice versa. My preference though, was that we share athletes. I suggested we let them focus on their respective sport while it was in season and let it be a free for all in the summer when we were both tugging at the kids to play our sport. He gave me good lip service, but I soon found that is all it was.

One fall, four of my top basketball players approached me and said they wanted to quit volleyball to focus their attention on a fall basketball league. I immediately told them I thought it was a bad idea. I said they would be better athletes and more prepared for the basketball season by practicing volleyball everyday rather than playing basketball once or twice a week. They insisted they would practice basketball every day. I knew better. In the end, I convinced them to stick with volleyball but told them that they could still play in the fall league in addition to volleyball if they really wanted to. That is the path they chose.

Three of these players ended up on the JV volleyball team. The fourth player became a key part of the varsity volleyball team. As the volleyball team approached their playoffs, I told this varsity volleyball player that she could not play in the upcoming fall league basketball games. In reality, I had no power to keep her from playing. I was

armed only with the influence I exerted as a head coach. When
she protested I replied "You can't jeopardize what your volleyball
teammates have been working towards all fall. If you twist an ankle
this weekend and miss their playoff games you will let them down and
you will have wasted all that hard work you and they put in these past
few months." She did not touch a basketball again until the volleyball
team's post season run came to a close.

I made it a point to tell the varsity volleyball coach about my
conversation with his key player. I also told him that I sincerely hoped
he would reciprocate should we find ourselves in a similar position that
winter. Sure enough, winter brought a strikingly similar scenario.

One of our starters in basketball was a girl that was also an outside
hitter in volleyball. Admittedly, she was a better volleyball player than
basketball player but she was a lockdown defender for us. I could put
her on the other team's best player and she would absolutely shut them
down. Just days before our first round playoff game, unbeknownst to
me, she went off to play in a weekend volleyball tournament. After 8
hours a day of swinging her arm down at a volleyball, she came in to
our trainer on Monday unable to lift her arm over her head. She was
unable to play in our playoff game.

The playoff game was a back and forth, high scoring affair. Both
teams traded buckets. We were unable to muster a key defensive stop
all night. The absence of our star defensive player was glaring. When
the game was over I went straight into the coach's office, called the
volleyball coach, and tore him a new asshole.

He said over and over again that he had no input or influence
over whether she played winter volleyball or not and that it wasn't
his place to tell her what to do. I reminded him what I had done for
his team that fall and that I had expected he would do the same. He
said he wasn't comfortable influencing a player in that way. I said he
didn't have any balls. Overall I thought the conversation was pretty
productive.

The point is, just like in politics, some coaches will seem to be on
your side and may even make you promises but when the chips are
down they are nowhere to be found. It is important to identify those
people early and do your best not to count on them. This volleyball
coach was a good person overall, but on this issue he and I were never
going to agree. I got burned and I learned. That is the best any of us
can ever do.

On the issue of sharing athletes the other thing a coach must
consider is which program is in a position of strength. If you are the

coach of the abundantly popular sport you can likely mandate that your athletes specialize. You may occasionally lose a good player to another sport, but you may consider it a worthwhile trade because your remaining athletes have improved greatly through their specialization.

If you are in the weaker position, leading the less popular program, your situation necessitates that you be far more flexible. You may have to accommodate an athletes' other practices or accept that they will miss an occasional game. Of course, you have to weigh the positives that could be derived for your program by having that athlete on your team versus what you risk by allowing them to miss practices or games. If you consider it most critical that you generate interest in your program via winning games, it is a bargain worth striking. Then, when your program reaches a position of strength and has more than adequate numbers you can then elect to advocate for specialization.

Again, personally I am not a fan of athletes specializing. Time and again I have seen players and parents put all their proverbial sports eggs in one basket only to get cut from the team as a sophomore having no other outlet or opportunities. The only scenario where I have endorsed an athlete specializing is when it becomes clear that their prowess in a certain sport will help the kid pay for college. No parent or player knows this scenario will be true in middle school so there is no excuse for specializing at that age. But if an athlete is a sophomore and division I or II schools are calling, I can fully support specializing because an athletic scholarship is a rare and special gift.

In contrast to my encounter with the volleyball coach, years ago there was a softball coach that I communicated with very well. We collaborated to arrange things so our athletes would not have to choose between our two sports in or out of season. We would meet in the spring to map out what nights I wanted to do basketball activities and when she wanted to have softball. If one of us had a very important summer tournament on a certain weekend, the other would avoid scheduling something that same weekend.

Just like nations form allies and hammer out treaties, coaches can do the same. Always endeavor for diplomacy first. Try to work things out with your fellow coaches not just because it helps your program and creates good will, but because it is in the best interest of your players too. But if someone wants to play hardball and try to damage your program to benefit their own, you had better not back down. You go toe to toe with that coach, whether you think they are the big bad bully on the block or not. If you don't stand up to them that coach will continue to treat your program as second rate. What is worse, that prominent coach's attitude may eventually be adopted by others in your community.

Dealing with Club or Personal Coaches

In recent years, high school coaches have been thrown into a competition they have never encountered before. High school coaches are no longer the only form of guidance an athlete receives. The exponential growth in offseason programs like club teams and AAU has created a climate where athletes are often exposed to a variety of coaching styles and philosophies. The end result can sometimes be that high school coaches are viewed as "inferior" to the club coach. This can be a frustrating and challenging development, but it is a new reality and it must be managed appropriately.

I have a colleague who is a top flight track coach. This coach competed collegiately and they have sent numerous athletes on to the state track meet and even to college competition. In the past few years, this outstanding coach has felt like they are now competing for their athletes' loyalty with AAU track coaches. As they attempt to tutor and coach their athletes during the high school track season, the coach will often hear that "my other coach tells me I should do this" or "that's now how I did it last summer."

This can be extremely frustrating to a coach who has no agenda but to try to help an athlete maximize their ability. But because the athlete has two or more coaches, inevitably the kid is going to consider one coach superior to the other and opt to listen to the instructions of that coach. There is no question that at times, the coach they opt to follow is the high school coach. But for a variety of reasons, high school coaches are becoming less credible in the eyes of athletes and parents. Here are just a few of the reasons:

High school coaches are usually teachers too.

Public education has been pummeled in the national media to the point that teaching is no longer a respected or admired profession in many regions of the country. Teachers have been vilified by talk radio hosts and others as the reason for the failure of some students and schools. As a result, a coach that is a teacher has damaged credibility from the beginning with a large number of parents and players. The logic goes they are teachers, so as coaches they must not know what they are talking about and they must be bad at their jobs. That is truly the mentality of some of the people coaches are working to help. There is no easy way to erase this ridiculous but growing stereotype. All we can do as coaches is continue to teach our athletes to the best of our ability and put kids first. Hopefully parents and players will eventually come to recognize that the vast majority of us are competent and we know what we are talking about.

High school coaches are employed by a school district, not by an "exclusive" club.

If you go on to the website of an AAU team or a club team it usually includes the profile and resume of its coaches. These profiles are often authored in such a way that it makes the club coach seem as though they should be coaching a professional team. These clubs have to promote their coaches in this manner because coaches are one of their key selling points. Many club sports operate like a business. The athletes and parents are the customers. Club teams need to make their service appear to be superior to all others, so they will enhance resumes and just generally self promote to a far greater extent than any high school coach ever feels compelled to do.

In recent years I have found myself doing a bit of self promotion at times in an attempt to generate a degree of credibility with the players and parents in my program. In an effort to diminish some of the "my AAU coach says to do this" comments, I sometimes advertise (in a subtle way) to parents and players that I have coached at the college level and that I have worked with some of the top division one coaches in the country at clinics and camps. My experience is not something I would prefer to make part of the discussion as I sometimes feel that I am boasting, but if I am competing for the attention of my athlete against the club coaches, sometimes it is what I am forced to do.

This new trend of divided loyalties can be particularly frustrating if you are a young, inexperienced coach. Without a resume or track record of your own, you can forever feel like you are viewed as a "second class coach" by your own players. When confronted with those feelings, do your best to keep them from getting you down. You can earn the trust and respect of your players if you work hard, if you really teach them, and if they experience some success under your direction.

High school coaches can afford to be honest with athletes because the athlete is not a customer.

Perhaps the greatest source of frustration for high school coaches dealing with athletes that play for club teams is the unrealistic expectations those athletes are often indoctrinated with after their club season comes to a close. I can't tell you the number of players I have had in recent years that come to me convinced they are going to get a basketball scholarship after their AAU coach spent the last four months stroking their ego on a regular basis.

The club coach and the high school coach would both like to see their player go on to the college level, but the club coach would like to see it for a different reason. For the club coach, one of their players moving on to the college level is a major boost for business. Now their brochures can say "12 of our players have earned athletic scholarships in the past three years." Parents read that and they can't write the check to the club team fast enough. If or when that parent's child fails to get a scholarship, in their mind it is obviously not the club team's fault. The club team has a track record of producing college players. Parents that are frustrated and confused at their child's lack of scholarship offers inevitably seek someone to blame and they often arrive at the high school coach.

As I mentioned previously, I have had players that had less than zero chance of playing college basketball come to me early in the season to ask why they aren't starting. When I explain that they aren't as good as the players ahead of them they often respond that their AAU coach told them all summer that they would be getting a scholarship to at least a division II school. The player and their parent then protest that not starting is going to cost them that scholarship. I become the bad guy because I can't deliver on someone else's reckless promises.

So why do club coaches pump these kids full of unrealistic expectations? Because it is good business. Tell a kid they are going to be a star, even if they aren't, and you have created a repeat customer. Many of these club teams cost thousands of dollars to play on. But the club team and the coach justify this exorbitant expense to parents by telling them their kid will get this money back and then some when they receive their athletic scholarship. In essence, the club coach is selling sunshine and rainbows. They tell the player and parents how great they are and as a result, the parents and players keep coming back and writing checks.

But when the scholarship offer doesn't come, who is the blame pinned on? Of course it is the high school coach. High school coaches are not selling a product so we can afford to be honest with kids. I prefer not to crush anyone's dreams, but if a player or parent asks me if they have a chance to play collegiately I will give them a very honest and accurate assessment. For those players that have very little chance of earning a scholarship, I become the bad guy. I am the only voice of reason the player and parents hear and I end up raining on their parade.

It is disappointing that high school coaches can be made into the enemy because of these club coaches and their profiteering. But they are a business and our job as high school coaches is to educate. By definition, they have to keep the customer happy and sometimes that means stroking their ego and selling them a bunch of bull. As educators, we want to inspire kids to achieve all that they can, but we also owe it to them to be honest along the way.

There is no sure fire way of altering this unfortunate climate that has developed between club and high school coaches. The best thing high school coaches can do is continue to advocate for their kids, help them maximize their abilities, and then ultimately be honest with the kids. It may be more fun to sell sunshine and there is certainly more money to be made doing it, but again, it is not in the long term best interest of your players so just tell them the truth.

And high school coaches should not be afraid to do a bit of self promotion. You are competing with club coaches for the loyalty and trust of your athletes. Outline to the people in your program exactly why you are a credible source of coaching. Parents and players are savvy consumers and high school coaches no longer have a monopoly. High school coaches can't just expect players to do things because they tell them to. Coaches have to adequately explain why executing the things they are asking are in the player and the team's best interest. Club teams have created a new environment and it is time for high school coaches to adapt.

Another interesting development in recent years has been the advent of personal coaches for athletes. Wealthy parents that don't feel their child is getting enough attention or instruction from their high school coach sometimes hire a coach or personal trainer to give their kid one on one instruction. This individualized attention is a luxury most high school coaches just can't afford to offer. Because a high school coach has a dozen or maybe even dozens of athletes to attend to, a player that is used to individual attention from a personal coach can feel ignored or unappreciated. This athlete's need for attention and validation and the inability of the head coach to deliver it will almost certainly lead to some form of drama. Based on conversations with coaches that have encountered these situations, the drama seems to manifest itself in the form of the athlete refusing to embrace the high school coach's teaching. The athlete instead announces that their personal coach or trainer tells them to do things a certain way and they are going to follow that coach's instruction.

When confronted with a conflict in how the club or personal

coach teaches things versus how you teach things, it can be very detrimental to diminish the teachings of the other coach. Regardless of how different your philosophy is from the club coach, you are better served to simply remind the athlete that there is more than one way to skin a cat and that while playing on your team or competing for you, you are expecting them to execute things the way you instruct them to. If they still don't comply, remind them that you aren't asking them to comply, you are telling them to. Of course the final straw is to sit them down or suspend them if they refuse to follow your instructions. In that case, it is clear they are so convinced their other coach is superior that they would be better served to go play for that coach year round anyway!

Dealing with College Coaches

One of the things I enjoy most about being a head coach is dealing with the college coaches that are recruiting my players. I enjoy it because I genuinely like the opportunity to help my players move on to the next level. I also recognize that if a college coach is talking to me about players, I must have some pretty good ones and that always makes for a better season!

My high school coaching career was interrupted by a brief stint as a college assistant. That time offered me excellent insight as to how high school coaches are perceived by recruiters and what high school coaches can do to best advocate for their players with college coaches.

Players and parents sometimes ask high school coaches to produce a "highlight" video that they can send out to various colleges. Something I learned during my time as a college assistant is the traditional "highlight video" is not well received by many recruiters. In the words of a couple of college coaches "You can make a highlight video of anyone and make them look decent. We want to see a full game or two. We want to see what the player does when they don't have the ball in their hands, whether they always hustle on defense, and how they respond to officials and teammates."

So in the future, your player may be better served by simply sending two of their game videos to college coaches with their jersey color and number marked on the DVD. A highlight tape may not get them very far.

Another thing I learned while at the college level is when a high school coach contacts a college coach to tell them they may want to look at recruiting one of their players, this is usually met with a certain degree of skepticism. A lot of college coaches don't respect a high school coach's ability to accurately assess the skill level required to compete at the college level. When a high school coach calls, the automatic assumption can be "this coach is just a rube." College coaches have seen hundreds of players promoted by their high school coach. These players may truly be the best player the coach has ever had, but they can still lack the skills and athleticism to play collegiately.

All this said, I still contact colleges on behalf of my players, but when I do I make it a point to explain that I have coached at the college level. I convey how this experience gives me a decent gauge on what kind of player is required to compete. There is no doubt this has helped me get my players increased attention from colleges in recent years. If I was lacking that college background, I would attempt to compare my player to other players from our conference that are currently playing collegiately in an effort to provide the college coach a better frame of reference.

Another thing high school coaches can do to enhance the chance a college coach will actually give their player a look is by focusing their sales pitch on the players' frame and athletic ability far more than emphasizing statistics. Statistics can be tremendously skewed and misleading based on the caliber of competition an athlete faces. If a player can bench 425 lbs. and has a 37 inch vertical, facts like that matter much more to a recruiter because they translate in a universal way.

One other move I have found to be quite helpful in dealing with college coaches is making sure I have my players contact information readily available. Recruiters want to know an athlete's home address, home phone number, cell phone number, e-mail address, ACT score, grade point average, and what other sports they play. I often also include the names and occupations of the athlete's parents. This can provide some immediate insight to the coach about what kind of financial package they can offer the player.

When a college coach contacts you about a player, be sure to have this important information handy. And if you contact a college coach, understand that they may approach your recommendation with a bit of skepticism. Offer your analysis of your player's athletic ability and attitude. Send full game tapes and then let the college coach determine whether your player is a fit for their program or not.

EIGHT
***

The Politics of
Winning and Losing

"Players win games. Coaches lose games."
— Anonymous

While politics is part of every aspect of the coaching profession, few things rival the political importance of the end result on a scoreboard. For far longer than factors like political correctness, activity fees, or club coaches have been around, wins and losses have been a determining factor in the future of coaches in every sport.

Often coaches assume that if their team is winning everything else will take care of itself. They believe winning will protect them from other issues. While that may have been true many years ago, merely winning games is no longer enough to insure job security. There is a proper way to manage the politics of winning games. We will address precisely how a coach should go about it in this chapter. Of course every coach understands that losing a lot of games is politically damaging and dangerous. This chapter will also offer ideas on how coaches can minimize the political damage incurred by losing, be it an isolated loss or a losing season.

How to Handle Winning

When you are winning games there is one simple but important rule to follow; give all credit to your players. Coaches should regularly and routinely deflect praise from themselves and make sure it is assigned to their players. Doing this actually benefits the coach in two ways. First, it is the gracious and mature thing to do. The players are the ones executing on the field and in turn, they deserve far more credit than the coach. But the other thing this constant deflection of praise does is elevate a coach's already growing reputation.

Receiving praise from the public demonstrates that people already think highly enough of you to compliment you on the job you are doing with your team. When you demonstrate a humble attitude those that are complimenting you will walk away even more impressed. Your willingness to put the spotlight on the kids will only enhance your own reputation. The more praise you give to others, the more you will actually get for yourself. Perhaps the praise will not be heaped on your directly but it will certainly accumulate in the all important court of public opinion.

One of the all time masters of this technique was former Minnesota Twins manager Tom Kelly. When he had great teams, teams that won world championships, he was always quick to point to the players as the key. "Having great players like Kirby Puckett and Kent Hrbek sure make a guy like me look smart" would be a typical thing you might hear him say. The way he deflected praise enhanced the image of his players and made him look like a class act.

But the real benefit of this technique came when Tom Kelly had a bad season. Because he was always so quick to credit his players and cite them as the ones responsible when the team was winning, the public was trained to expect that the success of the team was dependant on the players more than the manager. As a result, I never heard Tom Kelly get ripped by media or fans in the years his teams finished in the cellar. Everyone knew it was because the players were sub-par. Twins fans were trained to recognize that teams succeed and fail based on the performance of players, not coaches. To this day Tom Kelly is revered and respected all throughout the upper Midwest. His teams finished in first place and in last place, but he always deflected praise onto his players, maybe without consciously recognizing that he was simultaneously insulating himself from criticism when the lean years arrived.

Use "We" When Criticizing

Just as when the team wins it is politically prudent for the coach to praise in platitudes like "we did a great job of…" or "we executed the game plan to perfection" rather than heaping accolades on one or two individuals, it is equally wise to use the word "we" after a loss.

Rather than singling out a player or a play, no matter how obvious it might be that they contributed immensely to the outcome, it is always better to talk about what "we" could do better next time to achieve a more desirable outcome. Attacking a player or players on an individual level can create division on your team. There will be some in the locker room that agree with you and others that feel compelled to come to the defense of the player. Assigning blame to an individual is also dangerous as it teaches your team to point fingers after poor performances. Rather than focusing on what they could do better, they only focus on how Jake cost them the game. The use of the word "we" is just as important, and perhaps even more important, after a loss than after a win.

Beware of Blaming Bad Luck

Some coaches who have teams with wavering confidence or a fragile ego intentionally refuse to criticize their team's play, even with broad terms like "we." In an effort to keep spirits up these coaches will sometimes write off a loss to bad luck. "The ball didn't bounce our way" or "the refs cost us the game" can be effective, but only when used very sparingly. If a coach tells their team the reason for losses is "bad luck" on more than one or two occasions during a season, it can hurt far more than it helps.

During my second season in Red Wing, as we were trying to build the program to a level of respectability and competitiveness, we were scuffling along beating some good teams but still losing to poor teams from time to time. Through these highs and lows I worked hard to keep everything positive. In my effort to keep the teams' spirits up and confidence high, I found myself using the "bad luck" line on a pretty regular basis.

"The other team threw up a couple prayers that found the bottom of the net. We got great shots but they were just in and out" is what I told my team more than once. That season my other favorite target was the officiating. "We were playing five on seven out there tonight. We didn't get any calls and we still only lost by six" was a typical line I uttered after a loss.

My intention was to keep my teams' confidence level up and to keep them believing that they could win and be successful. What I didn't realize was that I was actually undermining our ability to improve. What was worse, I was creating a culture of frustration on our team. I didn't recognize it right away, but by late in the season I could see the frustration overwhelming us. When I sat down to diagnose what had created this team wide attitude I realized that I had created it by regularly writing off losses to bad luck.

My team had become frustrated because every time they lost a game they had come to feel like it was out of their hands. They hadn't lost because they were doing things inadequately. They were losing due to things beyond their control; things like officiating. At least that is what I had been telling them.

Because they thought it was the officials or other factors leading to their losing, subconsciously they felt like there was nothing they could do to help turn things around. They felt powerless to change things. I had been telling them to stay the course; that they were playing fine. What they heard was they were playing well and still not winning. After a while, that wears on a team.

The truth is we weren't playing that well and there was plenty we could improve on, but in my effort to stay positive I had ignored those areas and had never addressed them with my team. My crusade to keep positive had created a festering frustration and there was only one way to remedy it, but it wasn't going to be pleasant.

I called a team meeting where I laid out in detail many of the reasons we had not been successful in recent weeks. I acknowledged that yes, we could have got a break or a call here or there, but I followed that up by pointing out that truly good teams don't need the benefit of favorable officiating to win a game. Truly good teams can overcome a bad bounce and still pull out a win. We could have won those games if we had rebounded better, defended better, and shot better. The message of the meeting was that we were in control of our own destiny. There would be no more blaming officials or bad luck. If we lost a game, we were each going to look in the mirror afterwards and consider what we could have done better to alter the outcome. The point of my comments was to empower my players. It was to help them accept responsibility for their own success or failure. I didn't realize it right away, but accepting responsibility after a loss can actually be better in the long run for a team. It helps them recognize what they need to improve, but it also empowers them to know that if they do that thing better they can win!

There is something liberating about accepting responsibility for a loss. In your effort to lift your teams' spirits after a tough loss, don't deny them the satisfaction of knowing that they control their future fate. Don't lead them to believe their success will be determined by the bounce of the ball or by officials. Help them to recognize that no one has more control over their future than themselves.

Again, I do think there is a time and a place to write off a loss to bad luck. Maybe you really do feel your team played terrific and there is nothing you would have had them do differently. In that case, maybe you can help them move on from the loss a bit more quickly by assigning blame elsewhere. However, shifting blame more than once or twice in a season can cultivate the kind of frustration described above. Use the "bad luck" excuse for losing sparingly, if at all.

Shouldering the Blame

Just as there is an occasion for writing off a loss to a bad break there is also a time and a place to accept the full fault for the loss as a coach. Typically, the best time to do this is after a loss similar to the type just described in the previous passage. Your team played hard and played well but came up a bit short. You know that their confidence level is already low and it would be counterproductive to mentally punish them any further.

In that circumstance it can be helpful for the team to hear you say "that loss is on me." Especially if you have been particularly critical of your team in recent days or weeks it can be a great public relations move with your players for you to fall on the proverbial sword and criticize yourself.

I have found myself doing this about once a year. I don't usually know when I am going to do it in advance. It is either a sincere feeling after a loss or it is something I feel the team needs to hear for its own mental health. I don't make a big deal out of it. I usually just say "I get after you guys when you don't do things right. Well, tonight I made a mistake. This loss is on me and I'm sorry. You played hard. But I had a bad night tonight and I could have done a better job of putting you in a position to win. I point out when you make mistakes, so it's only fair I point out my own."

From a political perspective there are numerous benefits to be gained by making a statement like that to your team. Many players will immediately admire the fact that you are accepting responsibility for a loss and not always laying the blame on the team. It also serves as an excellent example. If you preach responsibility to your players and ask them to self evaluate after each game, it is wise to role model and demonstrate that you do the same. When the kids go home and tell mom and dad that coach said he screwed up tonight, there will even be some parents that appreciate and respect the candor.

But a coach must be careful not to make a habit of these types of admissions. When this is done more than once during a season you can create that same culture of frustration and powerlessness for your team that was referenced previously. The players will begin to think that you are the reason for their losing, not them. They will think you are the reason because you are the one that tells them so on a semi-regular basis. Again, this is a move to be used sparingly. And if you are already under fire from players and parents that accuse you of costing the team games, it is probably best not to use this technique at all. If you do, you are not going to garner any additional respect. You are merely throwing gas on an already burning fire.

There is a saying that "players win games and coaches lose games." There are plenty of people that already believe that. Especially at the high school level, when a team wins the parents think it's because their kids are immensely talented. When the team loses, many immediately feel it must be the coach's fault because the parents continue to be convinced that their kids are all stars. Accepting blame for a loss can be a risky move and timing is of the essence for it to be executed properly, but there is a proper time and place to take the fall.

Players Win Games

To expand on a point made above, it is wise for all coaches to keep the following fact near the front of their mind: as a coach you have never and will never make a basket, make a tackle, get a hit, serve an ace, or score a goal. It is up to your players do to all of those things. When the team wins it is truly because the players won the game. As coaches we can help players develop their skills so they are more proficient and we can help put them in position to be successful through the strategy we elect to implement, but ultimately the execution and the outcome is up to them.

Both winning and losing coaches can often lose sight of this fact. When a coach's team is winning it can be easy for the coach to get intoxicated by the success and to start to feel like they are brilliant. Conversely coaches that are confronted with chronic losing can have a tendency to beat themselves up and begin to question their ability to teach and their strategic decisions. I know both of these situations well as I have coached enough to experience both ends of the spectrum.

But now with 40 seasons of coaching under my belt I have come to understand that as a coach, I have far less control over the success or failure of my team than I sometimes care to admit. Being a coach is very much like being the President of the United States. When the economy does well the President gets far too much credit for it. When the country lapses into recession it is often the result of policies that were implemented as much as a decade earlier and the current President gets far too much blame. In truth, the President has a very marginal ability to impact the economy through their policy decisions. But the nature of the position is such that the President will collect the credit for the economy's success or accept the blame for its failure.

As coaches, we must learn to live with the same reality. When we come to terms with the fact that the team with the better players is going to win most of the games and that our implementation of strategy will win or lose just a few games a year, it helps us stay humble through the good times and sane through the bad times.

Perhaps the most egregious example I have ever seen of a coach's ego gone wild happened almost ten years ago on a cold, snowy, March evening. I was watching a section championship game in southeastern Minnesota. The game featured the number three seeded team versus the one seed. The coach of the three seed had made it known in a very public way that he felt his team had been insulted and disrespected by the other coaches in the section when they were assigned something less than the top seed. Though his team's record was not as good as the top two seeds this coach reasoned that his team played in a superior conference[4] and based on that fact alone they deserved the top seed.

Initially I assumed the coach was very vocal and public about this perceived slap in the face in an effort to motivate his team. He had created an "us against the world" mentality which I generally applaud. But when his team won the section championship it became obvious that the coach's politicking in the newspaper was not just a ploy.

As the final buzzer sounded his team congregated at half court and engaged in the traditional embracing and jumping up and down to celebrate their state tournament berth. While the players celebrated together, their coach proceeded to take a victory lap around the court. All by himself, the coach ran the entire sideline and baseline pointing his finger in the air and hollering. I had never seen a coach draw attention to themselves quite like that, but it got worse. After completing his one man victory lap the coach jumped up on the media table at courtside and started yelling at the opposing fans "Conference Respect!" He stood on this table, literally pounding his chest and taunting the opposing fans for the better part of a minute before one of his assistants came to usher him down. Very few of the thousands of people in attendance were even aware that the players were celebrating at center court. The coach had made himself the center of attention at a moment that should have belonged to his players.

This coach may have done a great job putting his team in position to win, but he didn't grab a single rebound or make even one basket the entire game. His players did all of that. In his exuberance, he forgot who did all the work. All coaches should endeavor to keep in the front of their mind that their players win games. As coaches we are just there to help them do it.

_____

4 *Have you ever heard a coach say they play in a bad conference? I never have. I always hear coaches talk about how loaded their league is.*

NINE
***

Surviving Race and Gender Issues

*"I am working for the time when unqualified blacks,
browns, and women join the unqualified white men in running our government."*
— Cissy Farenthold

While there are portions of books devoted to coaching the respective genders, those I have read always fail to confront the political pitfalls coaches can encounter as a result of the specific gender they coach. I thought it worth a few pages to address what, and what not to do when it comes to coaching boys and girls.

Males Coaching Males

It is often assumed that males can coach males without much trouble because every male coach was a teenage boy at one time. Therefore, the coach can easily ascertain what is going on inside their players' heads, then push the proper buttons to get the most out of their players. Of course, anyone that has coached youth or high school boys knows it has never been that simple. Beyond the psychology of coaching boys, what are some things coaches do that tend to create political problems when coaching adolescents?

With young male coaches, the mistake they most commonly commit is becoming more of a friend to their players than a coach. Young coaches can often connect and relate with their players better. As a result, they can sometimes get them to perform better. The trouble is helping both parties, the players and the coach, understand where the boundaries need to be in their player/coach relationship.

Whether it is on or off the field, young coaches will sometimes use language or discuss topics with their players that would make many of those players' parents blush. Young coaches need to be cautious about the language they use and the topics of discussion they broach with their players. For example, if an attractive girl is walking by and one of the players says something to their coach about how "hot" she is, while the initial reaction of the coach may be to simply agree, doing so is something that puts them on the same level as a teammate. I am not saying coaches can't discuss private matters with their players or council them, but those discussions should be done in precisely that manner; as counseling sessions. If the coach is acting as a mentor that is entirely appropriate. If they are acting as "buddy," that blurs the line between player and coach and can lead to problems down the road.

Another way young coaches commonly get in hot water is by confiding in certain players on their team. Maybe they feel like they have a strong relationship with a player and they talk to them about a specific situation involving another player on the team or perhaps even a conflict with a colleague at work. Coaches can't confide in players the same way they would confide in friends. These young men are still high school students and no matter how mature they might seem, they will make mistakes and say things they aren't supposed to. If a parent finds out that the coach told Tommy that Ben is the worst player on the team and he will likely get cut next year, when (not if) that is made public the coach will have a lot of explaining to do.

Middle aged and older coaches usually have the opposite issue. They can sometimes have a hard time connecting with the players on their team. The political battle they are forced to fight involves the kids tuning them out or trying to force them out. Older coaches can push a team just as hard as a younger coach, but the pushing by the younger coach is often more accepted because the coach is "cool" or he "gets" the players on the team. When the older coach pushes his players hard, to the players the older coach is just an asshole. Veteran coaches may need to work harder to communicate why it is they do what they do. What complicates this is when asked by players why they have to do something, older coaches are far more inclined to simply say "Because I say so, that's why." The older coach might feel their years of experience mean they are beyond questioning. They may not feel a need to offer explanations to their players. That can be a fatal miscalculation. Older coaches may have to convey to players why it is they are running certain drills or employing certain strategies to an even greater degree than a younger coach would because their players may be less likely to "buy in" right away due to the generational difference.

Finally, male coaches often think that because they are coaching males they can be more harsh and gruff. Increasingly that is not the case. Regardless of what gender you are coaching there are kids that respond best to a kick in the butt and others that will only respond to a pat on the back. The best coaches are those that can determine what button to push with each individual player, then address each player in the manner that gets the most out of them.

Females Coaching Males

First of all, any woman willing to coach a group of young boys deserves a tip of the hat. There is an enormous stereotype that a female coach must overcome to earn such a position. So what political problems does a woman need to be conscious of before directing these young men?

The first and most important thing to recognize is that nearly every pre-teen and teenage boy is incredibly sexist. From the moment you take control of the team, you will have a majority of your players immediately skeptical of your ability to teach and lead them. Most will be certain they know more about the game than you because you are "just a girl." I don't care how progressive their parents are, the culture kids grow up in helps promote this terribly ill informed attitude.

As a female coaching males, it would be wise to do something to demonstrate your superior knowledge or skill almost immediately. Depending on the age and ability of the athletes, perhaps you could challenge the guys to a foot race? If you coach baseball maybe you could challenge one of them to try to strike you out?

If you don't think a demonstration of physical skill is one you could sufficiently wow them with, attempt to dazzle them with your mastery of strategic situations. Create a late game scenario that you know they are unlikely to be familiar with or a situation where an often misunderstood rule would come into play. Ask them to write down what they would do in that situation. Have them turn in their answers, then without naming names read through some of their replies. Touch on the ridiculous ones and the utterly ill informed ones first. If you encounter one that is a correct diagnosis of the situation and what strategy should be employed, applaud them and then go on to explain why that is the right course of action.

Whether it is demonstrating physical skill or a command of strategy, the greatest challenge for a female coaching males is establishing a degree of credibility with this admittedly immature and sexist audience. In the mind of the players, a woman has got more to prove than any man that would walk into that same coaching position, even if that man had never seen a sporting event in his life. That said, a boys' respect and loyalty can be won. It may be a bit more challenging but once it is earned, a coach has won them over for good.

Females Coaching Females

The biggest obstacle encountered by females coaching females is overcoming what I call the "Bitch Factor." In the culture of adolescent males there is a clearly defined hierarchy. One or two boys tend to ascend to a leadership position either based on their physical prowess or the power of their personality. This leadership role is traditionally embraced and accepted by the other boys. For whatever reason, this ascension and acceptance of leadership is not nearly as prevalent among adolescent girls.

In my years of coaching girls' basketball I have learned that I have to define for my players the difference between being a leader and being a bitch. When a female teammate says to a group of average high school girls something like "Come on! Let's go! We gotta get this done!" the reaction among many of them is often "what a bitch!" The players have a difficult time delineating between leadership and someone telling them what to do. I recognize the tone with which things are said and they way words are delivered can make a major difference, but the fact of the matter is the captain of a male team can come in the locker room and chew some major ass at half time of a game and nearly no one on the team will recoil or consider the guy a jerk. They recognize the actions for what they are; a genuine attempt to motivate and get the team focused. There are girls (the truly competitive and athletic minded) that also have an intrinsic understanding of this, but many must be coached on discerning the difference between bitching at someone and leading someone.

Such is the challenge for a female coach. The first time she raises her voice or challenges her players in some way, there will be players that react negatively because they think coach is being bitchy. Oddly enough, girls are considerably less inclined to view a male coach in the same manner. Perhaps there is an odd expectation that a male coach is going to be a jerk from time to time so it is more easily accepted or dismissed by the players.

Regardless, the point is this; as a female coach you need to take some time to explain to your players the difference between leading, motivating, challenging, and being a bitch. If you do that early, you will avoid many of the problems that tend to crop up when women coach girls.

Males Coaching Females

I have saved this category for last as it is the most politically combustible coaching scenario of them all. There is no other situation where a coach's career can come to such an abrupt and crushing end as when a teenage girl accuses a male coach of some form of misconduct.

And I am not just talking about things of a sexual nature. When a coach yells, stomps, or throws a garbage can to make a point, there is far greater likelihood that a parent will complain to administration than if the coach were to behave in the same manner with a group of teenage boys. The reason is parents (both mothers and fathers) have a much stronger instinct to protect their "little girl" than their sons. If a girl on your team feels the least bit threatened because a male coach has raised their voice or demonstrated frustration, the instinctive reaction of the parent to protect their daughter can lead to all kinds of controversy.

For that matter, the coach doesn't really even have to raise their voice. Any reader that grew up with a sister can probably already relate to what I am about to say. In my years as a teacher and a coach I have learned that I can speak to a teenage girl in a completely conversational tone, but if I am saying something the girl doesn't want to hear she perceives it as me "yelling" at her. I can't tell you how many times I have talked with a female student or player days or weeks after a conversation where I offer some level of critique and they talk about how I "yelled at them." I am always quick to correct them on that statement. It is important they understand the difference between coaching or teaching and yelling. To demonstrate I usually tell them a quick story.

I learned the difference between coaching and yelling from my college baseball coach during my freshman season. During early season practices our hotshot shortstop was having a heck of a time throwing the ball successfully to first base. Every time the shortstop would fire the ball over the first baseman's head our coach would holler "Throw the damn baseball!"

After hearing our coach shout that out 50 times a day for the first two weeks of practice, I remember telling one of our assistants "Nate (our shortstop) <u>knows</u> he needs to throw the damn ball. Someone needs to tell him <u>how</u> to throw the damn ball." No matter the tone of voice, coaching occurs when you are offering instruction and genuine assistance designed to enhance a player's performance. If I am saying something instructive, my players need to recognize it for what it is. Regardless of gender, make sure your players understand the difference between coaching and yelling. Then make sure you are doing a lot more of the first and next to none of the latter.

Of course, the ultimate political nightmare for a male coach dealing with female players is to have one suggest that the coach conducted himself in an inappropriate manner as it pertains to sexual matters. It could be as simple as a comment or a joke that was deemed sexist or suggestive. Or it could be an accusation that the coach propositioned the player. Either situation can bring an immediate end to a coach's career. Even good, well intentioned coaches must be ever vigilant that they do not put themselves in a position for such an accusation to be made or substantiated.

A golf coach I became acquainted with experienced the ultimate nightmare scenario. He had been the girls golf coach for a few years at his school and he was in the midst of what he thought was a typical non-descript season. Suddenly, late in the school year and late in the golf season, he was summoned to the principal's office. The principal and AD explained that two players on the team had come to them and said that the coach (we'll call him Jeff) had been looking down their shirts when they bent over to line up putts and that he had been rubbing himself against them in an overtly sexual way when showing them how to putt.

Jeff was at a loss for words. He had never touched one of his players during the course of his instruction in an effort to avoid a situation such as this. And he couldn't recall a time he would have been in a position to peer down a golfer's shirt as he was accused of. He shared this with his administrators. They responded that these were very serious accusations and they would need to do a full investigation. He would be suspended with pay while they investigated.

Jeff contacted his union representative and he found the union rather cold to his plight. As is the case in our modern society, he was immediately presumed guilty by all that knew and worked with him. It didn't help that he was single and in his 20's. It was an easy leap for most to make that this young, bachelor coach would make a move on one of his players. The next several days were utter misery for Jeff.

He had been conversing with a lawyer and was preparing to head back in to visit with school administration when he got a call from the principal. The principal began with an apology then said "Jeff, we need you to come in and sit down with us. There has been a development that clears you of any wrong doing."

Jeff was relieved but he was also admittedly angry. Though he was going to be vindicated, his reputation was eternally tarnished. In his meeting with the principal Jeff was told that one of the girls on the team came to administration earlier that day and confessed that the whole story was concocted. The other golfer that had made the accusation was also a student in Jeff's math class. This girl had got an F in Jeff's class on a recent report card. As a result, the girl was grounded and had her car keys taken away. She decided to issue the harassment charge as a means to gain revenge on Jeff. The teammate that had agreed to corroborate the accuser's claim was eventually overwhelmed by a strong sense of conscience and she confessed to the set up. Jeff's teaching job was saved, but he immediately elected to end his coaching career for fear of being put in such a position again.

The frightening thing for male coaches is that a scenario such as the one just described could happen just as easily to anyone. It is not hard to imagine a player that isn't getting much playing time deciding to tell her parents or administration that the coach propositioned her and told her she would play more if she would perform sexual favors. It becomes a classic "he said, she said" and next to impossible to prove, but that is not the key. The scary thing for the coach is such an accusation is also next to impossible to disprove.

That is why it is absolutely vital that male coaches <u>never</u> put themselves in a position where a player can even suggest such a thing. If you are meeting with a player it should always be in public or in the presence of another adult, as outlined earlier in this book. If you have no choice but to meet with the player in a one on one situation, then make sure it is done with an open door or within view of others. Of course, the best and safest option is to avoid one on one meetings entirely.

Even if a male coach follows all protocol and conducts themselves in a manner that is beyond reproach, there is still the chance that nasty rumors can circulate. This is particularly true of the young, single male coach working with teenage girls. If the coach is liked by his players, there will be someone around the town or the school that will start a rumor that so and so and the coach seem way too chummy. That rumor will circulate until, in the minds of the pubic, it becomes an illicit affair. If a coach finds themselves the victim of such a rumor what is their best move?

Again, because such an accusation is virtually impossible to disprove, in most cases the coach is best served by ignoring the rumor entirely. On the rare occasion someone has the audacity to ask the coach directly if they are messing around with their player, the line used by so many politicians in the past; "I am not going to dignify that with a response" is probably best. There is a quote that the "only way to win a war is to make sure you don't get into it in the first place." That is true of rumors and accusations such as these. I am also reminded of another similar quote. "You can no more win a war than you can win an earthquake." No one "wins" an earthquake. You survive it, but no one wins. The same is true of character assassination like that described above. You can't win this situation. The best you can hope to do is survive it. So avoid it at all costs.

There were times when I was young, single, and coaching girls that I considered quitting the girls' basketball job simply because I feared the things described above. I had a couple of fellow coaches tell me "you need to get a wife" and they weren't just saying it because they were concerned about my long term best interest. They said it because they knew that a male coach with a wife has a certain degree of insulation from these kinds of accusations that a single man does not. When accusations are made against a man with a wife and kids, the reaction of many is to say "No, that can't be. He's got a wife and kids!" While that initial reaction can recede very rapidly, it is a benefit of the doubt that an unmarried male coach never enjoys.

Married or single, there is plenty of potential danger for a male coaching females. Men in this position must be consummate professionals and endeavor to avoid allowing even the suggestion of impropriety. Even then, a coach can only reduce the chance they become a victim of false charges or character assassination. Of course, the only way to avoid the threat entirely is to get out of coaching. Confronted with this fact, many men will continue to roll the dice because their passion for coaching supercedes their fear of false accusations.

The Politics of Race

Another area that can be radioactive for coaches is the issue of race. Occasionally, situations surface where coaches that are entirely well intentioned leave themselves vulnerable to an accusation of racism. Having the racist label attached can be the kiss of death for a coach's career.

Before I continue, I am compelled to explain that all of the following advice is offered with the assumption that the reader is not a racist. Certainly our society has progressed to a point where I can make this assumption with a certain degree of confidence. But should the reader harbor any racist inclinations, be they conscious or sub-conscious, I cannot offer a playbook to help that. The coaching profession has a way of filtering out those that cling to prejudicial or racist tendencies. Coaches that determine playing time based on artificial criteria like race usually don't last long in this line of work. There is no remedy for coaches embroiled in political problems created by the stupidity and ignorance of racism. The coaching profession always ends up giving those coaches what they deserve. With that in mind, let us examine some common issues well intentioned, intelligent coaches should be cognizant of.

We will begin with roster spots. Obviously this is essentially a non-issue for wrestling, track, golf, and tennis coaches to name a few. If one player triumphs over another in head to head competition or has a better time or score there is no debate. But in team sports, where there are tryouts and decisions about playing time, coaches are considerably more vulnerable to accusations.

In a tryout situation, one way coaches can insulate themselves from accusations of racism (and this is true regardless of race) is by having tangible, measureable criteria as part of their team selection process. Our basketball program implemented speed, strength, and vertical jump testing a few years ago in preparation for a season where we were going to have 40 juniors and seniors trying out for 18 spots. I knew that if I could point to statistics that clearly put one player ahead of another, I would be able to answer any accusations asserted by a disgruntled player or parent. If a parent had a beef with their kid not making the team, I first took the high road and explained that it wasn't that their child was a bad player, but rather it was the result of us having so many good players trying out. With all those good players and limited spots, it was inevitable that good players would get cut. This approach worked for most of the parents that wanted an explanation. However, one parent pushed things past that initial "high road" stage. I was happy to show him the results of our various tests. His daughter scored in the bottom five out of 40 in all three categories. Numbers don't lie, and the flames of his discontent were immediately extinguished.

In that case, the parent did not charge racism but he did suggest a bias or some form of discrimination and my data dismantled that claim. When prudent and possible, use statistics and measures to protect you from accusations of discrimination.

Of course, there are circumstances when the numbers may not work to your advantage. The player that you cut may have scored among the best in a couple of categories. We had that situation occur in a different season. A player that was on the borderline of whether she would make our team or not and was ultimately cut had scored among the top 18 in two of our three categories. The player was an OK athlete, but she just didn't have the shooting, passing, or dribbling skills to compete at the varsity level. In a sit down meeting with her parents my assistant coach and I had to explain how it worked out that the player could score near the top in a couple of categories but still fail to make the team. We pointed out that those measures were just one of many criteria we consider. We look at positional need. The player was a point guard and we had six that we rated ahead of her. We look at skills. While five of our other six point guards were adept three point shooters, the player we cut had very limited shooting range. We cited a few other examples of things this player didn't do quite as well as the ones we kept. The parents did not leave the meeting happy, but they did leave content.

The key to success in meetings such as the one just described is to enter the meeting prepared. Just like a lawyer attempting to prove their case to a jury by presenting evidence, I presented my case for cutting their kid. To be clear, coming in prepared requires more than having your bullet points on a piece of paper. Being totally prepared also means anticipating what your opponent might say in response to your claims. Just as a politician prepares for a debate, a coach needs to prepare for parent confrontations. Expect that an angry parent is not meeting you to get answers; they are coming to argue. Prepare yourself for every eventuality just as a candidate prepares for a debate and you will emerge from these meetings triumphant.

Do your best to establish grounds rules going in to the debate. Make it clear that you are there to talk about their child and no one else's. Keep the focus on their child and what their child needs to improve or areas they were inadequate in. Better yet, do as a polished politician does and dictate the topics of the debate by shifting their questions or comments back to areas that you can win on. Things like positional depth are rock solid topics that are hard for your opponent to argue effectively. When I explained to these parents that we had six point guards on a roster of 18 players and that typically no more than two will play in any one game, that conveyed that we were already saturated at that position and a few of the players we put ahead of their child weren't even going to play. The parent may enter the meeting upset, but as the confrontation unfolds it becomes clear to the parents that they are fighting a losing battle.

When it comes to the accusation of racism though, that becomes a difficult thing to for either side to prove or disprove. Not long ago we had a parent subtly suggested to others in our program that I clearly favored players of one race over another. To refute this accusation I was fortunate to have a long history of players of this particular race that had been starters and stars. These past players and I had a great relationship and it was widely known. So when the accusation was subtly made by one disgruntled parent, it was summarily dismissed by the rest of the parents in our program. But some coaches don't have the distinction of having a long track record. How do you deal with the accusations then?

For the young coach or the coach that has had no past experience with players of a different race or ethnicity, it is critically important that the coach is perceived by the majority of players and parents on the team as treating everyone equally. If your penalty for being late is running, then you make sure every player that is late pays that penalty, regardless of the reason or whether they are the star of the team or not.

I have always had players run for being late to practice. In the season that the parent tried to play the race card on me, one of the things they suggested is that their daughter had to run because she was late to practice and that it was an unfair punishment because I didn't understand "their culture." Fortunately some parents that over heard this were quick to point out that their daughters were late to practice earlier in the season and had to run just as much. Their daughters were of a different race than the accusatory parent. The charge was immediately diffused. The lesson here; being consistent in the way you treat and discipline players is the single best way to ward off accusations of racism.

The following story offers another example of how consistency can prevent frivolous charges from gaining traction.

I had a situation several years ago where I was taking my 9th grade baseball team to a one day tournament on a Saturday. The bus was to leave at 9am and when the clock struck nine we were minus two players. We pulled out of the parking lot and made the 45 minute drive to our destination. Just a few minutes before the first pitch, as we were finishing our pre-game warm-up, I saw a fancy Lincoln Navigator pull into the parking lot. Out tumbled my two missing players. They were in uniform and they jogged onto the field.

One player was my starting center fielder and lead-off hitter. The other was a platoon player. As they reached the dugout I told both boys that I appreciated them coming to support their teammates, but that neither would be playing in either game that day as they missed the team bus. They explained that they had a sleepover the night before and their alarm didn't go off. I said that was unfortunate, but school district policy said that if they didn't ride the team bus they needed clearance in writing from a school administrator ahead of time. It was liability issue and a legal matter. My hands were tied. They grumbled and pouted for a few minutes, but eventually they got over it and they were good teammates the rest of the day.

The next Monday, about mid-day, I got called down to our principal's office. He and the AD were there and the look on their faces told me I was in trouble.

"Carl, why didn't Steve Thompson play at all in your tournament last Saturday?" my principal asked.

"He missed the team bus. District policy is pretty clear on that, isn't it?" I replied.

"Well, you need to hear the voice mail I got this morning," the principal said.

It was the father of Steve Thompson calling to inform our school that he had already secured a lawyer and he would be pressing charges because of the racial discrimination his son had been subjected to on Saturday. Mid-way through the message I had a hard time holding back a smile.

"I don't consider this a laughing matter!" my principal barked.

I responded "If it was racial discrimination, then how are they going to explain Keith sitting out both games too? He is as blonde haired and blue eyed as they come."

I knew there was no case here and it was simply a pissed off parent trying to intimidate and throw their weight around. This father was miffed because the boys overslept, then he took the time to drive them almost an hour away to get to the games and they didn't play.

My administrators started to relax a bit, but before I left the office they added that in the future if I thought a kid was dropped off by a parent that I could use my discretion and go ahead and play the kid.

Our school had a policy designed to prevent lawsuits and when we implemented that policy we got threatened with a lawsuit! No matter how fair or unbiased a coach may be, there will occasionally be upset parents that attempt to implement the racial discrimination accusation as a means to the coach's end. To defend against this a coach must be able to document and explain their decisions and be consistent with their discipline. Understand that with every decision you make, you establish a precedent. Adhere to that precedent in all future situations and any attempt to smear your reputation or label you a racist will fall flat.

The other thing I would recommend to help coaches avoid potential charges of racial discrimination is probably going to be more controversial but remember, this book is about the politics of coaching, not the morals of coaching.

There have been seasons where members of different minority groups have been rather under-represented on my teams. This is primarily due to the demographics of the states I have coached in (South Dakota and Minnesota) and their overwhelmingly white populations. That said, with only one exception there has been at least a modest degree of racial diversity at every school I have coached at. Sometimes the small number of minorities on our team was due to a lack of kids trying out. Other times it was simply a lack of talent among those trying out. I am no different than any other coach in the sense that I want to win as many games as possible. I don't care what color a kid is, if they can help me win, they will be on my team. In all my years as a varsity coach I have had only one team that lacked any racial diversity.

However, there have been a few seasons where the final roster spot was a close call. One of the major factors that could lead a coach to keep the player of the under represented race on their team could be that the coach sees the value in bringing more diversity to their squad. Creating a better blend of backgrounds is certainly reason enough to keep the minority player when they are similar in ability with a player of the predominant race. But let's forget that very valid reason and look at the purely political perspective. When my final roster spot has been a toss-up between the mediocre white kid and the mediocre kid of another race, I have always filled that last roster spot with the kid of a different race. In doing so, I knew that the parents of the white kid would be considerably less likely to suggest "racism" as a reason their kid didn't make the team. Whereas if I took the white kid, I was giving the minority player's parents a chance to charge me with racism. One of the keys to surviving in coaching is doing everything you can to limit the ammunition would be enemies have to use against you. Never put bullets in their gun.

And before someone calls me "unfair" for taking the minority player merely to protect myself, please remember how I described the situation at the outset. If it's a "close call" is what I said. I am not talking about taking a player that is clearly inferior just to cover your ass. That would open you up to more criticism than it would prevent. I am saying if it is a coin toss situation, race can be a convenient tie breaker for the coach that is cognizant someone might try to play the race card against them.

Whether it is a Caucasian coach keeping a minority player or an

African-American coach taking a token white kid on their team, doing so is a prudent political move. You can bristle at this suggestion, you can even call it corrupt if you want, but the advice I have just offered is pure politics. Most importantly, it is winning politics.

TEN

***

All Politics Is Local

"There are two kinds of coaches. Them that's fired,
and them that's gonna be fired."
— Bum Phillips

Former Houston Oilers coach Bum Phillips was famous for his funny quips, but there was an enormous element of truth in the comment above. In the world of politics it is extremely rare for a candidate to complete their career undefeated, winning every election they have ever run. It is equally uncommon for a coach to last for years or decades in the same position at the same school. No matter how much you might love your job or how much you think the people in your program love you, the honeymoon will eventually come to an end.

Even if you employ all the political maneuvering you can imagine, sometimes the clock simply runs out and it is time to move on. It is hard not to take it personally. But if Abraham Lincoln had quit after his first or even his fourth political defeat, he would have never become one of our greatest presidents. As coaches, we often try to teach our players the value of persistence and perseverance. It is important we don't lose sight of that lesson if and when the time comes that we are dealt a career setback and our character is tested.

Coaches that come to accept that there will always be a person or a group of people that are unhappy with them are those that are best equipped to have a long, successful career in this profession. If you are a person that is preoccupied with pleasing others all of the time it is best to reconsider coaching, or at the very least you would be well advised to avoid becoming a head coach.

In this chapter we will examine some of the most combustible areas we encounter as coaches and we will address how to safely navigate through them. I will also offer what I consider to be the most positive and effective move any coach can execute if they hope to keep the majority of their "constituents" happy and on their side. Legendary

Speaker of the U.S. House of Representatives Tip O'Neill famously said that "all politics is local." In the coaching profession, that is particularly true. Coaches need to keep the items in this chapter near the front of their mind because the areas about to be covered are the proverbial front lines of every coach's political battlefield.

Picking Teams

Aside from playing time, selecting teams is the issue that puts coaches on the hot seat more than any other. When a coach is forced to cut players the coach is automatically put in a position where they will be considered an enormous villain by the player and the players' parents. This fact is virtually unavoidable. But if a coach lays the ground work ahead of time they can minimize the venom that is spewed at them and they can dull the pain experienced by the kids that are cut.

Ideally the foundation for making cuts begins in the offseason prior to tryouts. A coach that I know quite well was particularly adept at somewhat subtly conveying to kids which of them were likely to be on the team the next year and which didn't have much of a chance. During the summer when players would show up for open gym this coach would divide teams for scrimmaging. He would always sound as though he wasn't putting much thought into who would be on what team.

"Hmmm, Jim, you go over there. Bill, why don't you go with that group? Uhhh, Kevin you be a sub for this team, and that team needs a point guard so Zack, you go over with them." He couldn't have sounded less calculating as he "casually" created the teams. But by the time the teams were divided it was obvious to anyone that was paying attention that nearly all of the top players were together on the same team and that the "subs" for certain teams were always the bottom rung players. Again, lots of coaches do this but it was the way he did it. It was not menacing or harsh. He made it seem so unthreatening it was incredible. And by the end of the summer, many of the kids he would have cut began to connect the dots and they would inevitably decide not to try out that winter. The coach had quietly and subtly conveyed that they were not likely to make the team so the kids were spared the embarrassment of getting cut and the coach was spared the hostility of what would have been angry parents. The players elected on their own not to tryout. Certainly the coach helped them reach that decision, but ultimately he was not going to be the target of any irate parents because he did not cut the kids. By failing to tryout the kids basically cut themselves.

The next step in laying the foundation for cuts comes during a coach's pre-season parent/player meeting. On this evening I always make sure to announce exactly how many players we have trying out for our JV/Varsity team. I then remind everyone that the state only allows us to carry "X" number of players on our roster for post season. I acknowledge that while technically we can carry more players prior to the playoffs, that I have done that in years past with unfortunate results. Players we have had to leave off the playoff roster inevitably forget the great experience they may have had for the previous four months. Instead they are shattered by playing all season only to have to watch in street clothes as their teammates chase a championship. After expanding the roster a few times I do not do it any longer. We will keep no more than the max allowed by our state association. Sharing this information gives the players and parents time to do some math and let the challenge of making the team sink in. When there are 50 players trying out for 15 spots most should emerge from the meeting with an understanding that statistically the odds of making the team are certainly against them. After being confronted by those figures it is common that another half dozen to a dozen kids "cut themselves" and decide not to try out. Again, this makes the coach's job easier and it cuts down considerably on the number of people criticizing and complaining after cuts are made.

At our pre-season meeting I also explain the concept that our final team may not be comprised of the best players. If we have 12 tremendous guards we can't keep them all. There may be an awkward 6'9" player that makes the team and a guard that gets cut might honestly be able to say "I am a better player than that guy." But because opposing teams have tall players we are often forced to keep a tall player so we can match up defensively. Often it comes down to positional need and depth. It is not always about being the better player.

Further, I explain to my captive audience of prospective players and parents that we don't simply take the most talented players, we intend to take the players that make up the best team. The thing I often cite as an example is a description of what I am looking for out of the player that occupies our final roster spot. When confronted with the choice of a veteran player that may be lacking in skills but who understands their role, is a great teammate, works their tail off in practice, and genuinely wants the team to succeed versus a young, talented, ambitious player that might pout at a lack of playing time or who internally may be hoping the varsity player at their position does terrible so they can get a chance, I will opt for the less talented, good teammate every time.

Parents and players need to hear that it is not just about talent because quite honestly, most coaches understand and believe that to be true. By announcing that team selection is not solely based on talent that also allows a coach a certain amount of discretion in selecting their team. In addition, it makes it more challenging for a parent to debate the team selection because the coach clearly communicated the criteria going in to tryouts. When the parent doesn't complain about the policy prior to tryouts (and virtually no one ever will because they are all convinced their kid will make the team) and they find fault with it afterwards, the parent is immediately in a weakened position because their complaint can be easily characterized as "sour grapes."

I also provide a handout to all parents regarding our policies for picking teams so they have something in writing. I was very careful in crafting this policy to make sure I did not leave myself vulnerable to a parent attack. Remember, anything you put in writing always has the potential to be used against you. I have included a copy of my "Important Policies and Procedures for Parents and Players" in the appendix for you to peruse.

In terms of the hardcore politics of picking teams, rule number one is moving up younger players will <u>always</u> be an invitation for trouble. Even if moving up the younger players does not directly cost an older player a roster spot, it can create a culture of paranoia that you are going to have to deal with. Even when the younger player is clearly outstanding there can be a sense of entitlement that exists among junior and senior players and parents. They believe that because they are upperclassmen it is "their turn" to play. Even when they might acknowledge the younger player is superior, they can still cling to the notion that they deserve to play because of all the time and work they have put in over the years. This is not a belief even the shrewdest of political minds can easily alter. That is why coaches must consider all the possible political negatives of promoting younger players before they actually do it. Here are some of the repercussions that can result when a coach promotes a younger player to varsity or even junior varsity.

It can create a division on your team.

When an older player feels threatened by a younger players' presence, the veteran players' friends on the team will most often sympathize with their plight. As a result, you will find your team divided between those that abhor the younger player's presence and those that believe the player has every right to be there. When the younger player is clearly an impact player, one that can be the difference between winning and losing, you will usually find more consensus on your team in favor of having the younger player. A disgruntled upperclassmen will have only one or two teammates in their corner rather than half the team. Such a scenario is manageable. But if the majority of the team is against the younger players' presence it will lead to major problems. You will likely see the upper classmen "shun" the younger player, regardless of any efforts you employ to prevent or discourage such actions. That lack of acceptance amongst the older players can negatively impact your younger players' performance and future development.

Promotion can remove a younger players' incentive to work and improve.

I saw this happen with some players I inherited. They were starting on varsity in 8th grade and by the time I got them as juniors they had done nothing to improve themselves during the offseason for three consecutive years. In their mind they had made it. They were starters and there was no need to keep pushing to improve. Not every young player you promote will adopt this mentality, but it can be very hard to predict who will continue to work hard and who won't. Unless you are certain this underclassman is ready to make a major impact immediately and is good enough to do so for years to come, it may be too much of a gamble to move them up early.

Promoting younger players can cause older kids to quit, reducing your numbers and creating a vicious cycle that leads to promoting younger players even when they don't have the ability.

I also saw this in a program I inherited. It had been common practice for the previous coach to promote the top 9th graders to varsity and every time the coach did so, nearly the entire sophomore team and much of the junior varsity would elect not to play the following season. In the mind of the older players they had been passed up by some 9th graders so they didn't feel they would be given much of a chance the following season.

The major danger this creates for your program is not always immediate or obvious. Problems occur only after a year or two of losing nearly an entire class of players. That is when a coach will find themselves with only a handful of seniors and juniors on their roster. Then the coach is forced to promote younger players just to fill out the roster, whether those younger players have the ability to compete at the varsity level or not.

The reasons listed above are what have led me to develop my own personal philosophy on promoting younger players. I tell younger players that tryout for our combined JV/Varsity team that they can't merely be as good as an older player, they must be noticeably better. If I choose to keep a younger player because they are equally good as an upperclassman, I am ending the older players' career. Most often that upperclassman is a player that has worked hard and been very dedicated and loyal to our program. For me to end their career the younger player has to be markedly better than them. If we don't promote them, the younger player can continue to play and develop on an age appropriate team. The younger players' career is not over if I keep the older player. I genuinely feel that in the event of a tie, I will go with the older player. (Assuming they have a good attitude, work ethic, etc.) It just so happens that this philosophy is also best for preventing political problems.

While it is very common for the parent of an older player that is cut to go down kicking and screaming (largely because they have nothing left to lose) it is just as likely that the younger player you cut and their parents will give little more than a whimper when they are sent to their age appropriate team. The younger player and parent do this because if they hope to have a future in the program, they usually know better than to piss off the head coach by pouting and complaining about not making the varsity. Opting for the older player over the younger one is the politically astute move. But to be clear, if my choice is posting an 8 and 18 record with a bunch of older players or going 18 and 8 with a roster filled with a few younger players, I will absolutely move up the younger players.

Allow me to offer one more way to consider the difficult decision of whether to move a younger player up. There are times when our coaching staff is trying to decide between a junior and a freshman for a roster spot. I will often ask, "if we keep the freshman, will they be the difference between us going to the state tournament or not?" If the answer is "they could be" then we will almost always take the younger kid. There is a time and place to promote younger players. Just be cautious not to do it frivolously or you will eternally find yourself in the eye of a political storm.

Seniors: Cut 'Em or Keep 'Em?

For coaches that have to pick teams, an always difficult dilemma is what to do with marginal seniors. Many coaches would like to reward a player that has been loyal to the program and worked hard for many years but there is also the question about whether the coach can afford to carry "dead weight" on their roster. By dead weight I mean a player that will rarely play and is just wearing a uniform.

Beyond the logistical considerations of whether you can afford to sacrifice a roster spot to reward a senior, there are the political considerations. Before I address the political implications of cutting a senior, let me first share my own personal philosophy and experience.

I have never cut a senior that has been loyal to our program and that has demonstrated dedication at every level all the way through their career. If I am going to cut a player I am going to do it by the start of their junior year. If they are still a part of our program as a junior and want to be part of the team as a senior, I believe I owe them that much. There is a caveat to this though.

Before tryouts are complete and teams are announced I always have a very frank discussion with any senior that would take up a "loyalty" roster spot. I tell them in no uncertain terms that they are not likely to play very much, if at all. I tell them they will be expected to work hard in practice and demonstrate a team first attitude at all times. If they are unable to live up to either of those expectations, they will be removed from the team. I also ask them to imagine that they will not play a single minute of varsity all season long and to ask themselves if they would still be able to be a positive, contributing member of our team. If their answer to that question is yes, I always tell them we are happy to have them on the squad.

Some coaches are probably cringing as they read this and considering me a bleeding heart softy. Being "soft" has nothing to do with my reasoning for adopting this philosophy. I have always embraced the idea of having seniors on my team that truly accept their role and come to practice every day with the sole intention of doing whatever they can to help us win. This became my philosophy because I was given the chance to be precisely that kind of senior many years ago.

I was not a good basketball player. Some familiar with my skills might even suggest I am being rather kind to myself with that description. I was well aware of my limited ability to contribute on the court as I headed into my senior year so I went to our head coach and asked if I would be crazy to even bother trying out. He was rather ambiguous with his reply. He just gave your standard "it doesn't hurt to try" kind of line. He likely had dozens of kids come into his office over the years trying to pry some information out of him to better assess their chances of making the team. Accordingly, he gave a very politically correct answer.[5]

During my senior year I knew I wanted to be a head high school coach someday so I thought I had better at least have played varsity basketball. I expressed as much to our head coach. I told him that the only thing I wanted out of the season was to learn so I would be better prepared to be a coach myself. I explained that if I made the team he would never hear me whine or complain about playing time and that I would take great pride in beating the heck out of our other post players in practice. I closed by saying that I just wanted to be part of the team. I could not have been more sincere in my comments. I am not sure if he sensed my sincerity or if my comments had an impact on his decision to keep me on the team. All I can say for certain is it was not my stellar performance at tryouts that sealed the deal.

At any rate, the coach elected to keep players with more talent down on our JV and sophomore teams and he awarded a jersey to a kid with marginal skills, but a true team first attitude. His decision to keep me allowed me to be a part of a state championship team that season. It is a memory I will always treasure and I will forever feel grateful he afforded me that opportunity. Though my minutes were quite limited, I don't think anyone on the team would have characterized me as "dead weight." I was a ferocious competitor in practice, taking very seriously my job of preparing our starters for the next opponent. And I was an equally enthusiastic advocate for my teammates on game nights. No one wanted our team to win more than me and that attitude mattered. It is remarkable what a team can accomplish when everyone is truly pulling for each other. Myself and the other two guys that warmed the bench exemplified this team first attitude and it allowed all 12 players on our varsity team to be focused on a singular goal. There were no personal agendas, just a complete and total team focus on winning a championship.

---

5   *It is always dangerous to promise a player a spot on the team before the season begins. I don't care how talented the player might be. If the wrong parent hears that you have already started picking the team before tryouts and you are guaranteeing people spots that is excellent ammunition for them to raise holy hell with administration and/or the school board.*

If a coach can be sure that their "dead weight" senior will bring that same kind of attitude, I think the coach would be foolish not to keep them. But as I said, that is my personal opinion. Now let us examine the true politics of cutting or keeping a senior.

When you cut a sophomore or a junior there are often repercussions. Angry phone calls and e-mails to you, the AD, or the school board are par for the course. But when you cut an underclassmen there is always some sliver of hope left in the back of their (and their parent's) mind that they could still make the team next year. Or perhaps they hold on to the hope that you will die in a fiery car crash and the coach that replaces you will finally see their true talent that you obviously missed. The point is, cutting younger players will raise a ruckus but it never compares to the outrage that is unleashed when a senior is cut.

Shakespeare has been credited with saying "Hell hath no fury like a woman scorned" but I respectfully disagree. Hell hath no fury like the mother of a cut senior! When a player and their parents have put forth countless hours driving to and from practice, weekends away from home for youth tournaments, and thousands of dollars on camps and clinics, they will not go quietly into that good night. In the eyes of the parents you have done nothing short of crushing their child's dreams, forever tarnishing their sacred "senior year." You may even be accused of destroying the rest of their child's life. And because you destroyed their cherished child's life you can bet that this parent will make it their mission to destroy yours.

If there are any skeletons in your closet or any dirt they can possibly dig up on you, expect that they will dig with a vengeance. If you have no past incidents they could discover to damage your reputation they may even resort to making things up. There is no "next year" for the senior and their parents. There is no reason for them to hold back. They won't just burn bridges. They will "burn the boats" as the saying goes and fight to take you down until their last dying breath!

What I have just described is not true in every case mind you, but it is a scenario that is <u>far</u> more likely when you cut a senior than when you cut a kid of any other age. There is such a sense of sentimentality associated with the senior year that players and parents will react with considerably more vehemence and venom to perceived injustices perpetrated in that year than in any other. So, from a political perspective, what a coach must consider is simply this…is cutting the senior worth the war that will likely ensue?

To clarify, I am talking specifically about cutting a kid that has demonstrated or conveyed that they will accept whatever role they are assigned and there is ample evidence they will be a great teammate. If the senior-to-be would be pouting all year because a sophomore is playing ahead of them, then you have a carcinogenic toxin that would certainly become cancerous and you need to cut the kid, no question about it. That kind of cut is well worth the battle. But when the senior is a good kid, but not a good player, a coach really needs to give the decision careful consideration.

There is an administrative aspect to this scenario as well. Before you cut a senior that is widely considered to be a "good kid" and that has expressed they will play any role they are asked, you had better know where your AD, principal, superintendent, and school board stand on the matter. If any one of those superiors should over rule your decision you will instantly become impotent in the eyes of all of the parents and players in your program. On more than one occasion I have heard of coaches being told they must return a player to their team even after they have made their "final cuts." Needless to say, this is always the beginning of the end for the coach at that school, either at the coach's decision or the administration's.

The fact of the matter is, regardless of the sport, at the high school level most coaches can find room for at least one token senior that is a good kid with a good work ethic. In fact, one is usually all you will have to keep. By keeping one, you prove to your administration that you do in fact have a heart and that you will make room for a good kid whenever possible. You will also take away some of the ammunition from the pissed off parents of those that didn't make it because they cannot accuse you of "only caring about the younger players" or some other ridiculous charge.

In the final analysis, we all want to win as many games as we can and we will always be reluctant to keep a player on our team that might in some way hinder our chances to do that, but coaches have got to keep two things in mind:
1. We are educators and this isn't professional sports. We should endeavor to give kids great experiences whenever possible.
2. If you cut a dedicated, loyal senior you are unleashing a beast that will fight you to the death. Whether it is your death or theirs is the only thing that remains to be determined.

General Thoughts About Cutting Players
A wise old coach once told me "never cut a kid if you can get them to quit." What he meant by that is a coach that does things right

doesn't have to be the villain. If a player elects to quit or decides not to try out, the player made the decision to end their association with the team, not the coach. Sure, the kid will likely still blame the coach for their decision, but ultimately the coach can claim they were willing to give the kid a chance and the player is the one that chose to walk away. So aside from the ideas offered at the start of this chapter, how does a coach convince a kid to quit?

A high school baseball coach I worked with several years ago employed an interesting technique. At his pre-tryout player meeting he would encourage each prospective player to ask themselves three questions.

1. Did you help the team last year?
2. Will you help the team this year?
3. Can you help the team next year?

Then he would add that a player should be able to answer yes to at least two of those three questions. If they could not, it would be very difficult for the player to make the team.

These criteria do a particularly effective job of cutting down on the number of possible "dead weight" seniors you might have trying out because a kid that played JV as a junior could only answer yes to one question. Of course, if you have a kid that was on your JV team as junior but you still think they could play an important role on your varsity as a senior you can always visit with that kid individually and encourage them to tryout despite their answers to the three questions. The three questions are designed to preemptively and compassionately help players realize they are unlikely to make the team. This allows them to decide not to tryout on their own and hopefully it allows them to end their association with the sport with more dignity than the feeling of being cut by a coach.

Many coaches encourage players to "retire" from a sport by incorporating an exorbitant amount of conditioning during the initial tryout period. Some coaches call it "thinning out the herd." The theory goes that if you condition players to something bordering on the extreme it will become obvious who really wants to play and be a part of the team. Often after one or two days of vigorous conditioning, kids you would have been forced to cut end up "cutting themselves" when they decide not to continue with tryouts. This is advantageous because it keeps a coach's hands clean. The coach didn't have to do the direct dirty work. The kids did it themselves.

Of course, the drawback to this technique would occur when you have a player that you just can't keep, that does not walk away. Instead they work their tail off for three hellacious days at tryouts and survive the most grueling part of your season. It can be heart breaking to cut a kid that demonstrates they want to make the team that much. In my experience there are never more than one or two kids that fall into that category and I typically try to find a way to keep them if they make it through those difficult days.

Whether you incorporate the "three questions," extra conditioning, or some other system, the key for a coach is to implement something that puts players in a position where they must demonstrate or decide how much they want to make the team. Rather than making a lot of cuts, find a way to get the players to cut themselves. Doing this can significantly reduce the number of parent complaints when the final roster is arrived at after tryouts.

Most of the cuts that coaches make are not that difficult. You cut a kid that has never played the game at any organized level before and is light years behind where they need to be. Perhaps it's a kid trying out for the first time. Maybe it's a kid that is talented enough to make your team but one you are certain will grow into a cancer because they won't be content with their role. In that case, don't be blinded by their talent and keep in mind the wise move is always to cut them.

The best analogy I have heard to describe cutting a player is to imagine ripping off a band aid versus removing it slowly. When you rip a band aid off it stings like hell for two seconds but then the pain vanishes. When you take a band aid off ever so slowly you feel each and every hair getting plucked out of your flesh. The pain is nearly as intense and it lasts considerably longer. When you cut a kid, you rip off the band aid. Mom and dad will gripe at you for a couple of days and then they vanish. When you keep that same kid on the team and they aren't satisfied with their role you deal with the pain of putting up with their complaining for the entire season. Always rip off the band aid!

The Politics of Playing Time

Veteran coaches will read the next few paragraphs and immediately understand the message. This passage is primarily for younger, less experienced coaches.

When it comes to playing time, there is one key rule to remember: if you try to please everyone you will please no one.

As a young varsity coach I spent most of a season trying to play everyone on my team. The better players still played a little more than the less skilled players but everyone got to play. The result of this was that everyone on my team was at least moderately dissatisfied. Even the lower skilled players were unhappy. They got to play in every game but they were "insulted" by only getting to play a few minutes.

During that season I learned the math and politics of playing time. If a coach exclusively plays their top players there will be a few players at the end of the bench unhappy with their playing time. Obviously the top players that get all of the playing time will have no gripe. But if you try to play everyone equally or close to equal, now every player is at least a little bit unhappy. That has a dramatically negative impact on a coach's approval rating. When a politician does something that appeals to their strongest, most loyal supporters it is called "playing to their base." As a coach, remember that your best players are your "base." If there is any group on your team you had better keep happy it is them. Without your best players or your "base," it is impossible to continue to serve in your current position. Playing your best players is already the right move when it comes to wins and losses but it is actually the politically prudent move as well.

Another area where playing time can have powerful political ramifications is when a coach gives major playing time to a player that is a bad influence. If a coach has a player that is chronically late for practice, skips school, is lazy at practice, etc. and the coach continues to play this person a great deal, it can be extremely damaging to the coach and the team.

The team is tarnished because the players are given the strong impression that working hard at practice or being on time for practice is not a pre-requisite to play. Don Meyer, the all time wins leader in men's college basketball history, often said that "your best player has to be your hardest worker." If your top player goes half speed in practice the rest of your players will see that and follow that lead. As a coach, you can't afford to let the poor work ethic or attitude of your top player pollute the rest of your team. Playing the talented malcontent may pay short term dividends in the form of a few more wins here and there, but when the other players in your program adopt those bad habits (and they most certainly will) the long term negative impact will far outweigh any short term gain.

We have not even considered the degree to which playing the bad attitude player can damage a coach's image and reputation. When players and parents see that being on time, working hard, avoiding drugs and alcohol, etc. are of no importance to the head coach and that the coach's only concern is winning, that creates major negative consequences for the coach's public image. While every coach is expected to win, if a coach is perceived as caring only about winning there are few things more politically poisonous.

During my first season at Champlin Park we were in the midst of pre-game warm-ups for our second game of the season when the scoreboard operator approached me. He introduced himself and explained that he was a math teacher at the school. I did not teach in the building my first year as the coach there so I had never met this man before. The math teacher then shared that one of our starters and star players skipped his class that day. "I just thought you would like to know" he said, before returning to the scorer's table.

Honestly, with 10 minutes left in warm ups I would have preferred not to know! But I instantly recognized what the political fallout would be if I didn't act on the information he offered. If I did nothing this math teacher would go to the faculty and say "The new basketball coach only cares about winning. I told him that Jane Doe skipped my class and he still started her and played her the entire game!"

If I had any desire to teach at Champlin Park someday (and I did) I knew I had to address this issue. Of course, I only had 10 minutes to do so. I pulled the player in question out of warm ups and into the hallway outside the gym. I told her what the math teacher had shared and I asked her if the story was accurate. She explained that she was in class but her boyfriend came to her class shortly after the bell rang. They had been arguing and she left with him. She said they went to the cafeteria to try to sort things out.

"Did you ever come back to Mr. Johnson's class and explain where you went?" I asked.

"No" was her reply.

"You realize that if you had made an effort to communicate with him, he probably would have been fine with your absence, right?" I continued.

"I hope you also realize that I have got to punish you in some way. I want to be a teacher in this school and I can't have the staff here thinking I condone players skipping class."

I understood her situation and while I don't think there was any ill intent with her departure from class, I also knew I had to dispense some degree of discipline. I elected to sit her out for the first half of the game. That seemed agreeable to all parties involved.

The teacher was satisfied. My players and their parents learned that they had better be in class or there would be consequences. And most important of all, I had protected myself politically. Coaches can't just focus on winning the next game. They have to attempt to see the bigger political picture that can emanate from the decisions they make.

Playing Time During a Blowout

Coaches have different philosophies on when or if they clear their bench in a blowout. Whatever your philosophy is you are entitled to it, but be prepared to explain it.

A few years ago when we had a very talented team we found ourselves with a large lead by halftime of most games. My philosophy has always been that I would pull my top players about mid-way through the second half and give the reserves the final few minutes. I did this as much to protect my star players from injury in the closing minutes of a blowout as I did to reward the reserves with some varsity minutes.

About two thirds of the way through that season I had a parent contact me and ask why their child wasn't getting more playing time in the blowout games. I could have easily got this call from the parent of a starter as they were actually getting fewer minutes and racking up less in terms of statistics because they were winning by such wide margins all of the time. But the call came from the parent of a reserve. I explained that the reserves had already played a full JV game that evening and that if I were to take our top varsity players out early in the second half of each game they would not be getting the playing time they needed to develop appropriately. The parent seemed to understand this explanation and we said our good-byes but it made me realize that there were probably others out there wondering why I did things the way I did. I had never communicated my playing time policy for blowout games before but from that point forward I have done so.

Whether your team is involved on the right side or the wrong side of a blowout, there are a few constituencies a coach must consider when deciding to put in the reserves. The first consideration has to be winning the game. If you are well ahead but have a horrific bench, clearly you cannot insert the reserves until very late in the game. Conversely, a coach whose team is trailing by a wide margin must be careful about clearing the bench too early. Doing so can lead people to suggest that the coach "gave up" when the outcome of the game was still in the balance.

The second thing to weigh is the risk of injury to your star players. Whether you are blowing a team out or being blown out, you do not want to lose one of your top players to injury in a game that is all but decided. Experiencing an injury in a blow out could cost your team a chance to win the next several games. As soon as a coach gets the sense the outcome of the game is no longer in doubt, the key consideration should be the need for your top players to get playing time for conditioning, timing, etc. versus the risk of one of them suffering an injury. If you determine your starters have had their fill, sit them down so they are available to fight another day.

The final constituency to consider in a blowout game is the opposing team. If you are winning by a wide margin and you leave your starters in that can leave a very bad taste with the other team, especially if the opposing coach has already removed their starters. The same can be said when your team is trailing and your opponent has cleared their bench. Leaving your starters in when you are losing is certainly more widely understood and accepted, but it can make the opposing coach less inclined to clear their bench the next time they are kicking your teams' tail. The question a coach needs to ask themselves is how much they care about their reputation with opposing coaches. Some coaches could care less what their colleagues think of them. Other coaches recognize the value in having allies elsewhere in the coaching community.

Be sure you take some time to decide what kind of a message you want to send to each constituency when confronted with a blowout. Then do your best to communicate with each group (at the appropriate time) about why you are implementing a particular strategy. The mere act of communicating this can do wonders for protecting your public image with parents, players, and opposing teams.

Recruiting Players

Not every coach is so blessed with numbers that they are forced to cut players. If you are on the other end of the numbers spectrum and you are struggling for athletes you will need to wage a campaign of sorts just to build your program to a position of strength. There are two ways to get more players into your program. You can recruit from amongst the student population at your school or depending on the rules in your state (and your morals) you can recruit players from other programs to your school. But before we consider either of those options we must first examine why your program is lacking in participants in the first place. What follows is a list of some of the more common causes.

* The previous coaching staff was a bunch of idiots (or at least perceived to be that way) and they drove kids away.
* The program has a reputation for losing.
* You coach a sport that is not considered "high profile".
* Activity fees or socio-economic conditions in your area make participation in your sport cost prohibitive for many students.

In the case of the first three situations the basic answer is essentially the same. You need to engage in a big time public relations campaign. Get out and promote your program with all the salesmanship and pizzazz you can muster. To everyone that asks and to anyone that will listen, you must announce that you are going to build a championship program and you will not rest until it happens. You need to talk about this so matter of factly that you actually convince people you might just be crazy enough to pull it off. Tell kids that they can be the ones that are remembered for bringing the program to respectability and even to a championship. If they play other sports they can leave with a letter jacket. If they play your sport they can leave with a legacy!

Sell, sell, sell. But if your situation is specific to one of the first three circumstances on the list, let us now address each in a more detailed manner.

The previous coaching staff is blamed for chasing kids away.

Whether this perception is fair or not, the fact that the numbers in your program are low may not be your fault, but it is your problem. As a result, you have got to make it a point to demonstrate to students and to your community that you are not at all like the previous regime. In fact, you are quite the opposite.

If the previous coach was condemned for not being demanding or intense enough, you have got to show that you are willing to get after it and be fiery. If the previous coach was hated for being too heated and negative, you have got to be brimming with enthusiasm, optimism, and positivity. Some might say this would be awkward if you are in the same school as the previous coach, but that is simply not the case. I am not telling you to trash the former coach. Merely projecting a different persona can't be construed as insulting. If the previous coach is on the same teaching staff as you and harbors some ill will it is likely that they are simply bitter about their dismissal (and that they should have read this book!). Understand that because of their disgust, they would likely consider any attitude you project as insulting. While it is nice to try to be sensitive to the previous coach's feelings, especially if you work in the same district or in some proximity to each other, sympathizing with them cannot be anywhere near the top of your list of concerns. Your top priority has got to be winning the support and confidence of the kids at your school. Most sports rely on good numbers of participants to achieve any level of success. Keep your focus on what needs to be done to benefit your program. Worry about the feelings of the former coach if and only if that doesn't conflict with the top priority of strengthening your program.

In a situation where the former coach is long gone and you will never see or hear from them again, if you feel the need to trash them a bit it might be worth a try. If you think doing so will help you gain the confidence and support of the players, give it a whirl. I don't recommend this as a first option or even in general, but if you perceive that there is little downside and some major upside it is something you could at least consider doing.

Your program has a reputation as "losers"

Unfortunately I have confronted this situation first hand. When I was trying to get some of the better athletes in Red Wing to play basketball, more than a few said indirectly and some directly "Why would I want to get my ass kicked every game all winter long?"

As a coach and recruiter you can't show any weakness or hesitation when confronted with naysayers such as these. You need to convey unbridled confidence. My response to those students was "We are going to win games whether you are with us or not. And I'll tell you this…when it's all said and done you are going to wish you were a part of this historic turn around. Our players are going to be the talk of the town!"

I went beyond confident. I was flat out cocky. My efforts paid off in some respects. Our numbers improved dramatically in my first year and continued to improve each subsequent season. So did our win total. As mentioned in a previous chapter, you can only say you are going to shed the loser the label for so long before you have to deliver. But when you are starting out with a new program and you literally haven't lost a game, you need to take advantage of that lack of a track record and convince kids that things will be different from this point forward. Sell them on the chance to be the ones that turned the ship around. Sell them on the idea that they will be the biggest story at the school because they are going to do what everyone said couldn't be done. Sell them on making history. By doing that, you will get the kids you really want. You will get the hard-nosed competitors. Those fancy pants pre-madonna's that don't want to play for a "loser" wouldn't do you any good anyway. Sell your program in a way that attracts competitive kids willing to take on a challenge. And no matter what anyone says to you, continue to project confidence.

You coach a sport that isn't "high profile"

There is a book titled "Make the Big Time Where You Are" by Frosty Westering. I haven't read the book, but in my estimation the title says it all. Whatever sport you coach and wherever you coach it, you have got to give people the impression that it is important. Girls' basketball is certainly not widely considered to be a "fan favorite" in most areas of the country. Football, boys' basketball, and boys' hockey immediately come to mind as sports that will be considered more "high profile" in the media and within the school community. While boys' sports are most prominent in the town I coach in, I continue to project that our program is something that borders on the New York Yankees in terms of status and importance.

Among the first things I do when I get a new coaching job is create a professional looking letterhead and order a thousand pens with our team name and logo. I hand out pens to the students in my classes and to our players. This instantly conveys a degree of professionalism to the student body. It is simple marketing, but it is putting our program at the front of people's minds and that helps elevate our status in the mind of the student body.

The letterhead is something I use when corresponding with people in the community or with players and parents. Lately I have taken to having our team picture as a watermark in the background of the letterhead. The quality of the letterhead is something people would expect to see from a professional sports team, not from a high school program. Actions like these are all about making our program "the big time" in the eyes of the people that matter most, our players, parents, and community.

Another thing we do that is now becoming the norm among teams in various sports at our school and throughout our conference is the publishing of a professional team program. The program is patterned after the media guides or programs you might find at a division one sporting event. We have individual player profiles, team records, color photos, and everything else you would expect to find if you grabbed the media guide for any major college sport. We treat our players like they are a big deal, and in turn, the students at our school and the people in our community do the same.

These various promotional activities have helped us generate such a strong level of interest in our team among students that it has ultimately put us in a position where we now have to make cuts every year. I hate to cut kids, but the reality is it is a good problem to have. I would rather have too many kids interested in playing than have to go beg kids to be a part of my team. We will address the dangers of begging kids in a moment.

Activity fees or socio-economic conditions make participation cost prohibitive for some students

I had never heard of "activity fees" until I moved to Minnesota. I was stunned to learn that at nearly every school in the state kids had to pay well over a hundred dollars to play a sport. It continues to seem wrong to me on so many levels. Never mind the fact it makes life harder on coaches when it allows a parent to proclaim "I'm not paying money to watch my kid sit on the bench!"

The thing I find so disgraceful about paying to play is that while most schools encourage students to participate in extra-curricular activities because it helps keep them out of trouble and it gets them involved in something positive, schools are simultaneously putting their hand out and expecting them to pay for this thing we are so strongly encouraging them to do.

At my current school, athletes have to pay anywhere from $240 to over $400 to play a sport. Another number that stands out at our school is nearly 25% of the student body qualifies for free and reduced lunch due to the disadvantaged financial situation they have at home. Needless to say, out of those 25% of students a few of them would probably be pretty good players for our various athletic teams, but there are several that simply cannot afford to play.

Sure our school has a way to waive the activity fee for families that truly can't afford to pay, but the process involves the family asking for the fee to be waived. We all know that there are plenty of people that are just too proud to ask for a helping hand. Rather than seeking a free ride, their son or daughter simply does not play. When that happens everyone loses.

So how does a coach push past this challenging obstacle to getting more kids out for their team? Clearly it calls for creativity with a big dollop of discretion.

I saw a terrific idea for dealing with this situation when I was working a basketball camp for a prominent division one program. The college coach asked area businesses to donate money to provide a "scholarship" to kids that didn't have the funds to come to camp. If the cost of camp was $100, his staff asked area businesses to sponsor a kid by paying the $100 fee. After getting a couple of dozen sponsorships, they went to area elementary schools and asked guidance counselors and teachers to nominate kids that were in need and that would like to go to the camp. It proved to be a great way to get kids involved that otherwise would have never had a chance. When you call it a "scholarship" instead of a hand out, it can make all the difference.

Another idea I have seen some programs incorporate is having their booster club cover the cost of the activity fee for every player that makes the team. At the start of the season, families have to write out a check to the booster club equivalent to the activity fee. Then the booster club holds on to the check. If the player finishes the season in good standing with the team the booster club tears up the check and the athlete played for free. The only catch is that the player and their family might be expected to work a few hours at a weekend youth tournament or engage in some other form of fundraising.

The bottom line is coaches can keep making excuses for why their program is at a competitive disadvantage or they can get creative and find solutions to the problems that plague them. In the world of politics, blaming others or one's circumstances only gets a person so far. Creative solutions are the ultimate elixir for problems in politics and in coaching.

Make Players Feel Wanted But Never Needed

When I was out campaigning in the hallways to help get my program's numbers up, I learned that there is a huge difference between asking a kid to be a part of your program and begging them to play.

While coaches need to be enthusiastic and encouraging when talking to prospective players they must also be careful not to come off as really needing the player or "begging" them to play. I crossed that line with two players that I knew were good athletes and that I thought would help our team a great deal. After much arm twisting, flattering, coaxing, and cajoling, these athletes finally agreed to play for us.

Within the first few practices of the season it became evident that while one of these kids was a good athlete they weren't even close to being a good basketball player. They were relegated to the JV team and they were not at all happy about it. The player came to me shortly after the demotion and asked "If you wanted me on the team so bad, why am I on JV?" I was embarrassed. Through my full court press style of recruitment I had led this player to believe that they were going to be a starter and a star. When it didn't turn out that way they felt mislead and disgruntled.

The other player was indeed good but basketball was not their top priority. About a month into the season they were absent from

practice twice in the span of a week. I soon found out they had been
skipping practice because they had a practice for an offseason team
from their primary sport later that night and they wanted to "save their
energy." When I confronted the player about this they weren't the least
bit apologetic for missing practice. A short time into our discussion
it became obvious to me that this player had the strong belief that
we needed them more than they needed us. I also recognized that
I was the person that gave them that impression through my heavy
recruitment of them. The player believed that they were in a position of
strength and that they had a certain degree of leverage. They thought
they could dictate the terms of their spot on the team. They felt that
they could decide when they practiced and when they played because
they were led to believe they were that vital to the team.

    This was a monster of my own creation. In my zeal to add
the player to the roster I gave them an inflated sense of self worth.
While the player did make our team better, I decided the long term
detrimental impact of having a player practice whenever it was
convenient for them would be devastating to our program. In the
end, I apologized to the player for giving them a false sense of their
importance to the team and we made a mutual agreement to part ways.

    There is a fine line between making a player feel wanted as part of
your program and making them feel needed. Whenever you convince
a player that you "need" them you elevate them to a more powerful
position than you are in as the coach. You lead them to believe that
they can dictate terms. This is always a dangerous position to put a
player in. It is perfectly fine to let a player feel wanted, but be cautious
about begging them to play to the point that they feel needed.

    Also in the realm of recruiting kids from your school comes a
fairly new development. With the advent of open enrollment and the
recruitment of players by coaches at other schools, increasingly coaches
are put in a position where they need to "recruit" their own players
to stay in their school district. My first experience with this surfaced
several years ago. There was an excellent 5th grade player that was not
playing with our youth association. I had been told her mother felt she
was far too good to play for a local team so she had her daughter play
with something of an all star team. I had heard about the player and I
decided to go see just how good she was. Typically I haven't been able
to look at a 5th grader and say she'll be a star, but this girl was clearly
going to be very good. I visited with her mother a bit after the game to
make sure she knew I was there. The mother thanked me for coming
and commented that it was a good thing I had come because she and

her daughter would have some decisions to make in the next year or two about where she would be going to school. I didn't want to get into that particular discussion at the moment so we said our goodbyes and parted ways. A month later I got an e-mail from the mother. She wanted to know what type of a system we ran offensively and defensively. She said her daughter fit best in a particular style and that would factor into their decision. I explained what we do and left it at that. I wasn't going to try to convince a kid to stay in our school district and lead them to believe they had leverage. If they were going to threaten to transfer because we didn't run the right offense or defense I didn't want them anyway. That was a headache I did not need.

It turns out that the girl stayed a part of our program and helped us a great deal. Later her mother revealed to me exactly which other coaches had contacted them and what the coaches had said. These opposing high school coaches weren't just selling their program, they also trashed ours in an effort to convince the mother and daughter that their school would give her the best chance to showcase her skills. While most coaches reading this would consider these kinds of coaches corrupt, it is important to recognize this kind of activity is happening. You may disagree with how your opponents go about their business but it is always advantageous to understand their game plan.

The point is coaches are now competing for their own kids. Players that we help groom and develop through our camps, offseason activities, etc. are being pulled away by unscrupulous coaches. What we need to determine is how hard we are going to work to keep our kids from leaving. What I have come to decide is if a player wants to leave, I am going to let them. I have only lost three kids to transfers in the past 10 years but experience has taught me the players and parents that elect to leave have also tended to be rather high maintenance. They have had enormous egos and were a general pain in the ass to deal with. When you have a player or parent threatening to transfer if you don't accommodate their desires you would be wise to allow some other coach to be "blessed" with their presence.

Recruiting Players from Other Schools

Trying to convince players from other schools to transfer to your school is a ticking political time bomb for a number of reasons. If you are comfortable playing with fire and if you are particularly adept at disarming bombs the upside of bringing in these recruits can be significant, but it is certainly a high risk/high reward endeavor.

Most states currently allow students to open enroll in the school district or at the school of their choice for academic reasons. Of course, we all know that there are plenty of students that transfer to schools for "academic" reasons and that school also happens to have a stellar sports program that the student will be a part of. Most state high school athletic associations have included some policies or provisions to discourage or deter frivolous transfers. These associations have also announced that they will punish coaches that are caught recruiting athletes. But of course, we all know that there are still coaches that continue to engage in various forms of recruiting and the number that get caught is considerably less than the number that engage in it. For that reason, from a purely political perspective, coaches going out and recruiting these athletes is not particularly risky when weighed against the likelihood of possible sanctions that could be levied by a state governing body. Rather, the real political risks come from the following areas:

*   The leverage the player gains over the coach because they have been recruited (and often illegally).
*   The tarnished reputation the coach accumulates in the coaching community.
*   The alienation of players that have come up through your program, are displaced by these transfers and the subsequent parent and community uprising that ensues.

Let us first examine the player's leverage. When a player and their parents have been recruited to attend your school, and in particular when you have either bent or broken rules in the process, that player and their parents wield an incredible amount of power over you as a coach. If the player doesn't turn out to be as talented as you had expected or if they bring baggage like a poor work ethic or a rotten attitude that you did not anticipate, it will be very hard for you to bench or otherwise discipline that player. If they are not getting the playing time they want or expect, they can threaten to reveal to your state association or the media just how it is they came to be a part of your team. This can certainly put the coach in a compromising position. In a sense, the coach becomes held hostage by the player and their parents. The coach must comply with the players' wishes and keep the player happy or the coach risks being exposed and perhaps losing their job. The negative political consequences of a scenario like the one just described would suggest that coaches should not engage in illegally recruiting players from other schools to their program.

The programs that perennially get top flight athletes to transfer in often have surrogates that do the dirty work on behalf of the coach.

Sometimes it is a person loosely affiliated with the program, like a booster club president or a former coach that does the recruiting. Other times it is the parent of one of the team's players that goes out and tries to convince others players to come to the program. This means of recruiting is considerably less risky for the head coach. You then have something that Richard Nixon characterized as "plausible deniability".[6]

The coach can honestly say that they had nothing to do with the recruitment of that player. However, when the surrogate began to recruit the player the coach likely did nothing to discourage this action. From a political perspective, if a coach feels the need to recruit players they would be best advised to do it through the surrogate process to protect themselves from possible accusations of impropriety down the road. Using a surrogate would also help insure that no player or parent has the type of leverage that could lead to them dictating their playing time.

Of course, there is also one's reputation to consider. And whether a coach recruits directly or allows a surrogate to do it for them, the coach will be widely condemned by their fellow coaches either way. Let us not forget that the coaching community is a fraternity. A coach that is considered a recruiter will eventually become a pariah among their colleagues and be ostracized. Some coaches can accept this as long as they keep collecting championships. They don't want or need friends in the coaching community. But coaches that have that attitude don't fully appreciate the positive benefit that can be derived through the numerous connections the coaching community can create and the doors those connections can open. If you decide to be a recruiter, just be sure you are able to come to terms with the cold shoulder and lack of respect you will routinely receive from your coaching colleagues.

So far, there are still plenty of coaches that either recruit or intend to recruit that have read this and thought to themselves, "these are all chances I am more than willing to take in order to reap the rewards of having superior players and spectacular teams." But coaches that remain undeterred from recruiting for the first two reasons I have offered had better give plenty of thought and consideration to the third and final political issue I am about to present. It is by far, the most threatening both in terms of keeping a program strong and keeping a coaching job.

A program that consistently recruits players will have to be

---

6 *Before you pursue this policy, it might be wise to consider how things turned out for Richard Nixon.*

equipped to deal with the ire of the player and parent that the transfer displaces. Often, the displaced player has been in the program for a decade and during that time they have dreamed of being a varsity player. When that dream is denied by a "carpetbagger" or some player that may have arrived on the scene in an unscrupulous or illegal manner, you can be sure there will be shouting from the rooftops, and not only from the displaced player or that player's parents. If the recruiting happens on a consistent basis over the span of several years, you can bet there will be plenty of parents in your program that begin to feel threatened. They will worry that their child will somehow fail to be rewarded for all their years of preparation and dedication. Whether the coach's team is winning championships becomes immaterial to these parents and players. They will stop at nothing to expose the coach and they will fight ferociously for the coach's dismissal. I am not talking about a coach having to deal with a player here or some parents there. I am not talking about putting out a couple of fires. I am talking about a full blown mob mentality. I am talking about an entire youth association grabbing the proverbial pitchforks and torches to defend their child's perceived "right" to play varsity in that program someday.

If a coach is going to make a habit out of bringing in players that have been developed in other programs, then the coach had better be prepared to be under constant fire from a large group of people at all levels of their own program. The only way a coach can even begin to have a chance to survive such a barrage is with the full, unwavering support of their administrators. There are several schools in my home state that are notorious for bringing in recruits. One of the more prominent ones has an administrator that was equally famous for recruiting during his days as a high school coach. Thus, the coaches at that school can recruit with the confidence that they have the full support of their administration and no amount of parent or youth association complaining about recruits will threaten their job.

But even if a coach has the protection of a supportive administration, there is still the issue of reduced numbers that your program will eventually have to come to terms with. Programs that perennially bring in recruits tend to show reduced participation at the youth and middle school levels because players and parents begin to wonder why they should waste their time playing for a program for years and years only to be displaced during high school by a transfer player. The other practical consideration then, if you are going to recruit, is can you consistently bring in enough good recruits to offset the lack of players you will have in your program after you have alienated the kids from your own school district?

Again, I am not condoning recruiting players from other schools but this book would not be a comprehensive examination of the political elements of coaching if the subject was ignored. While I have attempted to outline the numerous risks involved should a coach engage in this unseemly activity, each coach must weigh the political risks versus the perceived benefits and conclude for themselves their philosophy on this eternally contentious issue.

Selecting Team Captains

In a previous chapter we addressed gender issues and how they can impact a coach's decisions. The selection of team captains is another realm where I have learned the gender can have a profound impact. When I have coached boys and allowed them to vote for captain I have never disagreed with their decision. My boys' teams tend to reward good leadership with the title of captain. In my experience, girls are far more inclined to vote for the players they consider "nice." Nice does not always make for a good captain.

Beyond the stereotype I just made, at its best having your players vote for captains offers an opportunity to rightfully anoint the leader or leaders that the team already recognizes as such. At its worst, it is a popularity contest and the title "captain" is as hollow and empty as a beer can in the hospitality room at a hockey coaches convention.

In a perfect world, we would allow our players to pick their captains. Frequently leaders develop naturally over the course of a season and players, usually subconsciously, determine who they will follow. But we don't live in a perfect world and players and parents can sometimes attach an obscene level of importance to the title of "captain." In an effort to prevent one more miniature crisis for you to deal with during your season, let us examine your two primary options for arriving at captains and the political ramifications of both.

Option 1: Voting for Captains

Even if allowing players to vote does not end up a popularity contest and your players select the player or players you consider best equipped to lead your team, the fact that there was a vote means that a player that aspired to be named captain may have their feelings hurt when they discover that their teammates don't hold them in as much regard as they previously believed. This can lead to chemistry issues when Billy or Becky fall into a mini mental funk for a couple of weeks because their teammates "don't like them."

Of course, this can also prompt mom or dad to pick up the phone and question the voting or the process of picking captains. Many coaches have answered a ringing phone to hear a parent saying "Why do you only have two captains? If Jimmy got third in the voting why can't you have three captains when you know how important this was to Jimmy? And don't get me started on how much this is going to hurt him when he doesn't have it on his college applications."

That is just one example of something you could anticipate hearing from the parent of a jilted player. Of course there will be those players and parents that accuse you of "rigging" the vote, suggesting that the whole thing is a fraud. They will insist that you just picked who you wanted because they "know" that a long list of players all voted for their child.

It is because of the possibility of those types of accusations that I hold on to all ballots filled out by my players for team honors for about a year after the season ends. Players don't put their names on the ballots as they vote, but each ballot clearly has different handwriting. It would be hard for a parent pushing a conspiracy to continue their quest when I produce the ballots. I never reveal the final tally of captain or award votes because that can typically make kids feel even worse if they find out they were one vote short of claiming a particular accolade. However, if someone is going to question my integrity I am going to hold on to those ballots so I can shove them up the accuser's nose!

In summary, if you elect to have your team vote for captains be prepared to manage the hurt feelings and accusations that can follow.

Option 2: The Coach Picks the Captains

One way to eliminate all conspiracy theories is for the coach to choose the captains. There are two obvious advantages to this. First, you can be certain that you are going to get the captain or captains that you feel would be best for your team. Second, you cut down on some of the "so and so voted for so and so" drama that can divide your team. There will still be players upset after the announcement of captains, but at least they are upset at you and not at each other.

Of course, the downside is there is nowhere to hide when the parents come calling and questioning your choices. A coach cannot point to the ballots and throw up their hands saying there is nothing they can do. If you are prepared to take any potential heat for the choice you make, then picking captains yourself leads to the least amount of drama.

There are other options of course; things I would characterize as "compromise" options.

One thing I have heard of some coaches doing is allowing their players to vote, but also telling their players that the coaching staff gets a vote as well. Some coaches tell their players that the coach's votes count double. This is clearly a blend of the two options above. It seems to me by compromising you open yourself up to all the possible criticisms, but this has worked for many coaches.

A few years ago we had 12 seniors on our team and all of them were fantastic people. I selected two permanent captains, but every game we had a rotating third captain that would go out before the game and represent our team. The way I pitched this was that as seniors they all had to be leaders, so I wanted to make sure that all of them were recognized as a captain throughout the season. I also told them all that they could all list themselves as "team captain" on their college applications because in my mind, every single senior must share in that leadership role. This proved to be the least controversial approach I ever took and it was very well received by all.

The emphasis placed on the role of team captain varies a great deal from coach to coach. But no matter how little a coach cares about who their captains are, a coach had better take a few moments to consider the possible repercussions of who is picked and how they are picked. Coaches have enough battles when it comes to playing time and other issues. They do not need to create another crisis when they go through the ceremony of picking captains.

My Proudest Moment in Coaching

Just to further demonstrate that no matter what we do as coaches we will always make half of our constituents unhappy, I offer you a story about the moment in my coaching career I have always been most proud of and the improbable fallout that ensued.

It was the summer before my third season at Red Wing. I had a group of soon to be seniors that I had been coaching since they were in ninth grade. I truly loved the kids like they were my own family. Earlier that spring I had begun hearing rumors that some of them were making bad decisions on weekends. This information compelled me to meet with the three specific players whose names had been brought to my attention. I told them what I had been hearing and asked them if it was true. All three denied any wrong doing. I didn't accept their answer that easily. I pressed them a bit, asking "what incentive do the people that are telling me these things have to lie?" They didn't have an answer to that other than to say they must have been accidently lumped in with a group of people because they have some close friends that drink. I reminded them of how seriously I took their position as a role model to the young people in the community. I added that if they were to betray that trust there would be hell to pay.

In my heart I wanted to believe they were telling the truth. In my head I had a strong suspicion they had indeed been drinking and violating state activity association rules, but I hoped my direct discussion of the matter with them would deter any future violations.

About six weeks after these meetings, in the midst of summer, the guy that was soon to be my JV coach approached me and asked if I had heard the news. The concern his question conjured up within me was warranted. He explained that two of my seniors had been busted at a party for drinking and a couple of other players had escaped before the cops could catch them. My first reaction was outrage. These kids that I have known and cared about for three years lied right to my face! Within an hour, my emotions morphed into a mix of disappointment and depression.

That night I contacted all of our players entering 10th through 12th grades and told them to be at the school for a very important meeting the next afternoon. I didn't sleep much that night. I spent most of the evening reflecting on what I must have done wrong the previous three years that made me unable to reach these kids and convince them to abstain from alcohol. I did a lot of soul searching that night. And by sunrise I knew exactly what I was going to tell my team.

As the players filed in for the meeting they looked like they were arriving for a funeral. There were lots of long faces and serious looks. The room was utterly silent. Thirty players lined the benches in the locker room as I began one of the most heartfelt and passionate speeches of my life.

I began by explaining to everyone why they were there. Some of the players genuinely did not yet know about the transgressions of their teammates. I explained my immense disappointment and reiterated what the players had heard me say so many times before, that there is nothing I take more seriously than their position as role models to the young people in our program and in our community. But then I threw them all a bit of a curveball. While I am certain they expected a red faced, profanity laced tirade, what they got was a side of me they had never seen.

I shared that I had spent much of the last evening awake and contemplating what I had truly emphasized and promoted as their head coach. This reflection led me to conclude that I had put so much emphasis on winning and rebuilding the program back to a level of respectability that I had lost sight of what is really important. As I examined things in earnest during the wee hours of the morning I realized what it was that I really wanted. I wanted to win. That would not change. But I discovered winning wasn't what I wanted most.

The thing I wanted above all was for my players to become great people. I wanted my players to invite me to their wedding some day, to send me a Christmas card with a photo of their family, and to always consider me someone they could count on if they ever needed a helping hand. Through sports, I wanted them to learn the importance of things like self discipline and sacrifice so when they had to decide between taking a week long cruise with their spouse or buying braces for their kid, they would do what a great parent does; they would sacrifice and put their child first. I wanted my players to be exceptional people. Average kids drink alcohol on weekends. I wanted them to have the self discipline to be exceptional people, not average people.

I wanted them to learn the importance of honesty so they could someday have a relationship with their spouse built on a strong foundation of openness and trust. In summary, I wanted them to be great people far more than I wanted them to be great players.

And in that spirit I asked each of them to do the right thing. I asked them to admit to themselves, their teammates, and their families if they had ever drank alcohol, and not just on this occasion but at any other time in the past. I insisted the incident that led to the meeting that day was not about who got caught, it was about who did the wrong thing by drinking. If they drank alcohol I was asking them to do the right thing, the responsible thing, the mature thing, and admit their mistake. I was asking them to go beyond what the average person would do and be exceptional.

I was stunned when almost half of the players in the room stood up to acknowledge their wrong doing and to make a very public confession to their teammates and to me as a coach. But in the same moment I felt stunned, I was also overwhelmed with an immense sense of pride. I genuinely felt like I was seeing these girls I had known since 7th, 8th, and 9th grade grow up right before my eyes.

There were a lot of tears and hugs in that locker room for the next several minutes. I reminded the players that being honest with their loved ones is the most important thing of all, and I implored them to go home and come clean to their parents. Every one of them did. And that is when the shit hit the fan.

In my emotional plea, I had completely forgotten and ignored my position as a school district employee. I was so consumed with emotion that I failed to realize that when all those players confessed to violating state high school association rules I was mandated to report it to our administration. That was not at all my intention when I called the meeting. I did not bring the girls together that day in an effort to get a mass confession and get a bunch of them punished. When my administration first told me that I would have to turn kids in I was quite adamant that I would not tell them a single name. I tried to explain that this was about kids being honest with themselves, their teammates, and their family. I tried to explain that this was a monumentally important "teachable" moment where I was attempting to instill the importance of trust and integrity. To force me to turn them all in and get them punished would be a betrayal of the trust they bestowed upon me when they confessed.

Over the next several days, as I butted heads with administration, I got two distinctly different types of phone calls and e-mails from parents. One group of parents was abundantly supportive and extremely appreciative. This was not limited to the parents of kids that were innocent. A number of parents whose daughters had confessed to drinking thanked me for convincing their kid to come forward. They explained that their daughter's decision to be honest with them about her indiscretions strengthened their relationship immensely. I had other parents tell me it was "about time a coach stopped turning a blind eye to what everyone knew was going on" and they applauded me for addressing the underage drinking "epidemic" in the community.

Then there was the other group of parents. About half of the kids that came forward and did what I considered the "right thing" had parents that were angry to the point of outrage that I had "coerced their kids into confessing." They accused me of entrapment and they insisted that their child's behavior was none of my or anyone else's business. This was a ridiculous suggestion that I took them to task on every time. But the real reason for most parents' objection was that their child was going to have to sit out some games and they, the parents, would be subjected to a degree of scrutiny within the community that they did not want.

While praise and criticism from parents began to die down after a few days, my clash with school administration continued. I even contacted the administration at our state high school association asking for them to demonstrate some level of discretion in this case. I insisted that coming forward and doing the right thing was something we should be applauding our students for. If these players were punished I felt the lesson our association was going to instill in them was that it would have been better to continue to live a lie. I was adamant that punishing these players in exactly the manner that a player caught by the police is punished would be immoral and wrong. I pleaded for a lighter sentence. My pleas fell on deaf ears.

I still feel a distinction should be made between athletes that do the right thing and confess to their crimes and those that hide their sins and are eventually caught. But I did not win in this situation. Perhaps still in the spirit of doing the right thing, all of my players came forward to administration on their own except one. While I still feel a degree of guilt to this day, in the end I conceded. I gave administrators the name of the final player that refused to turn herself in.

Every now and again I reflect back on that emotional meeting. In the moments after I saw these players step forward, admit their mistake, and take a major step toward becoming responsible adults, I was absolutely as proud as any coach has ever been of a group of players. The weeks of controversy that followed clouded that feeling of pride to a degree, but only for a few months. By the end of that season, and especially when those seniors graduated, I was again abundantly proud of what took place in our locker room on that late June day. And though I have moved on to coach at two different schools since then, there is no question I still have a stronger bond with those players than I have had with any group I have coached since then.

The moral of the story is even when coaches do what seems so clearly to be the right thing, there will be critics and complainers. It is impossible to please everyone in this profession. So just do the right thing and populate your coaching career with great memories and moments you can be proud of.

The Impact of the Classroom on Coaching

When I was a student teacher one of the guys I taught with was a former head football coach. He was a <u>former</u> head football coach because he had been fired. I remember him telling me that he was grateful he was considered a strong teacher in the classroom because it saved his teaching job when the school board fired him as the football coach. Beyond that obvious reason, there are other examples of how your coaching career is directly impacted by your conduct and performance in the classroom.

We all know the stereotype that coaches are PE teachers that just throw out a ball to their students then sit down and draw up plays or

0

242   ALL POLITICS IS LOCAL

that they are social studies teachers that just pop in a video and go back to their desk and work on practice plans. Coaches that fit this stereotype had better win games because if they don't, they will have no one coming to their defense when the vultures start circling over head.

Politically, the best thing any coach can do is be an excellent classroom teacher above all else. The benefits derived from this go beyond what you might originally expect. The single biggest benefit I have noticed is that at schools where I have been liked and respected as a teacher by my students, I have been liked and respected by the players and parents in my program. We encounter far more kids in the classroom than in the athletic arena and we may not have many, if any, of our athletes in our class. As a result, what our athletes hear about us as a teacher from their friends helps to shape their opinion of us as a coach.

At my first two head coaching stops I was widely considered a "fun" teacher with a good sense of humor. As a result, my players entered the season with a perspective that I was an overall nice guy that they could relate to. So even when I hollered and yelled, they believed that at my core I was a nice guy. They believed it because it is what they had been told by dozens of people prior to playing for me. My reputation as a coach had been established before I ever ran a practice based solely on my conduct in the classroom.

During the first year of my third coaching stop I did not teach in the same building as the kids I coached. This made all the difference when it came to my reputation with the players and their perception of me. They did not have first-hand experience seeing me in the more relaxed environment of my classroom and none of their friends or classmates could convey stories about the funny jokes I told or the pranks I pulled. All that my players saw of me was the rather intense, focused person I am at practice and during games. For this reason I garnered a reputation with the players in my new program as an intense, scary guy. Though I started teaching in the same building as my players the following year, the reputation had already been established. Many of my players genuinely feared me. I did not completely understand it at first. Upon further examination I established it was the disconnect of not having students convey to players that I was actually a decent guy and a good teacher. Only after three years at the school had I taught enough students and finally had enough players in class that my younger players did not demonstrate the same obvious intimidation factor their predecessors projected.

What your students think of you matters because it affects what your players will think of you. I am not saying you need to be the cool, nice teacher to win over your players. I am just saying you need to acknowledge that your demeanor and performance in the classroom will have an impact on how you are perceived by your players. If your students think you are a jerk that word will get to your players and they will likely adopt the same attitude before you have even had a single practice with them.

The Coaching Crossroads: Recognizing When to Move On, Resign, or Stand and Fight

Niccolo Machiavelli was a pioneer of political study. In his legendary treatise on leadership titled "The Prince" Machiavelli offers a comment that could not be more relevant to the modern coaching climate.

"Men change their leaders gladly with the belief that they will better themselves by the change."

In youth and high school sports we can't sign free agents or make trades. When a team flounders, parents and administrators often elect to make a coaching change with "the belief they will better themselves by the change." Of course it is rare that a team's skill level improves over night because a coaching change is made. But because it is human nature for players and parents to explore every possible reason for failure before finally arriving at the conclusion that they themselves are the cause, coaches will continue to be confronted with pressure to resign their position.

Though these calls for dismissal have become a common occurrence, one of the consistent causes of consternation in the coaching community is an almost universal failure to recognize when it is time to step down or move on. By their very nature coaches are competitive people, so acknowledging that it is time to throw in the towel or raise the white flag is contrary to all of a coach's instincts. However, the ability to accurately diagnose when to walk away can actually mean greater longevity and greater success in a coach's career. So let us examine when it's time to "hold 'em" and when it's time to "fold 'em" in terms of a coaching position.

In politics, one of the most important statistics for elected officials to consider is their public approval rating. This number is of particular importance to the President. When the President's approval rating is above 50% they have the ability to accomplish much of what they would like to. Conversely, when the President's approval rating dips below the 50% threshold they find it considerably more difficult, if not altogether impossible, to get anything done. This fact of Presidential politics equates to head coaching quite well.

Just as every President will always have at least 25% of people in the country dissatisfied with their performance, a coach can usually count on at least that many players and parents to feel the same way about them. This consistent and sometimes vocal minority can create little fires from time to time, but they can rarely derail what it is the President or the head coach intends to accomplish. With this in mind, coaches should not get too concerned or obsess over the 25% of people they will never change.

So whose opinion should a coach consider when trying to informally gauge their own approval rating? It cannot only be the players on their team. A coach's constituency extends well beyond that. A coach must also consider their level of support among parents, administration, fellow teaching staff, players and parents in their youth program, and depending on where they live, the opinion of key community members.

In politics, some demographic groups are more important than others when gauging public opinion and approval ratings. For example, elderly people vote in disproportionate numbers compared to young people so politicians pay considerably more attention to their approval rating with the 60 and older crowd than they do to the 18 to 25 year old demographic. A head coach would be just as wise to focus their attention on a couple of key groups. While all of the constituencies listed above are important to a certain degree, there is no doubt a coach's key demographic is players and parents. When a coach's approval rating with players and parents drops below 50% the coach will find it increasingly difficult to direct their program and lead their team. The resistance and roadblocks presented by this key constituency effectively prevents the coach from enacting initiatives intended to further the program. When a majority of players and parents are working against a coach rather than working with them, it is time for the coach to start exploring other options.

What are these options? Below are some scenarios every coach should consider when they sense the tide of public opinion turning against them.

1. Begin casually exploring coaching positions at other schools.
2. Explore the pros and cons of resigning as a pre-emptive move.

3. Embark on a major public relations campaign in an attempt to turn the tide and win back support.
4. Make a triumphant last stand and go out with your guns blazing.

Now, we will examine each of these options and the positives and negatives they bring.

Many people admire the violin players on board the Titanic that kept on playing even as the ship was sinking. I am not among their admirers. When a ship is sinking, I am looking for a life raft or a means of escape. If you feel your ship sinking, it would be wise to start looking for a new coaching opportunity in another district.

The advantage to this is you can leave before your resume or reputation is tarnished by being fired or forced to resign. It is far more likely your administration will give you strong recommendations at this early stage of political unrest than after they are forced to drop the axe on you. Administrators are also adept at recognizing when the vultures are circling and most don't want to see their coach become the victim of an angry mob. Odds are the AD and principal would like to see you get out of town before things get any worse. You moving on takes heat off of them and they don't have to fend off parents clamoring for your dismissal. With these things in mind, your administration will usually be very supportive and helpful as you pursue a new position.

The disadvantages to this course of action include the inconvenience of moving your family to a new town and a new situation, but this inconvenience must be weighed against the sometimes more devastating result of being fired and shunned in the community you continue to call home. The other disadvantage for coaches with a competitive streak is the fear that if they move on to another school the players and parents they leave behind will gloat and pound their chest proclaiming that they successfully pushed the coach out. While none of us want to give jerks like that the satisfaction of leaving, it is very much like folding a pair of kings when there is an ace on the board in Texas Hold 'Em. You might have a good hand, but your brain is telling you if you stay in you will be throwing your money away. Early in my card playing days I hated to concede defeat so much that I would toss my money into a pot I knew I was certain to lose. There is no benefit derived from that. Do not let your stubborn, competitive streak cost you the chance to continue your coaching career. Know when to fold your cards and walk away.

Another thing coaches should consider when they feel their support slipping away is resigning on their own before they are asked to or forced to do so. The advantage of this pre-emptive action is that you get to go out on your own terms. A resignation can be somewhat of a red flag on your resume if you should elect to move on and try to coach again somewhere else, but it is still easier to explain and looks far better than being fired and having that albatross around your neck. Coaches that should most seriously consider resigning are those that have been in a community for a long time and have no desire to move. Maybe they have been thinking about retiring from coaching anyway. Resigning is not typically a great option for a younger coach, but for the coach that has been at it for a decade or more there is usually very little stigma attached to a resignation.

In fact, I have seen it happen more than once that a coach resigns and after a couple of years with a new coach, the players, parents, and community are all clamoring for the old coach to return. Sometimes people don't know how good they have it until it's gone. Whether a coach that has resigned ever wants to throw themselves back into the same meat grinder is a purely personal consideration, but just know it is not unprecedented for a coach to come back with a much higher level of support than they left with.[7]

Coaches on the hot seat might also mull over launching the equivalent of a major public relations campaign. I would only recommend this in certain circumstances. The situation where this would be the best and most viable play for the coach is when they have a group of disgruntled parents at one particular level of their program but adequate or strong support at the other levels. For example, if a coach has a group of very vocal and upset sophomores but above average support in the senior, junior, and freshman classes as well as in the youth program, the coach should not be discouraged by this vocal minority. The coach would be well advised though to engage in some damage control. If the vocal minority is allowed to spew unchecked their anti-coach propaganda it could infect others in your program. In this case, the coach needs to "shore up their base." Reach out to the players and parents that support you and do things to strengthen those existing positive relationships. Shoring up the group that supports you will help keep them from falling into the negative abyss. If a coach can ascertain that their opposition is not nearly as large in numbers as it might originally seem it would be wise to weather the storm while working to strengthen the relationships that will keep you employed.

7 *We have had a President go through a similar situation. Grover Cleveland is the only President to serve two non-consecutive terms. He was defeated in his first attempt at re-election but four years later the voters decided President Cleveland wasn't so bad after all and they elected him for another term.*

If a coach has accumulated far more enemies than just one specific group or if the coach has allowed a vocal minority to grow into a majority, then embarking on a public relations campaign can be considerably more difficult. While Presidents can go on a tour around the country speaking to throngs of supporters or have their message broadcast on nationwide television to raise their approval ratings, coaches do not enjoy an equivalent opportunity. Coaches that try to restore support against a rising tide of opposing sentiment are relegated to something referred to as "retail politics." For a candidate, this means going door to door and connecting with constituents on a very personal level. For coaches, it would have to be something similar. Perhaps you could have individual sit down meetings with players and/ or parents in your program to let them speak their mind and share their concerns. It is remarkable how much merely listening to your critics can alleviate some of their anger and alter their opinion. However, a coach that is intent on having these meetings must be prepared to truly listen. If the meetings erode into arguments or the coach attempts to dismantle or dismiss the player or parents' concerns, it will prove to be more damaging than having no meetings at all. In this format the coach must listen and must validate some of the concerns expressed. If a coach does this they will put themselves in a position where they are at least treading water and they will buy themselves perhaps a few more months or another season. Should such a public relations campaign prove effective, a coach should never consider the campaign to win back the hearts and souls of the people in their program a cure all. At best, it is a temporary fix. To alter opinions permanently your opponents in the program would have to see whole sale changes in whatever it was that caused the controversy in the first place. Short of that, to use another political analogy, you may have some time left on your term but you are nothing more than a lame duck.

When a coach is under fire their final option would be to dig in their heels and accept the fact that they are going down, but to develop a mindset that they are going down swinging. These are the confrontations that often make headlines in the local newspaper. A coach gives a dramatic, emotional speech at a meeting where the school board is voting to remove the coach from their position. There are letters to the editor from people that support the coach and from those that condemn them. Tears are shed and bridges are burned in this final showdown scenario. This is the exit of choice for the most stubborn among us. Coaches that choose to go down fighting are often holding on to some sliver of hope that a sudden public outcry of support will overwhelm the administration or the school board and their job will be spared at the last moment. While there is indeed a chance this can occur, what these coaches fail to consider is the aftermath. The coup attempt may be thwarted and their coaching job might remain intact, but at what cost?

After such an emotional battle is waged this much is certain; things will never be the same again. While the coach may rejoice that their job was saved their celebration will be short lived when they realize their program has been torn apart by the civil war it just endured. The players and parents that pushed hard for the coach's ouster might fade into the background, but they will not disappear. And their kids most certainly won't continue to play in the program. There is always a hit in terms of the total number of kids a coach has participating in their program after a showdown like this. Of the players that remain in the program, some certainly were supporters but the others were likely indifferent. There are always kids that simply enjoy the sport and they are going to play regardless of who the coach is.

And lurking in the background there will always be those opponents that fought so vigorously for the coach's removal. Rather than waging their battle in the public arena through letters to the editor and speeches at school board meetings, these people are now relegated to an underground, shadow campaign. They may not be in the public eye but you can be sure they will continue to work for your dismissal. In some ways, this can be even more dangerous for a coach because in the previous situation at least the coach was aware of who their enemies were and what they were up to. When the enemy goes underground and resorts to a whisper campaign it is markedly more difficult for a coach to manage or defend against.

As coaches, we should all consider how we might react or respond when the parent posse comes calling for our job because Bum Phillips was right when he said there are two kinds of coaches "them that's fired and them that's gonna be fired." We can choose to stay one step ahead of the posse or we can stand and fight. There is no clearly defined right answer. It depends on what a coach wants to be known for. Some coaches want to continue coaching and they will get out of town before the posse catches up to them. Other coaches decide to make a last stand. Theses coaches usually find their career hanging from the gallows, but they might consider it worth it because they went down with a fight.

The Single Smartest Political
Move Any Coach Can Make

After all the analysis and suggestions offered in this book, it might seem odd that I can offer coaches just one single bit of advice that can help them not only survive but thrive in the coaching profession. The thing that every coach can do to help them stay on top in the increasingly political world of coaching sounds simple, but it is not as easy as it may appear.

Make it your top priority to make all of your players feel valued and feel important.

If a coach can convince the worst player on their team that they are as important to them and to the team as the star player is, that coach will last in the coaching profession for as long as they like. Yes, even coaches adept at doing this will have their critics and create enemies along the way, but coaches that attempt to make every player feel valued and important will always have an approval rating well above 50%.

Earlier in this book I told you about my old high school basketball coach. He was frequently immersed in controversy but he seemed to capture championships just as frequently. However, collecting trophies is not what truly protected him from his critics. The bond he created with his players and their parents, a coach's most important constituency, is what allowed him to coach in the same community for nearly 40 years.

I was the worst player on our basketball team but he treated me with as much respect as our best player, and he made sure that I knew and believed that what I was doing (even if it was mostly waving a towel on the bench) was important to our team. I remember him saying that "a chain is only as strong as its weakest link." Well, I was fully aware that I was our weakest link, but his words convinced me that I was also among the most important components of our team.

Today, when people ask, I make no illusion of the fact that I was the worst player on my high school basketball team. But I am always quick to add that a team is only as good as its worst player, and when we won the state championship that made me the best worst player in the state!

I have tried to incorporate the way Coach Munsen treated his players into my own coaching style. But one thing I have also learned is you can't fake it. Coach Munsen didn't have to make a concerted effort to demonstrate that he cared about his players. It was clear to all of us that he did. And he didn't write us birthday cards or come watch us play other sports. He didn't have individual meetings with us to find out how we were doing emotionally. He just had a genuine concern and caring for his players and when it's real, kids know. When it's manufactured, kids know that too.

There will be the occasional kid, or maybe even an entire team every few years, that we just have a hard time liking. But you can dislike someone and still care about them. It is a lot harder, no doubt, but it can be done.

If a coach makes every effort to make their players feel valued, respected, and important, and if the coach can convey a genuine sense that they care about each player as a person, that is the single most effective political technique that any coach can ever employ. The way you respond to the various political issues that pop up will be of considerably less consequence if you consistently demonstrate that you truly care about your players.

At its core, politics is the art of understanding and communicating with people. When coach's endeavor to be empathetic and they attempt to relate to the people they are working with or leading, they can be immensely effective. Listening to your constituents, putting yourself in their shoes, and attempting to anticipate the impact of your words and actions are all habits that will help a person survive in coaching, but there is no substitute for compassion and exhibiting a genuine concern.

Care about the kids you coach and you will not only survive, you will thrive in this incredibly demanding and rewarding profession.

Afterword

I t is my sincere hope that the scenarios and ideas presented in the previous pages have inspired you to consider how you will react and respond when confronted with the many difficult decisions coaches face on a daily basis. The situations and subsequent suggestions have been offered with the intention of helping coaches preserve and maintain their position in our increasingly challenging profession.

While I am quick to concede that not all players and parents are out to get us, this book wasn't written to protect coaches from the many quality kids and parents we encounter. Obviously we don't need protection from them. This book was intended to arm coaches with the necessary tools to withstand the attacks mounted by the small but dangerous group of people that don't give a second thought to destroying a coach's career if it could further their own agenda.

It is not my intent to discourage young or aspiring coaches from pursuing the profession. Please don't let this book lead you to believe that a career in coaching will only cultivate enemies. The truth is, the vast majority of players and parents we encounter are outstanding, inspiring people and we benefit immensely by having shared a season or a period of our lives with them. Even though they make up a small percentage of people we deal with, it is the trouble makers that create controversy and garner a good majority of our time, focus, and attention. Hopefully the ideas put forth in the previous pages empower coaches to reduce or eliminate much of the drama these people create that can damage and diminish this otherwise remarkably rewarding profession.

The stories I have shared are not unique. Most coaches will eventually encounter similar situations. With that in mind I would love to learn from my fellow coaches. If you have a situation that confounded you or an experience you learned from and you would like to share it, I would love to hear from you.

I can be reached via e-mail at coach@politicsofcoaching.com.

I am also available to present on the Politics of Coaching at coaching clinics or to consult in a small group setting with the coaching staff at individual high schools. Again, I can be reached at the e-mail address above and my other contact info is available at www.politicsofcoaching.com

Thank you for enhancing the lives of the kids you coach and for improving the communities you live in by giving your time, your heart, and your soul to coaching.

APPENDIX 1

THE REBEL WAY

What it means to be a Rebel girls basketball player

Coaches and athletes are role models. We will not debate whether they should or should not be. It is an undeniable fact that people at high levels of athletics are admired by others, especially young people. This is a responsibility our athletes will not run from; rather they will embrace it. Every athlete in our program will be acutely aware that their actions will have a tremendous impact on the lives of people around them. As role models, there are certain values and character traits athletes and coaches should demonstrate and possess.

Among these are a positive attitude, sportsmanship, competitiveness, team concept, a good work ethic, and an understanding of what success is. These are the things more than offenses and defenses that will be stressed in our program. These are the things that are essential to achievement in athletics and in life.

Positive Attitude- There are two things an athlete can always control. One of them is their attitude. A positive attitude can help you overcome seemingly impossible obstacles. Positive people see challenges, not problems. It's not always easy to be positive. There will be people who criticize you and there will be times when things don't turn out the way you'd hoped or planned. Positive people will bounce back from these difficult situations more quickly and once success is achieved, they will remain successful longer. The best thing about a positive attitude is that it's contagious. If just one player is positive, the feeling can permeate through an entire team. A team with a positive attitude is taking the first step toward being a good team.

Work Ethic- Little in athletics or in life comes easy. It's the people that are willing to put in the extra time and effort that most often come out on top. We will never ask ourselves at the end of a game "what if we'd just practiced a little harder?." We will never lose due to a lack of effort or preparation. High intensity and hard work will be a trademark of our team, and knowing the value of hard work will help you well beyond your years in athletics.

Competitiveness- This cannot be overemphasized. A competitive spirit is the thing that most separates the successful from the rest. Almost everything in life is a competition and everything in athletics is. The thing we all must be aware of is that our toughest competition will rarely come from an opponent. Most often as athletes we are competing against ourselves. There is a voice inside each of us that tells us to take a break, or to take it easy. The voice may tell us we're not good enough or that we'll never make it. Sometimes the voice even tells us that we should give up or quit. Successful athletes are those that can ignore that voice and consistently overcome that part of themselves that wants the easy way out. The other characteristic of a great competitor is that they hate losing as much or more than they love winning. Everyone likes to win. The trademark of a true competitor is an unwillingness to tolerate losing.

Sportsmanship- In victory or defeat, athletes should maintain dignity and demonstrate respect for their opponents, their program, their fans, their sport, their school, the officials, and themselves. We will play within the rules at all times, period. Players will be allowed and encouraged to display emotion, but it must be directed in the right way. Showmanship does not make you a better player and it shows no respect. Again, athletes must keep in mind that they are role models and they must act accordingly.

Team Concept- A team is a group of people that share a common goal and work together to achieve it. Everyone must genuinely care for the well being and success of the group. Individual accomplishments and achievements must always be secondary to the success of the team. Good teams will almost always beat groups of talented individuals. We will first be good teammates, and by doing so, we will develop into a good team.

Understanding Success- I mean it when I say that for us success will not be measured in wins and losses, though we will pursue winning in a vigorous manner. We are successful when we have put forth our absolute best effort. Anything less than our best effort in practice, in a game, or in life is unacceptable. Only when you give something less than your best effort are you a failure. Effort is that other thing that every athlete can control. If we as a team can look back after every practice and game and say to ourselves "I did the best I could" then everything else, including the score is irrelevant. That being said, I am thoroughly convinced that if we honestly give our best effort every day, when we look up at the scoreboard, most of the time we will like what we see!

Being an athlete is not easy, but that's what makes it so rewarding. That is also why people look up to athletes as role models. It takes a special kind of person to succeed in athletics and in life. It is through athletics that we hope to instill these values and help to mold and create special people.

APPENDIX 2

<u>**Important Policies and Procedures for Players and Parents**</u>

We are truly happy to have you and your family as a part of this program. The support and involvement of players and parents are what make great programs. Of course being a part of this program requires a great commitment from everyone involved. The following paragraphs will outline some expectations for players and parents and explain important policies that pertain to your role in the program.

Time commitment

No matter what the activity, family comes first. When a player has family commitments, we want and expect the player to make the family their first priority. That being said, it is our hope that when planning family vacations or excursions that you will also consider the impact the player's absence will have on our basketball family. When a player in our program is absent, it almost always impacts their teammates in a negative way. Whether it means a less productive practice or a loss in a game, please keep in mind that there are always several other players and coaches counting on you. At the varsity level there are times when an entire school and community are counting on you. Again, we recognize that family emergencies do come up and no player will be faulted for absences related to such a situation. All we ask is that you recognize and respect that there are others counting on you when you commit to being part of a team and that your presence at practice and games is of great importance to your teammates and the program.

Academics

We want our players to excel in everything they do. This includes performing at a high level in the classroom. Players may occasionally miss class time when we are on road trips. Our players must be responsible and always ask for assignments ahead of time. We will not ask for special privileges or exceptions. We will be leaders in the classroom. Get assignments ahead of time and turn in assignments on time or ahead of schedule.

Players that are deficient in more than one class may be suspended from playing in games at the coach's discretion. If parents ask the coaches to keep players that are failing academically out of games, we will comply with the parent's wishes. The top priority for players is to get a good education. Basketball can be a part of that learning process, but only when the traditional academic areas are adequately addressed.

On and off court behavior

Our players will take their position as role models very seriously. Rebel basketball players will be expected to conduct themselves in a class manner on and off the court. No taunting or inappropriate gestures will be allowed on the floor.

Off the court, we expect that our players will be leaders and that they will NEVER use drugs, alcohol, or tobacco. Players that are unwilling to sacrifice such things are demonstrating a selfish attitude and a lack of commitment to their teammates. They are also directly violating the trust and admiration that is given them by the young people in our community. Such abuses will be dealt with harshly. The school's policy will be followed and enforced. Upon completion of the suspension we will not promise to treat the player as though nothing happened. When trust has been violated and a team has been betrayed it is extremely difficult to heal those wounds.

In short, do not do anything to embarrass yourself, your family, this program, or this school, or your actions will result in severe repercussions for an extended period of time.

Emphasis on winning and playing time policy

At every level in the program below the varsity level, the primary emphasis will be on player development. However, as players climb up the competitive ladder there will be an increased emphasis on winning. Upon reaching the varsity level, winning will absolutely be a primary goal. While we recognize winning is not the most important aspect of athletics, it certainly enhances the experience for all involved so we will pursue winning in a vigorous manner.

When it comes to choosing the JV/Varsity team we will abide by the following criteria: Seniors will be given first consideration when selecting the team. I am not suggesting that every senior that tries out will make the team, but seniors that have displayed a good attitude and loyalty to the program will be given considerable consideration. After selecting seniors, underclassmen will be given an equal chance to make the team and they will be assigned a level based on two things. First, they will play at a level that will benefit the program the most. Second they will play at a level that will allow them to develop to their fullest potential as a player. Often these levels are one and the same. We will carry 18 players on our JV/Varsity. When it comes to playing time there are no guarantees. Because you are a senior or because you are on varsity does not guarantee that you will play. We will play the players that give us the best chance to win, period. As coaches we are charged with the task of doing what is best for the team. Sometimes what is best for the team is not what is best for an individual player. Every player and every parent has the right to an explanation if they are not comfortable with their role on the team. They may not like the explanation or the situation but again, it is our job to do what is best for the group at large, not what is best for an individual.

As coaches we encourage players to discuss concerns and questions with us. When a player is unclear of their role or of where they stand it can lead to a great deal of turmoil and stress. All conversations relating to a player's role or playing time must be had in private. If a player is unclear on their role the coach will explain it to them. If a player is not satisfied with their role they should ask the coach what they can work on to improve their position on the team.

Teams where everyone understands and accepts their role usually turn out to be special teams. Unfortunately those teams are usually rare. We will do our best to accommodate every player on our team, but we will never accommodate one player at the expense of the rest of the team.

Elastic Clause

Recognize that the above list of policies and procedures is not comprehensive. As coaches, we reserve the right to add or adapt policies as we deem necessary. All district and administrative policies and decisions supercede the policies listed above.

Now that we have dispensed with the policy and formality, let me again thank you for being part of the Rebel Girls Basketball family. We look forward to an exciting, productive, and rewarding season! GO REBELS!!!

APPENDIX 3

REBEL OFFENSIVE FOCUS AND PHILOSOPHY

The aggressive, attacking demeanor we demonstrate at the defensive end will also be our attitude on offense. From the instant we gain possession of the ball we want to be the aggressor and make the defense react to us. We will be a fastbreak first offense. We don't want to allow the defense to get settled in so we will attack every time with a primary break.

When teams respond to our aggressiveness by hustling back on D, we will continue our attack with a secondary break designed to create a quick, high percentage shot. In the event that we must execute our motion or zone offense in the half court, we will do so in an equally agressive manner by setting a number of screens with quick ball movement.

Other important offensive principles:

1. Set good screens all of the time

I am convinced that setting good, aggressive screens is the most important component of productive offense. This will require our players to be physical. If you're not comfortable being physical, you'd better learn.

Someone that sets a good screen leading to a score by their teammate should feel just as good as the person that scored. We will applaud the screener as much as the scorer. Good screens equal good offense!

2. Always be a threat with the ball

Defenders cannot play us as aggressively if we do two things consistently. First, do not give up your dribble unless you are going to get something out of it. You should only dribble to get a better angle on a pass, to create a better shot for yourself, or to avoid a five second call. Many players have a habit of dribbling as soon as they get the ball. We want to use our dribble wisely because once our dribble is dead, teams can play us as aggressively as we want to play them.

Second, avoid holding the ball over your head. There is only one thing you can do from that position (pass) and the defender knows it. We want to remain in triple threat position as much as possible. That means having the ball down by our side so we can pass, dribble, or shoot.

3. Move without the ball

Good shots don't come when everyone is standing around. Be hard to gaurd! Cutting or screening when you don't have the ball will make the defense move and cause a breakdown, leading to a better shot for you or a teammate.

4. Recognize when and when not to shoot in transition

We want to push the ball up the floor and take advantage of slow or lazy defensive teams. When we run our fast break, it is the job of the point guard (also called the 1) or whomever has the ball, to attack the basket, pass ahead to an open teammate, or decide that we don't have a numbers advantage and slow it down to execute our half court offense.

5. Be patient in the half court offense

Good shot selection is one of the most crucial aspects of good offensive basketball. We never want to force a shot for the sake of shooting. We must be willing to set several screens and make several passes if that's what it takes to create a defensive breakdown and a high percentage shot.

6. Get to the line and concentrate on free throws

Because we will be a physical team, we should expect to make frequent trips to the free throw line. Success at the free throw line eminates from concentration and repetition. Develop a routine, focus your eyes on the rim, and keep your hand up maintaining your follow through until the ball hits the rim or goes in. And do these things every time.

Several studies have shown that the team that attempts (not makes) the most free throws in a game wins over 70% of the time. Let's be the team attempting the most free throws 100% of the time. Be physical and aggressive on offense!

APPENDIX 4

REBEL DEFENSIVE FOCUS AND PHILOSOPHY

Defense wins championships. This statement, while uttered by coaches in every sport is most true in basketball. In no other sport can good defense turn into instant offense as quickly. It is for that reason that we consider our defense the starting point for our offense. Because we will play an aggressive, up-tempo brand of basketball, it is essential that our defense sets the tone by creating easy offensive opportunities. With constant ball pressure, people in every passing lane, and a commitment to contest every shot, we can insure that not only will teams struggle to score against us, they will in fact help us to score via turnovers.

This defense demands an incredible amount of energy, but as much as that it requires intense desire. Our defense cannot be played at less than 100% effort. There will never be a question about what component of basketball is most important in our program. If champions are what we aspire to be, then it is aggressive, attacking, team defense that will make us champions. Other important defensive principles:

1. Talk, Talk, Talk

There is a tremendous difference between five good one on one defenders and a good defensive team. The thing that makes that difference is communication. By talking to each other on the floor, we evolve from five individuals to one team. Even the best individual defender will sometimes get beat one on one. By playing good TEAM defense, no opponent will beat us one on one. They will have to beat us one on five.

2. Turn The Ball And Keep It In The Corner

We want to push the ball towards the sideline and baseline, using the out of bounds line as an extra defender. Through use of stance, we will influence opponents into corners. Once there, we must keep the ball in the corner or on the same side of the floor. Offenses that can't reverse the ball aren't offenses at all.

3. Know Opponents Strengths and Weaknesses

This can be difficult to do when your playing an opponent for the first time, but by being perceptive before and during the game you can sometimes discover something that gives you a decisive edge. Does the player your guarding favor one hand when they dribble? Do they always turn over the same shoulder to shoot in the post? Identify the things your opponent is most comfortable doing, then take those things away!

4. Contest Every Shot

Teams will probably score on us every game, but we want to make our opponents work hard for every basket they get. If we are successful at this, we will frustrate teams into bad shots and wear them down mentally as much as physically. Nothing will ever come easy against our defense!

5. BOX OUT!!!

I list this last, but by no means is it the least important thing. We want to hold our opponents to none or one shot every time we're on defense. An important step to making this happen is boxing out every time our opponent shoots. Again, this goes back to communication. When an opponent shoots, the defender guarding them must yell "shot!." This alerts the other four players to box out. Offensive rebounds must be kept to a minimum. We will rebound better than every team we play, regardless of height.